New Inside Out

Sue Kay & Vaughan Jones

with Peter Maggs & Catherine Smith

Intermediate

Student's Book

MACMILLAN

WB = **Workbook**. Each unit of the Workbook contains a one-page section which develops practical writing skills.

1 Friends

Grammar Question forms. Tense review. Adverbs of frequency
Vocabulary Friendship expressions
Useful phrases Meeting friends unexpectedly

Speaking & Reading

1 Write down the names of three people who are important to you:
a) a relative; b) a friend; c) a famous person.

Ask a partner about the people they have chosen. Find out as much as you can.

2 Read the questionnaire about the American actor, David Schwimmer. According to his answers, which of these famous people is the odd one out?

> Dostoevsky   Sophia Loren   Mahatma Gandhi   Martin Luther King
> Leonardo da Vinci   Charlie Chaplin   Michael Jackson

Q&A

David Schwimmer

David Schwimmer was born in New York and grew up in Los Angeles. He appeared as Ross Geller in the popular TV show, *Friends*. He's also a stage actor and a film director.

When were you happiest?
Before I realised my parents, sister and I were all mortal.

What is your greatest fear?
Besides death? Standing on stage in front of thousands of people, forgetting what happens next, but knowing I'm supposed to be doing it. Also, being in the ocean alone and feeling something large brush against my leg.

What is your earliest memory?
Diving off a piece of furniture and onto my parents' bed.

What or who is the greatest love of your life?
The theatre.

Is it better to give or to receive?
I am always happier giving, rather than receiving, a gift – and happiest when I give anonymously.

Where would you like to live?
Near the ocean, one day.

What is your guiltiest pleasure?
Pizza and television, hopefully together.

Who would you invite to your dream dinner party?
Dostoevsky, Sophia Loren, Mahatma Gandhi, Gene Kelly, Martin Luther King Jr, Leonardo da Vinci, Charlie Chaplin, Cole Porter, Sade, my family, my friends, my lady and a translator.

When did you last cry, and why?
Three days ago, when I saw the film, *La Vie en Rose*. It reminded me how brief our time is here, and how wonderful it is to fall in love.

What song would you like played at your funeral?
Don't Stop 'Til You Get Enough by Michael Jackson.

3 Work with a partner. Look at the questionnaire and discuss what David Schwimmer says about the following subjects.

a)   The theatre *It's the greatest love of his life.*
b)   The ocean   c)   Gifts   d)   Pizza and television   e)   *La Vie en Rose*   f)   Love

4 Choose the five most interesting questions from the questionnaire and think about your own answers. Work with a partner and compare your questions and answers.

Speaking & Grammar

1 Work with a partner. Match the beginnings (*a–l*) with the endings (*1–12*) of these questions.

About you: Q&A

a) Where …
b) How many …
c) What does …
d) Are …
e) How often do you …
f) What do …
g) What kind of …
h) How long …
i) Have you ever …
j) When did …
k) What were …
l) Who …

1 you do for a living?
2 music do you listen to?
3 been to an English-speaking country?
4 you doing at this time yesterday?
5 do you come from?
6 you last go on holiday?
7 you studying for any exams at the moment?
8 brothers and sisters have you got?
9 do you admire most?
10 your name mean?
11 have you been learning English?
12 see your parents?

Ask each other the questions. How many of your answers are the same?

Question forms

Where **does** he **come** from?

Has he **been** here long?

What **was** he **doing**?

Who **saw** him first?

2 Classify the questions *a–l* from the Q&A above in the following table of tenses.

	simple	continuous	perfect	perfect continuous
Present	*a, b, …*			
Past				

Which two tenses are not included in the Q&A?

3 Questions sometimes end in a preposition, for example questions *a* and *g* in the Q&A above. Rewrite these questions in the correct order.

a) learning / English / What / you / for / are / ?
   What are you learning English for?
b) are / at / you / sort of things / What / good / ?
c) kind of things / What / in / are / interested / you / ?
d) money / you / on / do / spend / most / What / ?
e) clubs or groups / What / to / belong / you / do / ?
f) What / about/ kind of things / you / do / worry / ?
g) lunch / you / usually / Who / have / do / with / ?
h) in / you / do / confide / Who / ?

Ask your partner the questions.

4 Look at these questions and answers. In which question is *Who* the subject?

a) '**Who** do you confide in?' 'I confide in **John**.'
b) '**Who** confides in you?' '**John** confides in me.'

Do you use the auxiliary *do* when *Who*, *What* or *Which* is the subject?

5 Grammar *Extra* **1** page 126. Read the explanations and do the exercises.

6 Look at these sentences. Write questions with *Who*.

a) Jenny talks the most.
   Who talks the most?
b) Tom always remembers my birthday.
c) Brad wears the best clothes.
d) Becky texts me the most.
e) David lives the closest to me.
f) Rick has known me the longest.

Think about your close friends and answer the questions (*a–f*). Ask your partner.

Pronunciation

1 🌐 1.01 **Listen and repeat the fractions in the box.**

½	⅓	¼	¾	⅘	⅛	³⁄₁₀	¹⁄₂₀

2 **Match each percentage with the equivalent fraction.**

a) 5% – ¹⁄₂₀   c) 25%   e) 33.3%   g) 75%
b) 12.5%   d) 30%   f) 50%   h) 80%

🌐 1.02 **Listen, check and repeat.**

Reading

1 **Write down the names of five friends. When was the last time you were in touch? How did you communicate (face-to-face / by phone / online messaging / ...)? Tell a partner.**

2 **Work with your partner. Read the results of a survey about keeping in touch with friends. Read each statement (a–j) and decide which alternative is most likely to be true.**

Keeping in touch

A global poll was conducted into how young people communicate with friends. 18,000 people between the ages of fourteen and twenty-four in sixteen countries were interviewed. These were some of the key results of the survey.

a) The average young person has **94 / 48** numbers in their mobile phone.

b) On average, young people communicate regularly online and face-to-face with **5 / 53** friends.

c) The group who has the largest number of friends are **girls / boys** aged 14–21.

d) Of all the people surveyed, those who spend the most time online (31 hours per week) are **women / men** aged 22–24.

e) Over half of young people said that they like messaging because **they can talk about more things than face-to-face / it's cheap**.

f) The top messaging topic is **work or school / gossip**.

g) Technology has resulted in young people having **more / fewer** close friendships.

h) Technology has **replaced / improved** face-to-face interaction.

i) Technology makes young people **happier / more stressed**.

j) **59% / 29%** of young people prefer television to their computer.

🌐 1.03 **Listen and check your ideas. Which are the most/least surprising results?**

Listening

1 Three people (Adam, Carole and Sharon) were asked, 'How do you usually contact your friends?' Guess their answers and complete their responses with the words in the box.

| emails letters online phone Skype text |

Adam

'I (1) _____ from time to time. I usually speak on the (2) _____ . I check my (3) _____ twice a day.'

Carole

'I check my (4) _____ once a week. I use (5) _____ now and again. I rarely write (6) _____ nowadays.'

Sharon

'I never send (7) _____ . I (8) _____ all the time. I don't often speak on the (9) _____ . I'm always (10) _____ .'

2 🌐 1.04–1.06 Listen and check your ideas for Exercise 1. How many of the sentences are true for you?

Grammar

Adverbs of frequency

Adverbs

be + adverb
I'm always online.

auxiliary + adverb + main verb
She doesn't often phone me.

adverb + main verb
I rarely write letters.

Adverb phrases

I'm on the phone all the time.
They contact me from time to time.
He uses Skype now and again.

1 Add more adverbs of frequency from the sentences in the Listening section.

Always	Often	Sometimes	Not often	Never
	normally regularly	occasionally	hardly ever	

2 Look at the sentence below. Decide which adverbs in the table normally go in position *A* and which ones normally go in position *B*.

I A contact my friends by phone B .

Position A: always, …

3 Guess which adverbs from the table would make these statements true for your partner. Rewrite the sentences with the adverbs you have chosen.

a) He/She writes letters.
b) He/She listens to classical music.
c) He/She is late for appointments.
d) He/She remembers friends' birthdays.
e) He/She goes to the theatre.
f) He/She buys chocolate.

Ask your partner questions to check your ideas.

'Do you ever write letters?'   'How often do you listen to classical music?'

4 **Pairwork Student A:** page 116 **Student B:** page 121

Reading

1 Look at the photos of Tina and Will at university and Tina and Will now. Discuss whether you think the following statements are true or false.

a) Tina and Will had similar interests when they were at university.
b) They chose similar careers when they finished their studies.
c) They have similar jobs and lifestyles now.

Read the article and check your ideas.

That
was then

**This
is now**

Tina and Will met when they were both studying at the same university. Three years later, we contacted them and asked them to take part in a survey to find out how many people had stayed friends. Here is what we found out.

Tina

5 **'How did you meet Will?'**
'I first met Will when I was looking for someone to share the house I was renting. I put an advertisement in the local newspaper, and he answered it. When we met, we clicked straightaway, and I told him he could move in.'
'What was it like living with Will?'
10 'It was fun. We soon found out that we had a lot in common and quickly became close friends. We had the same ideas about politics and other less important things like cooking. We also liked the same music, and that's important when you're sharing a house. We fell out a couple of times about the housework. Will thinks I'm untidy, but I think life's too short to worry about things like that.'
15 **'What happened when you left university?'**
'When we graduated three years ago, we went our separate ways, and since then our lives have been very different. I went back to my home town and got a job as a production assistant for art exhibitions. I love my job but I'm living with my parents because I'm not earning very much. Will thinks I'm crazy, because money
20 is very important to him now, but I get a lot of satisfaction from my job. He's earning a lot of money, but he doesn't have time to spend with his family. Our lifestyles are so different now that when he comes for the weekend we have a laugh, but we don't have very much to talk about.'

Will

25 **'What kind of relationship did you have with Tina at university?'**
'Tina and I got on very well together. When we first met, we hit it off immediately and we ended up sharing a house for nearly three years. We had our ups and downs but we had the same attitude to the important things in life, and the only thing we argued about was the housework. I'm a Virgo, so I'm very tidy,
30 whereas Tina's the opposite. I don't think she ever found out where we kept the vacuum cleaner!'
'What did you do when you left university?'
'When I left university, I moved to London and got a job in a finance company. I have to work long hours and I don't really enjoy what I'm doing but I earn a
35 very good salary. I'm very ambitious and I enjoy spending money on CDs, clothes and a nice car. Tina's working really hard as well, but she's not earning much. I don't understand why she's doing it.'
'Are you still in touch with one another?'
'Our lifestyles are very different now, so we've drifted apart. We still talk on the
40 phone, and when I go down to visit her, we have a laugh. I know she'll always be there for me.'

2 Underline the correct name.

a) <u>Tina</u> / Will was looking for someone to share the house with.
b) **Tina / Will** is a very tidy person.
c) **Tina / Will** lives at home now.
d) **Tina / Will** has a well-paid job.
e) **Tina / Will** loves her/his job.
f) **Tina / Will** has a nice car.

Vocabulary

1 Complete these expressions to talk about friendship from the article on page 8.

a) 'we liked one another as soon as we first met' = *we clicked _____ / we hit it _____*

b) 'we had similar interests' = *we had a lot _____*

c) 'we got to know one another very well' = *we became _____*

d) 'we argued' = *we fell _____*

e) 'we became / have become more distant from each other' = *we went our separate _____ / we've drifted _____*

f) 'we enjoyed one another's company' = *we got on _____*

g) 'we had good moments and bad moments' = *we had our _____*

h) 'I know I can count on her when I need a friend' = *I know she'll always be _____*

Look again at the text and check your answers.

2 The following is a summary of Tina and Will's friendship. Put the lines of the summary in the correct order.

☐	met. They became close
☐	separate ways and they've drifted
☐	friends and got on
1	Tina and Will hit it
☐	in common. Now they have gone their
2	off immediately when they first
☐	out and they say that they are still
☐	there for each other.
☐	apart. They haven't fallen
☐	well together. They had a lot

3 How many friends have you stayed in touch with from:
a) primary school; b) secondary school; c) university? Compare with a partner.

Speaking: anecdote

▲ Antonia

▲ Antonia's friend

1 🌐 1.07 Listen to Antonia talking about a friend who is different from her and look at the questions. Which two questions does she not answer?

a) What is your friend's name?
b) How long have you known each other?
c) Where did you meet?
d) Why did you become friends?
e) In what ways are you different?
f) What do you have in common?
g) Have you ever fallen out?
h) How often do you see one another?
i) What sort of things do you do together?
j) When was the last time you saw your friend?

1 In Paris.
2 Backgrounds, tastes, personalities, looks.
3 We support Chelsea.
4 Jackie.
5 Three or four times a year.
6 We go out for lunch; talk about football or Paris.
7 Ten years.
8 We were both in the same situation; both from England.

Match the questions with the answers (1–8). Listen again and check.

2 You're going to tell your partner about a friend who is different from you.
- Ask yourself the questions in Exercise 1.
- Think about *what* to say and *how* to say it.
- Tell your partner about a close friend.

Useful phrases

1 🔊 1.08 **Listen to three conversations between friends. Are the following statements true or false?**

a) Cathy meets her friends by chance.
b) The friends are all in a hurry.
c) Cathy makes plans to meet her friends again.

2 **Work with a partner. Underline the most natural sounding alternatives (1–5).**

a)

Cathy:	Hey! How's it going?
Harry:	Not bad.
Cathy:	What have you been up to lately?
Harry:	(1) **I haven't done a lot really. / Not a lot, really.** What about you?
Cathy:	(2) **Oh, I've been doing this and that. / Oh, this and that.**
Harry:	Look, I must dash – I'll give you a call.

b)

Cathy:	Hello, stranger!
Jim:	Cathy! How's life?
Cathy:	Great! What are you up to these days?
Jim:	(3) **Oh, keeping busy, you know. / Oh, I'm keeping busy, you know.**
Cathy:	You must come over for dinner some time.
Jim:	That would be lovely. Better get back to the office. See you.

c)

Cathy:	Hi. How are things?
Ed:	Fine. What about you?
Cathy:	(4) **Oh, things are pretty good. / Oh, pretty good.** Are you doing anything special at the weekend?
Ed:	(5) **No, just taking it easy. / No, I'm just taking it easy.**
Cathy:	Me too.
Ed:	Look, I'm afraid I can't stop. Take care.

Listen again and check.

3 **Complete the table with the highlighted useful phrases from the conversations.**

Greetings	How's it going? a) *How's life?* b) _____
Saying things are OK	Not bad. c) _____ d) _____
Asking for news	What have you been up to lately? e) _____
Saying you're in a hurry	Look, I must dash. f) _____ g) _____
Goodbyes	I'll give you a call. h) _____ i) _____

🔊 1.09 **Listen and repeat all the useful phrases in the table.**

4 **Work with a partner. Practise the conversations.**

Vocabulary *Extra*

Using a dictionary

1 Work with a partner. What kinds of information about words can you find in a good dictionary?

Look at this dictionary page and discuss the questions.

a) How many different words are defined?

b) Which words are more frequent: the red words (eg *friend*) or the black words (eg *frigate*)?

c) Which words do you already know?

d) Which words are completely new to you (you've never seen them before)?

e) Which new words can you understand?

f) In your opinion, which new words would be most useful to learn?

2 Match the following dictionary abbreviations/symbols with their meanings.

a)	abbrev	adverb
b)	adj	uncountable noun
c)	adv	synonym
d)	noun [C]	abbreviation
e)	noun [U]	transitive verb
f)	verb [I]	adjective
g)	verb [T]	opposite
h)	sb/sth	countable noun
i)	=	intransitive verb
j)	≠	somebody / something

Find an example of each abbreviation or symbol on the dictionary page.

a) abbrev – *Fri. abbrev Friday*

3 Refer to the dictionary page and discuss these questions with your partner.

a) How many phrasal verbs are there?

b) What are the eight most frequent adjective collocations for *friend*?

c) Which of the following grammar patterns is *not* possible?

I'm frightened about … I'm frightened of … I'm frightened that … I'm frightened to … I'm frightened with …

d) Identify the seven words with the letter combination *ie*. Which three of these vowel sounds – /aɪ/, /e/, /iː/, /eɪ/, /ɪə/, /ɪ/ – are possible ways of pronouncing *ie*?

Write an example word for each of the three sounds.

e) What is the difference between *frightened* and *frightening*?

4 Check your own dictionary. How does it give the kinds of information discussed on this page?

F

6 if you feel fresh, you have a lot of energy =REFRESHED
7 fresh flowers have been recently PICKED (=taken from the place that they were growing in)
8 fresh water is water in lakes and rivers that does not contain any salt
PHRASE **fresh from/out of sth** if someone is fresh from a particular place or situation, they have recently come from there: *He was just a kid, fresh out of law school.*
—**freshness** noun [U]

fresh ˈair noun [U] the air outside that is nice to breathe → BREATH

freshen /ˈfreʃ(ə)n/ verb [T] to make something fresher, cleaner, or more attractive: *She quickly freshened her make-up.*
PHRASAL VERBS **freshen ˈup** to wash your hands and face and make yourself cleaner and tidier
ˌfreshen sth ˈup same as freshen: *Freshen up your room with a coat of paint.*

fresher /ˈfreʃə/ noun [C] British a student in their first year at university

freshly /ˈfreʃli/ adv recently

freshman /ˈfreʃmən/ (plural **freshmen** /ˈfreʃmən/) noun [C] American a FRESHER

freshwater /ˈfreʃˌwɔːtə/ adj living in water that does not contain salt

fret /fret/ verb [I] to worry about something continuously

fretful /ˈfretf(ə)l/ adj someone who is fretful is worried and unhappy

Fri. abbrev Friday

friar /ˈfraɪə/ noun [C] a man who is a type of MONK (=a member of a Christian religious community)

friction /ˈfrɪkʃ(ə)n/ noun [U] **1** disagreement: *There is some friction between the various departments in the organization.* **2** the fact that one surface rubs against another

Friday /ˈfraɪdeɪ/ noun [C/U] ★★★ the day after Thursday and before Saturday: *Let's go swimming on Friday.* ♦ *We usually meet on Fridays* (=every Friday). ♦ *My birthday is on a Friday this year.*

fridge /frɪdʒ/ noun [C] ★ a piece of equipment that is used for storing food at low temperatures =REFRIGERATOR

ˌfridge-ˈfreezer noun [C] British a machine that consists of a FRIDGE and a FREEZER —picture → C2

fried /fraɪd/ adj cooked in hot oil

friend /frend/ noun [C] ★★★ someone who you know well and like who is not a member of your family: *She's visiting friends in Scotland.* ♦ *Helga is a close friend of mine.* ♦ *I'm having lunch with an old friend* (=someone who has been a friend for a long time). ♦ *May I introduce Peter Flint, a very old friend of the family.* ♦ *She has a wide circle of friends* (=group of friends). ♦ *They used to be friends* (=with each other). ♦ *They made friends with the children next door* (=started to be their friends).

Words often used with friend
Adjectives often used with friend
■ best, close, dear, good, great, lifelong, old, trusted + FRIEND: someone who you know very well

friendly /ˈfren(d)li/ adj ★★
1 someone who is friendly is always pleasant and helpful towards other people ≠ UNFRIENDLY: *He will be remembered as a kind, friendly person.* ♦ *The local people were very friendly towards us.* → SYMPATHETIC
2 if you are friendly with someone, you are their friend: *Janet and I used to be very friendly.* ♦ *Doctors shouldn't get too friendly with their patients.*

-friendly /ˈfren(d)li/ suffix **1** used for showing that something does not harm something else: *wildlife-friendly farming methods* ♦ *environmentally-friendly cleaning materials* **2** suitable for a particular type of person: *child-friendly restaurants*

friendship /ˈfren(d)ʃɪp/ noun [C/U] ★ a relationship between people who are friends: *Whatever happened, I did not want to lose Sarah's friendship.* ♦ *his friendship with a local businessman* ♦ *She formed a close friendship with Vera Brittain.*

fries /fraɪz/ noun [plural] FRENCH FRIES

frieze /friːz/ noun [C] a line of decoration around the walls of a room or building

frigate /ˈfrɪgət/ noun [C] a small fast ship that is used by a navy

fright /fraɪt/ noun [singular/U] a sudden strong feeling of being afraid: *He was shaking with fright.* ♦ *Kelly cried out in fright.*

frighten /ˈfraɪt(ə)n/ verb [T] ★ to make someone feel afraid =SCARE: *The thought of war frightens me.* ♦ *It frightens me how quickly children grow up these days.* ♦ **frighten sb into doing sth** *adverts that frighten people into buying expensive security equipment*
PHRASAL VERB **frighten sb/sth aˈway** or **frighten sb/sth ˈoff** to make a person or animal so afraid that they run away

frightened /ˈfraɪt(ə)nd/ adj ★ feeling or showing fear =SCARED: *The puppy looked cold and frightened.* ♦ *Bruckner was watching him with wide, frightened eyes.* ♦ *There's nothing to be frightened about.* ♦ *I've always been frightened of snakes.* ♦ +(that) *I was frightened that he might see us.* ♦ **frightened to do sth** *Now he is frightened to go out at night.*

■ **Frightened** describes how you feel: *I am frightened of spiders.* ♦ *She looked very frightened.*
■ **Frightening** describes things or situations that make you feel frightened: *The look on his face was frightening.* ♦ *It was a very frightening experience.*

frightening /ˈfraɪt(ə)nɪŋ/ adj ★ making you feel afraid, nervous, or worried: *a frightening noise/thought/experience* ♦ *It was supposed to be a horror film but it wasn't very frightening.* ♦ *It's frightening that people like him get elected.*
—**frighteningly** adv

From the Macmillan Essential Dictionary (reduced to 85%)

---

2 Adrenalin

Grammar Present perfect simple. Past simple and continuous. Comparatives and superlatives
Vocabulary Gradable and non-gradable adjectives. Sports
Useful phrases Giving advice about complaints or injuries

Reading

1 Read Mike's blog. Choose the best description of his attitude towards skydiving.

a) Mike never wants to go skydiving again.
b) Mike can't live without skydiving.
c) Mike thinks skydiving is too dangerous.

I've just done my first jump since the accident that nearly killed me just over a year ago. As I was lying in hospital after the accident, I wasn't feeling glad to be alive. Instead, I was wondering how I could
5 possibly live without skydiving again.

It all started one evening after another typical nine-to-five day. I was sitting at home thinking, 'There has to be more to life than this,' when an advert came on the television. 'Try skydiving,' it
10 said. The next day, I called my local skydiving centre and booked my first jump. At the end of a day's training, I signed a document to say that I understood I was taking part in an activity that could end in serious injury. At that moment I
15 wondered if I was completely mad.

I will never forget my first jump. Five of us walked to the runway and got into a tiny plane. I was beginning to feel nervous, but the others were chatting and joking, and I started to feel more
20 relaxed. It was a beautiful, cloudless day and the sun was just going down.

We climbed to 11,000 feet, and then the trainer opened the plane door. Suddenly, it was time to jump, and as
25 I pushed myself away from the plane, my mind went blank.

Words cannot describe the rush of adrenalin I experienced while I was free-falling. At 5,500 feet I pulled the cord, and the parachute opened immediately.
30 Suddenly, everything was silent and peaceful. Twice I shouted, 'This is absolutely incredible!' It was the most amazing four minutes of my life.

From the first jump, I was hooked. I started spending every free moment I had skydiving. It became my
35 reason for living, and nothing else mattered.

Things were going really well. Then disaster struck on my 1,040th jump. Another skydiver collided with my parachute. I fell and hit the ground at about 30 mph. I broke both legs, my right foot, left elbow, right arm, my
40 nose and my jaw. I lost 10 pints of blood, 19 teeth and 25 pounds of fat. I was lucky to survive.

People who have never experienced skydiving will find it hard to understand that my only motivation to get better was so that I could do it again. All I can say
45 is that for me, skydiving is life, and life is skydiving.

2 These sentences summarise Mike's story. Correct the factual mistake in each sentence.

a) Mike was ~~reading a newspaper~~ one evening when he saw an advert for skydiving.
   Mike was watching the television …
b) A month later, he phoned the skydiving centre and booked a jump.
c) After a week's training he wondered if he was completely mad.
d) His first jump was unforgettable. It was a beautiful, cloudless morning.
e) When he jumped out of the plane he was conscious of everything.
f) After his first jump he stopped thinking about skydiving.
g) On his 1,040th jump he had an accident because his parachute didn't open.
h) He nearly died. His motivation to get better was so that he could see his family.

3 Have you ever done a parachute jump? Would you consider doing a jump? Choose a response from the box and tell your partner.

Yes, for charity. Yes, for fun. Yes, for money. No way!

Vocabulary

1 Look at the adverbs in the box and the sentences in the table. Answer the questions.

> absolutely   extremely   fairly   really   very

With 'gradable' adjectives	With 'non-gradable' adjectives
a) 'This is _____ good!'	b) 'This is _____ incredible!'

1 Which adverbs can you use to complete sentence *a*?
2 Which adverbs can you use to complete sentence *b*?
3 Which adverb can you use in both sentences?
4 Which sentence did Mike use to describe his first parachute jump?

2 Find pairs of adjectives in the box that have similar meanings. List them in the table under the appropriate headings. Use your dictionary if necessary.

> ~~angry~~ astonished boiling cold dirty exciting exhausted fascinating
> filthy freezing frightened funny ~~furious~~ gorgeous hilarious hot
> interesting pretty surprised terrified thrilling tired

Gradable	Non-gradable
angry	*furious*

3 Combine adverbs from Exercise 1 with adjectives from Exercise 2 to make five sentences that are true for you.

The last time I went to Madrid was in August, and it was absolutely boiling – over 40 degrees!

Pronunciation

1 🎧 1.10 Listen and repeat the exchanges. Copy the intonation.

a) 'It's very cold.' 'Cold? It's absolutely freezing!'
b) 'She's very funny.' 'Funny? She's absolutely hilarious!'

2 🎧 1.11 Listen and respond to more prompts.

a) 'It's very hot in here.' *'Hot? It's absolutely boiling!'*

Make up similar exchanges. Use adjectives from Vocabulary Exercise 2 above.

Speaking

1 Imagine you are in the following situations. What emotions would you feel? Use words in the box or your own ideas. Tell a partner.

> angry bored embarrassed excited frightened nervous thrilled worried

a) Going on a roller coaster at the fair.
   'I'd feel nervous.' 'Oh, I'd feel really excited.'
b) Galloping on a horse.
c) Being stuck in a traffic jam.
d) Being stopped by the police.
e) Taking off in a plane.
f) Giving a speech in front of an audience.
g) Talking to someone you fancy.
h) Watching your national football team.
i) Realising that you have been robbed.
j) Looking down from a high place.
k) Taking an exam.

Tick the situations you have experienced personally.

2 Work with your partner. How many experiences do you have in common? Which experience was the most exciting?

Adrenalin

Grammar

Present perfect simple

We**'ve swum** with dolphins.
She **hasn't been** to Alaska.

Have you ever **ridden** a camel?
Yes, I **have**.
No, I **haven't**.

1 Match each question beginning with the most appropriate endings.

a) Have you ever ridden
b) Have you ever given
c) Have you ever met
d) Have you ever swum
e) Have you ever won
f) Have you ever slept

1 a famous person? / a person from Japan?
2 a competition? / a race?
3 a horse? / a motorbike?
4 a speech? / a lecture?
5 in a tent? / on a boat?
6 in a river? / with dolphins?

Choose the correct meaning of *ever*: a) usually; b) always; c) in your life.

2 Underline the responses in the box that are possible answers to the questions in Exercise 1.

> Yes, I have.   Yes, I do.   No, I haven't but I'd like to.   No, I didn't.
> No, never, and I wouldn't like to.

Ask and answer the questions with a partner.

3 Complete each sentence (*a–d*) with three different time expressions from the box. Use each time expression only once.

> ~~already~~   before   for ages   in 2004   just   last May   lately   many times   never
> three weeks ago   twice   yet

a) I've *already* / _____ / _____ been to Egypt.
b) I've been to Egypt _____ / _____ / _____ .
c) I haven't been to Egypt _____ / _____ / _____ .
d) I went to Egypt _____ / _____ / _____ .

Which of the twelve possible sentences in *a–d* are true for you?

4 **Pairwork** **Student A:** page 116 **Student B:** page 121

Listening

1 🔘 1.12–1.14 Listen to Andy, Beth and Cindy being interviewed about past experiences. Connect the key information from each person's story.

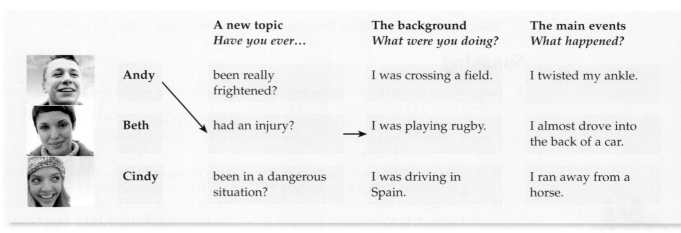

	A new topic *Have you ever...*	The background *What were you doing?*	The main events *What happened?*
Andy	been really frightened?	I was crossing a field.	I twisted my ankle.
Beth	had an injury?	I was playing rugby.	I almost drove into the back of a car.
Cindy	been in a dangerous situation?	I was driving in Spain.	I ran away from a horse.

Work with a partner. What other details can you remember? Listen again.

2 When you tell a story, which tense can you use for each of these functions:
a) introduce a new topic; b) give the background; c) talk about the main events?

Ask and answer the questions in Exercise 1 with your partner. Give as many details as you can.

Grammar

Past simple and continuous

He **was playing** rugby when he **fell** heavily on his left leg and **twisted** his ankle.

1 Complete the rule with *simple* or *continuous*.

The past (1) *continuous* is almost always used in contrast with the past (2) _____ . You use the past (3) _____ to describe a 'longer' activity that was in progress when other past events happened. You use the past (4) _____ to describe single, completed actions – usually the main events of a story.

2 Complete the sentences with the past simple or the past continuous.

a) We (move) *moved* house several times when I (be) _____ a child.
b) My parents (meet) _____ when they (travel) _____ abroad.
c) I (have) _____ a small accident while I (learn) _____ to drive.
d) When I (wake up) _____ this morning, the sun (shine) _____ .
e) While I (walk) _____ to work, I (bump into) _____ an old friend.
f) I (break) _____ my leg once while I (play) _____ football for the school team.

Are any of the sentences true for you?

3 Grammar *Extra* 2, Part 1 page 128. Read the explanations and do the exercises.

Speaking: anecdote

1 🔊 1.15 **Listen to Jake talking about a time when he was in a dangerous situation. Read the questions. Tick the answers that are correct.**

a) 'What was the situation?' 'A dog attacked me.' ✔
b) 'When did it happen?' 'A few ~~months~~ years ago.'
c) 'Where were you?' 'In the garden.'
d) 'Who were you with?' 'My older brother.'
e) 'What were you doing?' 'Playing tennis.'
f) 'What happened?' 'Someone kicked the ball through a window.'
g) 'What happened next?' 'I climbed over the fence and saw a dog.'
h) 'How did you feel?' 'I was very surprised.'
i) 'What were the consequences?' 'I climbed back over the fence with the ball.'
j) 'What happened in the end?' 'My brother never found out about the football.'

Listen again and change the incorrect answers.

2 **Stories are often told in five stages. Put the headings below in the appropriate places to show the five stages of Jake's story.**

> The background   How you felt   The problem   The resolution   ~~Introduction~~

The stages of a story	The summary of Jake's story
1 *Introduction*	Have I ever told you about the time a dog nearly attacked me?
2 _____	It was a few years ago. It was the weekend and it was summer. The sun was shining and we were playing football. We were using my older brother's football.
3 _____	We were having a laugh, when suddenly one of my friends kicked the ball over the fence. I had to climb over the fence. An enormous dog was running towards me.
4 _____	I've never been so frightened in my life! I was absolutely terrified.
5 _____	Fortunately, the neighbours came home before my brother did. In the end he never knew about the football.

3 **You're going to tell your partner about when you were in a dangerous or exciting situation.**

- Ask yourself the questions in Exercise 1.
- Think about *what* to say and *how* to say it.
- Tell your partner about a time when you were in a dangerous or exciting situation.

Vocabulary & Speaking

1 Work with a partner. List the sports in the box in different groups according to the criteria *a–f*. A sport might belong to more than one group.

> athletics badminton baseball basketball boxing bungee jumping
> cycling fishing football golf horse-riding ice hockey judo karate
> kite surfing rock climbing rugby running sailing scuba diving
> skating skiing skydiving snowboarding surfing swimming
> table tennis tennis volleyball windsurfing

a) Water sports *fishing, …*
b) Team sports
c) Indoor sports
d) Sports that collocate with *play*
e) Sports that are hardly ever shown on TV
f) Sports that need special footwear

2 Work with your partner. Tell each other about the following.

a) Sports you have tried   c) Sports you watch
b) Sports you do   d) Sports you don't like

Listening & Vocabulary

1 🔵 1.16–1.17 Listen and guess which sports Toby and Kate are talking about.

2 Complete the table with words from the conversations.

	Sport	Place	Equipment
Toby		*the sea*	*a board*
Kate			

▲ the sea

▲ a wetsuit

▲ a harness

▲ a kite

▲ a board

▲ mountains

▲ waterproof clothes

▲ climbing shoes

▲ cliffs

▲ ropes

Listen again and check your answers.

3 Work with your partner. Choose five more sports to add to the table and complete the 'place' and 'equipment' columns for each one. Use your dictionary if necessary.

Grammar

Comparative and superlative structures

He's **slightly taller than** me.
She's **much more mature than** he is.
They're **just as good as** we are.
It's **by far the biggest** one I've ever seen.

1 Group the words in the box into four groups of three adjectives according to how their comparative and superlative forms are made.

<del>cold</del>   fat   happy   interesting   <del>high</del>   hot   lucky   popular   pretty   <del>quiet</del>   relaxed   sad

Group 1: cold – colder – coldest; high – higher – highest; quiet – quieter – quietest

Complete these rules for forming comparative and superlative adjectives.

1   For most one-syllable adjectives and some two-syllable adjectives, you add *er / est*.

2   For one-syllable adjectives which end in one vowel + one consonant you double the consonant and add _____ .

3   For two-syllable adjectives which end in *y*, you replace *y* with _____ .

4   For most other two-syllable adjectives and for all three-syllable adjectives, you use _____ .

What are the comparative and superlative forms for *bad, good* and *far*?

2 Look at the table and complete the sentences (*a–f*) to make true statements.

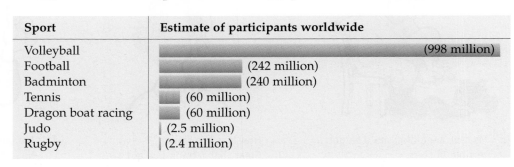

Sport	Estimate of participants worldwide	
Volleyball		(998 million)
Football		(242 million)
Badminton		(240 million)
Tennis		(60 million)
Dragon boat racing		(60 million)
Judo		(2.5 million)
Rugby		(2.4 million)

a)   *Football* is much more popular than *rugby*.
b)   _____ is slightly more popular than _____ .
c)   _____ is just as popular as _____ .
d)   _____ is a bit less popular than _____ .
e)   _____ is a lot less popular than _____ .
f)   _____ is by far the most popular sport in the world.

3 Complete the following sentences with your own opinions about different sports.

a)   _____ is much _____ than _____ .   d)   _____ is the _____ I've ever _____ .
b)   _____ isn't nearly as _____ as _____ .   e)   _____ is much _____ than _____ .
c)   _____ is just as _____ as _____ .   f)   _____ is by far the _____ in the world.

Now find other people in the class who share your opinions.

4   Grammar *Extra* 2, Part 2 page 128. Read the explanations and do the exercises.

Speaking

1 How well do you know the town/city where you are studying English? Discuss these questions with your partner.

Where is …

- the nearest ski resort?
- the nicest swimming pool?
- the biggest football stadium?
- the best-equipped sports shop?

- the most difficult street to park in?
- the most fashionable clothes store?
- the tallest/oldest/most famous building?
- the best shop to find English books?

2 Note your answers down. Now discuss in groups and decide how well you know the place where you are studying English.

Useful phrases

1 Read the conversations. Underline the injury or complaint in each case.

A: How did you get that <u>black</u> <u>eye</u>?
B: I was playing cricket yesterday, and the ball hit me in the face.
A: *You'd better put a bag of ice on it.* It looks terrible.

C: Why are you limping?
D: I've got a twisted ankle.
C: Oh dear. It looks really painful. _____

E: Did you have a good swim?
F: It was OK at first, but then I got cramp and I had to stop.
E: Oh, that's horrible. You're probably dehydrated. _____

G: My feet are killing me. I've got terrible blisters.
H: _____ . And then you should wear sandals for a while.
G: But it's winter.

I: How was the sailing?
J: Great, but I think I've got sunburn. My nose is really red.
I: _____

K: Are you OK?
L: No, I think I've got a broken thumb.
K: Oh dear. You probably need an x-ray. _____

2 Read the conversations again. Match the following useful phrases with the appropriate conversations.

1 You'd better put a bag of ice on it. *a*
2 You need to drink more water.
3 You'd better go to the hospital.
4 You need to put some cream on it immediately.
5 You really should lie down and keep your leg up.
6 You need to put some plasters on them.

🌐 1.18 **Listen and check**.

3 🌐 1.19 **Listen and repeat the useful phrases.**

4 Work with a partner. Discuss what advice you would give to these people.

a) I think my nose is broken.
b) My wrist is swollen – I think I've twisted it.
c) My two front teeth are loose.
d) I've got a terrible headache.
e) A wasp has stung me on my neck.
f) I've hurt my back.

Choose one injury/complaint. Write a short conversation like the ones in Exercise 1. Practise your conversation.

Vocabulary *Extra*

Adjectives: exploring synonyms

1 Look at the table below. In each column, cross out the word that is not usually a synonym of either *important* or *nice*.

important /ɪmˈpɔːtənt/ adj ★★★ =	nice /naɪs/ adj ★★★ =
big essential key main major necessary significant top	fine good great kind lovely pleasant sympathetic wonderful

Check your ideas with the two dictionary extracts.

2 Complete the diagram with headings from the dictionary extract for *nice*.

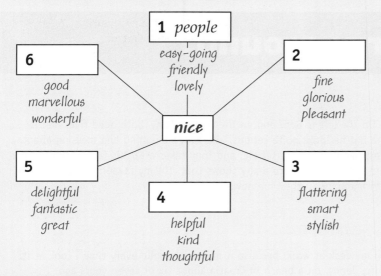

1 *people*
easy-going
friendly
lovely

6
good
marvellous
wonderful

2
fine
glorious
pleasant

nice

5
delightful
fantastic
great

4
helpful
kind
thoughtful

3
flattering
smart
stylish

Make a similar diagram for *important*.

3 Cross out the adjective that is not possible in each sentence.

a) The president is the most **influential / ~~landmark~~** politician in my country.

b) Global warming has very few **far-reaching / senior** effects on the environment.

c) Traffic congestion is a **major / top** problem in my city.

d) The world wide web was the most **main / significant** invention of the 20^(th) century.

e) 1945 was a/an **historic / groundbreaking** year in the development of my country.

f) It's **major / vital** that we find a cure for cancer.

Which of the above statements do you agree with?

4 Complete each sentence with an appropriate synonym of *important* or *nice*.

a) My mother is a/an _____ person.

b) We had really _____ weather on holiday.

c) My best friend always wears _____ clothes.

d) I had a _____ time last weekend.

e) My favourite restaurant serves _____ food.

f) It's _____ that I devote more time to learning vocabulary.

Tick the sentences that are true for you.

5 Check your own dictionary. What information can you find about the words *important* and *nice*?

Words you can use instead of **important**

Important is a very general word. Here are some words with more specific meanings that sound more natural and appropriate in particular situations.

people	influential, leading, prominent, senior, top
events	key, historic, landmark, major, main, momentous
issues/problems	critical, major, significant
achievements/ discoveries	groundbreaking, historic, landmark, significant
effects	far-reaching, lasting, main, major, significant
facts	notable, noteworthy, significant
things that are important because you must have or do them	critical, crucial, essential, necessary, urgent, vital

Words that you can use instead of **nice**

Nice is a very general word. Here are some words with more specific meanings that sound more natural and appropriate in particular situations.

people	easy-going, easy to get on with, friendly, good fun, kind, lovely, sweet
behaviour	helpful, kind, thoughtful
something that happens or something that you do	good, great, lovely, marvellous, wonderful
weather	fantastic, fine, glorious, good, lovely, pleasant
clothes	beautiful, flattering, smart, stylish
food/flowers/gifts/ places	beautiful, delightful, fantastic, great, lovely

'Thank you for holding. Your call is important to us ...'

3 Relationships

Grammar Dynamic and stative meanings. Present perfect simple and continuous
Vocabulary Family. Relationships. Describing character
Useful phrases 'Less direct' language

Reading

1   Look at the photographs. What do you think the relationship is between the people and the people in the photos that they're holding? Discuss with a partner.

Read the article and check your ideas.

Who do you **carry around?**

Alison

'These are my twins. On the left is Ben, and on the right is Tony, both aged five. Ben is looking at the camera but he looks quite serious, and Tony's laughing and messing about. They're identical twins, but Ben takes after me, and Tony takes after his father. They're like chalk and cheese, and I think this photo really shows that. It's my favourite photo of the boys, and I carry it in my diary all the time now.'

Bruce

'I keep this photo on my desk at work, because it makes me smile every time I look at it. It's a photo of my wife, Jenny, on a beach in Croatia about six or seven years ago. I remember it was just after breakfast, and she was sitting with her face in the sun. We were the only people on the beach, and it was a nice moment. I like it, because she isn't frowning at me for once.'

Chris

'This was taken a couple of months after I met my girlfriend. She's an actor too, and we were working on a television series. We were playing the part of a couple, so it was quite interesting on the set! I have lots of photos of her on my phone, but this is the only one with both of us in it. I think everyone has photos on their phone these days.'

Debra

'Ananda is a child in India who I'm sponsoring through Action Aid, and this is the first photo I ever saw of her. I carry this photo, because she isn't smiling in it. Every photo I've seen since I started sponsoring her shows her smiling. To me, this photo is precious, because it reminds me of why I'm sponsoring her.'

2   Read the article again and match each person with their reason for carrying the photo.

a) 'It makes me smile.' *Bruce*
b) 'It's the only one I have of us together.'
c) 'It's my favourite photo.'
d) 'It reminds me of why I'm sponsoring her.'

Whose photo do you carry around with you and why? Tell your partner.

Grammar

Dynamic and stative meanings

Dynamic meaning
(Use simple or continuous forms)
He usually **smiles** all the time but he **isn't smiling** now.

Stative meaning
(Use only simple forms)
She **likes** taking photos. (NOT ~~She's liking~~ ...)
Did you **understand**? (NOT ~~Were you understanding?~~)

Note: Some verbs (eg *have, look, think*) can have both meanings:
I **think** my camera is useless. (stative: *think = have an opinion*)
I**'m thinking** of getting a new one. (dynamic: *think = plan*)

1 **Look at this sentence from the article on page 20. Match each example of *look* (1 and 2) with the correct meaning. Then answer the questions.**
   '*Ben (1) **is looking** at the camera but he (2) **looks** quite serious.*'
   look = to have a particular appearance   *look* = to direct your eyes towards something
   a) Which example of *look* (1 or 2) describes an action – something 'happens'?
   b) Which example of *look* (1 or 2) describes a state – nothing 'happens'?
   c) Can you use continuous tenses with verbs when they describe a state?

2 **Complete the descriptions using the present simple or the present continuous.**
   a) She (look) *looks* like a kind woman. She (not be) _____ related to the child in the photo. The child (come) _____ from India.
   b) He (pose) _____ with his girlfriend. They (seem) _____ very happy together.
   c) She (smile) _____ and (show) _____ us a photo of her twin boys.
   d) He (hold) _____ a photo of his wife. It (remind) _____ him of a lovely holiday.

   Match the descriptions (*a–d*) with the people (*1–4*) on page 20.

3 **Do these verbs describe actions or states? Underline the correct verb forms.**
   a) I **think** / **'m thinking** photos of friends and family **are** / **are being** important.
   b) I **have** / **'m having** lots of photos on my phone.
   c) Photos **remind** / **are reminding** me of special occasions.
   d) I **hate** / **'m hating** photos of me.
   e) People **think** / **are thinking** that I **look** / **'m looking** like my mother.
   f) I **think** / **'m thinking** that I **take** / **'m taking** after my father.

   Are any of the sentences true for you?

Vocabulary

1 **Combine these words and part-words to form at least ten more family words.**

aunt	boyfriend	brother	child	cousin	daughter	ex-	father	girlfriend
grand	great-	half-	husband	-in-law	mother	nephew	niece	only
parent	partner	second	single	sister	son	step	uncle	wife

   great-aunt, ex-boyfriend, brother-in-law, stepchild …

2 **Which family words in Exercise 1 can you use to describe yourself? Draw a diagram.**

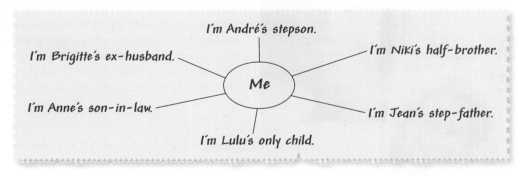

   I'm André's stepson.
   I'm Brigitte's ex-husband.
   I'm Niki's half-brother.
   Me
   I'm Anne's son-in-law.
   I'm Jean's step-father.
   I'm Lulu's only child.

3 **Refer to the people in your diagram in Exercise 2 and complete the following task.**
   • <u>Underline</u> the people who live nearest to you.
   • ~~Cross out~~ the people who you see least.
   • (Circle) the person who you saw most recently.
   • Put an asterisk ✱ by the oldest person and two asterisks ✱✱ by the youngest.
   • Put a tick ✔ next to the person who you get on best with.

4 **Tell your partner about some of the people in your diagram.**
   Brigitte is in her forties. She lives in a small flat in Paris with her partner, René. She …

Speaking

1 Which of these 'firsts' do you remember best?

> your first home   your first friend   your first hero   your first crush
> your first date   your first love   your first English lesson   your first kiss
> your first dance   your first holiday   your first broken heart

2 Choose three 'firsts' and tell your partner about them.

'I remember my first hero – Jonny Wilkinson. He kicked the winning points for England in the 2003 Rugby World Cup final. It was …'

Reading & Listening

1 Read about these first dates. In your opinion, which relationship has the best chance of success? Why? Tell your partner.

Bill It was love at first sight for Ruth and me, which was lucky because we met for the first time on our wedding day! A radio station was running a competition called 'Two strangers and a wedding', and I won the title of 'Most Eligible Bachelor'. Ruth was one of 300 single women who offered to marry me! The first time we spoke to one another was when I proposed to her on the radio with 50,000 people listening. It wasn't exactly intimate, but she said yes anyway. My mother was not amused – in fact, she told a newspaper that she was shocked and appalled. But we knew we were doing the right thing.

Bill and Ruth

TWENTY-FIRST CENTURY **DATING**

Clare

Stan

Clare I've finally found the man of my dreams. We have so much in common. We laugh at the same things and we talk for hours. There's only one problem. We've never met. Stan lives in Canada, and I live in Scotland.

We got in touch through an online dating site. In the first week, I had about twenty-five responses, but nobody I was particularly interested in. Then, two months ago, I received an email from this guy in Canada. He sounded interesting, so I decided to write back. Soon I found myself rushing back home after work to check my emails. Stan made me laugh. He challenged my opinions. We talked about everything, and I just knew this one was different. I'm really excited, because we've decided to meet!

2 Complete the sentences with *Ruth and Bill* or *Clare and Stan*.

a) _____ spoke to one another for the first time on the radio.
b) _____ met on their wedding day.
c) _____ are sure they are doing the right thing.
d) _____ live in different countries.
e) _____ started writing to each other two months ago.
f) _____ haven't actually met yet.

3 🔘 1.20–1.21 Listen to Ruth and Clare talking about the relationships one year later. Which relationship didn't work out? Why?

4 Work with a partner. What do you think are the secrets of a successful relationship?

Vocabulary

1 Complete the statements with words from the box.

> dating   dreams   ~~love~~   propose   relationships   sight   split up

a) I don't believe in *love* at first _____ .

b) Online _____ is the best way to find a new partner.

c) A man should _____ to a woman. It isn't natural for a woman to ask a man to marry her.

d) A marriage is more likely to succeed if both partners have had _____ before getting married.

e) People don't usually marry the man or woman of their _____ .

f) Couples soon _____ and go their separate ways if they don't have anything in common.

2 Work with a partner. Which statements in Exercise 1 do you agree with?

Grammar

Present perfect simple & continuous

I've **known** her for a few weeks.
She's **been going out** with my brother.
He's **asked** her to marry him.

1 Complete the table with these example sentences (*a–c*) from Ruth's story.

a) 'We've **been** together for a year now.'
b) 'We've **been trying** to live a normal life.'
c) 'We've **decided** to move away from our home town.'

	What does the verb describe?	Verb form	Sentence *a, b* or *c*?
1	A continued or repeated *action* that started in the past and is still happening now.	Present perfect continuous	
2	A *state* that started in the past and continues now.	Present perfect simple	
3	A *finished action* that happened some time in the past. (You don't say when.)	Present perfect simple	

2 Underline the correct verb form. What does the verb describe in each case? Refer to the table in Exercise 1 and discuss your ideas with your partner.

a) I've learnt / 've been learning English for three years.

b) I've had / 've been having the same hairstyle since I was a teenager.

c) My sister has gone out / has been going out with the same guy since university.

d) I've been / 've been going to London three times.

e) I've known / 've been knowing my best friend for over ten years.

f) I've stopped / 've been stopping using online dating sites. They don't work!

Are any of the sentences true for you?

3 Make questions using the present perfect simple or continuous.

a) ever / cry / at the cinema?
   Have you ever cried at the cinema?

b) How many times / travel / by air?

c) ever / read / the same book twice?

d) How long / have / your watch?

e) How many times / go / to the USA?

f) How long / go / to the same dentist?

g) ever / own / a pet?

Ask and answer the questions with a partner.

4 Pairwork **Student A:** page 116 **Student B:** page 121

5 Grammar *Extra* 3 page 130. Read the explanations and do the exercises.

Vocabulary

1 🌐 1.22 **Read and listen to six people talking about the qualities they look for in an ideal partner. Which person is most/least like you?**

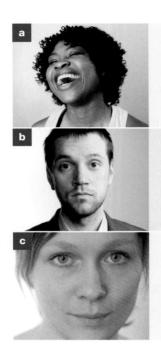

a 'I like a man who can look after me. My ideal man has to be athletic, hardworking, down-to-earth , reliable and romantic.'

b 'Well, I'm quite shy and sensitive. So I'm usually attracted to women who are outgoing and self-assured .'

c 'I think the most important thing is a good sense of humour and a kind heart. My ideal partner is witty , generous and thoughtful .'

d 'I couldn't live with a miserable, narrow-minded person. The person I share my life with has to be cheerful , broad-minded and optimistic.'

e 'I'm looking for a good-looking, kind, faithful partner who can cook really well.'

f 'My ex-partner was big-headed , demanding and self-centred . So next time I'd like someone modest, easygoing and considerate.'

2 **Complete the table with the highlighted words from Exercise 1. Use your dictionary if necessary.**

Words from the interviews		Words with similar meanings		Words with opposite meanings
a) *faithful*	=	loyal	≠	unfaithful
b)	=	considerate	≠	thoughtless
c)	=	arrogant	≠	modest
d)	=	realistic/practical	≠	unrealistic/impractical
e)	=	confident	≠	unconfident
f)	=	sociable	≠	shy
g)	=	optimistic	≠	miserable
h)	=	selfish	≠	unselfish
i)	=	trustworthy	≠	unreliable
j)	=	amusing	≠	dull
k)	=	tolerant	≠	narrow-minded
l)	=	relaxed	≠	demanding

3 **What qualities do you look for in your ideal partner? List the six most important qualities. Find someone else in the class who has chosen the same qualities.**

Pronunciation

1 🌐 1.23 **Listen and repeat the words. Underline the stressed syllable for each word.**
   a) loyal cheerful faithful impractical
   b) interesting sociable miserable considerate
   c) ambitious demanding creative intelligent

2 🌐 1.24 **Look again at the words in Exercise 1. Circle the word in each group that has more syllables than the other words. Listen, check and repeat.**

Reading & Speaking

1 Do the questionnaire. Choose only one answer (*a–e*) for each question.

What's your type?

What your score means

1 The quality you admire most in other people is their ...
a) artistic talent.
b) ambition.
c) love of nature.
d) intellect.
e) sense of humour.

2 In a relationship it's important to ...
a) give each other space.
b) respect each other's career.
c) enjoy the same outdoor activities.
d) discuss things.
e) laugh together.

3 Your favourite place for dinner is ...
a) a trendy new restaurant.
b) somewhere the rich and famous go.
c) a barbecue in the garden.
d) a quiet place where you can talk.
e) a crowded place with loud music.

4 Your ideal weekend is ...
a) going to a jazz festival.
b) shopping in designer boutiques.
c) walking in the mountains.
d) going to the theatre.
e) clubbing.

5 On a Saturday night, you're most likely to be ...
a) at the opening of a new art gallery.
b) making important new work contacts.
c) halfway up a mountain.
d) at home reading a novel.
e) in a crowded bar or nightclub.

6 You're most comfortable wearing ...
a) black clothes.
b) smart clothes.
c) sports clothes.
d) jeans and a T-shirt.
e) colourful clothes.

7 On television you most like watching ...
a) foreign films.
b) business news.
c) nature documentaries.
d) political debates.
e) comedies.

8 Which phrase best describes you?
a) I don't like following the crowd.
b) I live to work.
c) My idea of heaven is sleeping in a tent in the middle of nowhere.
d) I love a good argument.
e) Life's too short to stay at home – let's party!

Mostly *a*: your ideal partner is the artistic type. The artistic type is sensitive, creative, confident and independent *but* can be unreliable.

Mostly *b*: your ideal partner is the career type. The career type is ambitious, sociable, serious and hard-working *but* sometimes dull.

Mostly *c*: your ideal partner is the outdoor type. The outdoor type is down-to-earth, reliable, easygoing and optimistic *but* can be demanding

Mostly *d*: your ideal partner is the brainy type. The brainy type is intelligent, witty, interesting and broad-minded *but* can be big-headed.

Mostly *e*: your ideal partner is the party type. The party type is cheerful, funny, sociable and outgoing *but* sometimes selfish.

2 What does your score mean? Do you agree? Compare with a partner.

Useful phrases

1 🔊 1.25 **Listen to the conversation. Are the following statements true or false?**

    a) Milly and Rita know John very well.
    b) Milly and Rita know Liz very well.
    c) Milly is more critical than Rita.

2   **Read the conversation. Match the highlighted phrases (1–9) with their more direct meanings (a–i) below.**

Milly: So what do you think of Liz's new man?
Rita: John? He seems nice. I don't really know. (1) He wasn't very talkative .
Milly: Well, (2) he's a bit shy . And (3) Liz tends to dominate the conversation , doesn't she?
Rita: Yes, I suppose so. But when John *did* say something, (4) it wasn't particularly interesting .
Milly: Oh dear. (5) You can be so mean .
Rita: I'm not mean – just honest.
Milly: But (6) he's not bad-looking , is he?
Rita: He's OK. Isn't he a bit young for her?
Milly: Young? (7) Liz isn't exactly old .
Rita: That's true. But she looks older than she is.
Milly: Yes, I know what you mean. But she's so lovely – she deserves someone really special.
Rita: Actually, (8) she can be rather difficult .
Milly: Really?
Rita: Yes, (9) she can be a bit bossy .
Milly: Oh dear. Why can't everybody be perfect, like us?
Rita: And so modest. Ha, ha!

    a) it was boring *4*
    b) You're horrible
    c) Liz is young
    d) He was very quiet
    e) she's controlling
    f) he's under-confident
    g) she's impossible
    h) Liz talks too much
    i) he's good-looking

3 🔊 1.26 **Listen and repeat the useful phrases (1–9) from the conversation.**

4   **Match the comments (a–j) with their less direct versions (1–10).**

    a) She never stops talking.
    b) The restaurant was awful.
    c) He prefers older women.
    d) She's rude.
    e) He's big-headed.
    f) They're unfriendly.
    g) He never gets up before midday.
    h) Sometimes she looks exhausted.
    i) They're well-off.
    j) She didn't help me at all.

    1 She isn't particularly/exactly polite.
    2 He tends to get up rather late.
    3 They're not particularly/exactly friendly.
    4 She can be a bit talkative.
    5 The restaurant wasn't very/particularly good.
    6 She can look a bit tired.
    7 They're not particularly/exactly poor.
    8 He tends to go out with older women.
    9 She wasn't particularly/exactly helpful.
    10 He's not particularly/exactly modest.

Vocabulary *Extra*

Sounds and spelling

1 Say the words in the box. Look at the phonemic chart and find the symbols for the vowel sounds in red.

> beige /beɪʒ/   check /tʃek/   jump /dʒʌmp/   mother /ˈmʌðə/
> mouth /maʊθ/   ring /rɪŋ/   shop /ʃɒp/   year /jɪə/

Use the words in the box above to complete the table. Make sure the vowel sounds are in the same order as they appear in the chart.

need	(1)	put	fool	(2)	(3) *beige*	
(4)	(5)	verb	saw	tour	boy	go
back	(6)	arm	(7)	hair	white	(8)

See the full list of phonetic symbols and spellings on page 158.

See the full list of phonetic symbols and spellings on page 158.

2 Say the five words beginning with *hea* in the dictionary extracts. What do you notice about the pronunciation of the letters *ea*?

Complete the table with the words in the box according to the pronunciation of the letters *ea*. There are two words for each sound. Check your answers in a dictionary.

> ~~bear~~ break breath dream dear great health idea learn
> meat search wear

/iː/	/e/	/ɜː/	/ɪə/	/eɪ/	/eə/
					bear

3 Say the seven words (*bought – warm*) in the dictionary extracts. Which vowel sound do all the words have in common? What do you notice about the spellings?

Connect the words according to their vowel sounds. Check your answers in a dictionary.

a) /ə/ —— arrive —— colour —— husband ⟍ people
b) /iː/ —— bean   dirty   niece   ⟋police
c) /uː/ —— blew   fruit   shoe   through
d) /ɜː/ —— burn   key   spinach   women
e) /ɪ/ —— busy   pretty   term   work

4 Read the six words (*economical – politician*) in the dictionary extracts. How is the main stress indicated? Underline the stressed syllables in the noun phrases below and practise saying the phrases.

a) an eco<u>nom</u>ical <u>eco</u>nomist
b) a philosophical philosopher
c) a political politician

5 Look at the phonetic transcriptions for six words from Units 1–3. Say the words and complete the spellings. Check in a dictionary.

a) /ɔːlˈðəʊ/ *although*
b) /ˈdɔːtə/ d_ _gh_ _ _
c) /ɪˈnʌf/ e_ _ _gh
d) /lɑːf/ _ _ _gh
e) /ˈneɪbə/ _ _ _gh_ _ _ _
f) /ˈθɔːtləs/ _ _ _ _gh_ _ _ _ _

6 Check your own dictionary. Find six more words from Units 1–3 that are difficult to spell or pronounce. Practise saying them.

---

single vowel
sounds   diphthongs

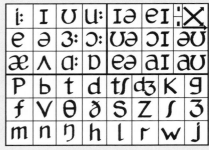

consonant sounds

---

head /hed/ noun ★★★

hear /hɪə/ verb ★★★

heard /hɜːd/ verb ★★★

heart /hɑːt/ noun ★★★

heat /hiːt/ noun ★★★

---

bought /bɔːt/ verb ★★★

caught /kɔːt/ verb ★★★

draw /drɔː/ verb ★★★

floor /flɔː/ noun ★★★

horse /hɔːs/ noun ★★★

talk /tɔːk/ verb ★★★

warm /wɔːm/ adj ★★★

---

economical /iːkəˈnɒmɪkəl/ adj

economist /ɪˈkɒnəmɪst/ noun

philosopher /fɪˈlɒsəfə/ noun

philosophical /fɪləˈsɒfɪkəl/ adj

political /pəˈlɪtɪkəl/ adj ★★★

politician /pɒləˈtɪʃən/ noun ★★

Review A

▶ **Grammar *Extra*** pages 126–131

Grammar

1 **Complete the sentences. Use *about, at, in, on, with*.**

a) What sports are you good _____ ?
b) What have you spent the most money _____ ?
c) Who were you having dinner _____ yesterday?
d) What kind of music are you interested _____ ?
e) What sort of things do you worry _____ ?

Ask and answer the questions with a partner.

2 **Complete the questions for these answers.**

a) 'Who *loves cooking*?' 'My father loves cooking.'
b) 'What _____ ?' 'I saw the new George Clooney film.'
c) 'Who _____ ?' 'I spoke to my brother yesterday.'
d) 'Who _____ ?' 'Josh gave her that watch.'
e) 'Which _____ ?' 'She chose the red car.'
f) 'What _____ ?' 'A parcel arrived this morning.'

3 **Write the sentences in the correct order.**

a) at home / work / I / usually
   I usually work at home.
b) I / from time to time / travel abroad
c) come / I / hardly ever / to my English class
d) I / a hat / all the time / like wearing
e) often / I / by car / come to school / don't
f) I / very fast / always / walk

Tick the sentences that are true for you.

4 **Complete with the past simple, present perfect or present perfect continuous form of the verbs.**

Jed: Have you ever (1 go) *been* on a horse before?
Bob: Well, I (2 go) _____ on a camel, but I (3 not ride) _____ a horse.
Jed: Really? A camel?
Bob: Yes. We (4 go) _____ to Egypt a few years ago, and we (5 do) _____ a camel trek into the desert.
Jed: Wow! What (6 be) _____ that like?
Bob: Wonderful. We (7 sleep) _____ under the stars. I (8 never see) _____ anything so beautiful in all my life. What about you?
Jed: Oh, I love horse-riding. I (9 do) _____ it since I was ten years old. My grandfather (10 teach) _____ me.

5 **Underline the correct form of the verbs.**

Last year a group of friends (1) **invited / were inviting** me to go skiing with them. They (2) **were / were being** very experienced skiers, but I wasn't so I (3) **had to / was having to** go to boring ski school every day, while the others (4) **had / were having** a good time up in the mountains. One day, after my ski lesson, I (5) **decided / was deciding** to meet them at the top of the mountain. While I (6) **went / was going** up in the ski lift I (7) **started / was starting** to feel really nervous, but it was too late. I was at the top of the mountain, and there was only one way to get down!

The sun (8) **shone / was shining**, and everyone (9) **talked and laughed / was talking and laughing** as we started to ski down. Suddenly, one of my friends (10) **shouted / was shouting**, 'Look out!', because I (11) **went / was going** towards a group of trees. I (12) **tried / was trying** to stop, but I couldn't and when I (13) **fell / was falling** down into the snow, one of my skis (14) **came / was coming** off and (15) **hit / was hitting** me on the head. I (16) **spent / was spending** the rest of the week in hospital. Great!

6 **Complete the sentences with the words in the box and the correct form of the adjectives.**

> by far the most   most   ~~much~~   not as
> slightly   the

a) I'm 1.60 metres tall. Di is 1.80 metres. She's (tall) *much taller* than me.
b) Russia is (big) _____ country in the world.
c) I don't like my new bike. It's (good) _____ as my old one.
d) Skydiving is (exciting) _____ thing I've ever done.
e) This book is (easy) _____ than the last one … but not much.
f) What is the (popular) _____ sport in the world?

7 **Spot the mistake! Cross out the incorrect sentence.**

1 a) Did you go shopping yesterday?
   b) ~~Have you been shopping yesterday?~~
2 a) Who does like chocolate?
   b) Who likes chocolate?
3 a) They met while they taught together in Spain.
   b) They met while they were teaching together in Spain.
4 a) He is by far the most intelligent boy in the class.
   b) He is by far the more intelligent boy in the class.
5 a) Why are you hating football so much?
   b) Why do you hate football so much?
6 a) I've known Olivia for two years.
   b) I've been knowing Olivia for two years.

Vocabulary

1 Replace the underlined words with the expressions in the box.

> clicked straightaway   drifted apart
> ~~got on well with~~   have fallen out
> have a lot in common

a) Have you always <u>enjoyed the company of</u> your sister?
   Have you always got on well with your sister?
b) Jo and Rob <u>argued and aren't friends any more</u>.
c) He likes football. She likes reading. They don't really <u>have similar interests</u>.
d) They got divorced because over the years they found they had <u>become distant from each other</u>.
e) Don and I <u>liked one another the very first time we met</u>.

2 Match the gradable adjectives (*a–f*) with their equivalent non-gradable adjectives (*1–6*).

a) good   1 terrified
b) funny   2 hilarious
c) dirty   3 boiling
d) tired   4 fantastic
e) frightened   5 filthy
f) hot   6 exhausted

3 Complete the sentences with adjectives from Exercise 2.

a) That film was absolutely *hilarious*. I laughed so much!
b) She doesn't like dogs. In fact she's very _____ of them.
c) This wine is not bad. Actually, it's fairly _____ !
d) I need to wash the car. It's absolutely _____ .
e) I've been working very hard, and I'm extremely _____ .
f) Can we open a window? It's absolutely _____ in here.

4 Complete the words for sports with *a, e, i, o, u*.

a) sw*i*mm*i*ng
b) k_t_ s_rf_ng
c) b_dm_nt_n
d) v_ll_yb_ll
e) s_ _l_ng
f) f_ _tb_ll
g) t_bl_ t_nn_s
h) skyd_v_ng
i) f_sh_ng
j) sk_ _ng
k) t_nn_s
l) sn_wb_ _rd_ng
m) b_sk_tb_ll
n) _c_ h_ck_y

5 Put the sports in Exercise 4 into these groups.

a) Sports you can play with a partner *badminton, …*
b) Water sports
c) Sports you play in a team
d) Sports you do up in the air
e) Sports you can only do outside in winter

6 Complete the text with the words in the box.

> online dating   love at first sight   meet
> proposed   relationship   ~~split up with~~
> the woman of his dreams

Four months ago, Rob (1) *split up with* his girlfriend, Jane, after four years together. Rob felt lonely. He wanted to start a new (2) _____ , but it was difficult to (3) _____ anyone in the small town where he lived. So he decided to try (4) _____ . During the first week five women emailed him, but one woman, Rosa, sounded like (5) _____ . They arranged to meet, and, as soon as Rob saw Rosa it was (6) _____ . After only two months together, he invited Rosa out to a romantic restaurant and (7) _____ to her.

7 Underline the correct word.

a) Jill is very <u>**considerate**</u> / **confident**. She always remembers my birthday.
b) I've never seen Cary sad. She's always smiling and **miserable** / **cheerful**.
c) Is Theo late again? He's so **unreliable** / **unfaithful**.
d) Katy is so **dull** / **shy**. I nearly fell asleep when she was telling me about her work.
e) Lee didn't give me any of his chocolates. He's so **impractical** / **selfish**.
f) Ken didn't tell me he'd won that big prize for his book. He's very **modest** / **arrogant**, isn't he?

Pronunciation

1 Look at some words from Units 1–3. Say the words and add them to the table.

> ~~answer~~   ~~appointment~~   athletics   extremely
> friendship   mobile   ~~normally~~   often
> personal   really   remember   similar
> somebody   theatre   together

A: ■□	B: □■□	C: ■□□
answer	*appointment*	*normally*

2 Underline the stressed syllable in each word.

🔊 1.27 Listen, check and repeat.

Reading & Listening

1 Read about five young people who share a house talking about each other. Who is each person's favourite housemate?

Happy house

Pete 'I suppose the person in the house I get on best with is Ned. We have a lot in common. We like the same sort of music – we both play the guitar. We have the same sense of humour. We're the same age and we have the same friends. We've known each other for three years, but it feels like we've known each other all our lives. Ned's a good-looking guy, and women love him.'

Alicia 'I've lived in the house for four years. I get on well with everyone. Grace and I are good friends. Ned and Pete are really nice but they're like schoolboys. Pete thinks women love Ned, but it's just not true. Ned thinks he's really good-looking, but it's not true either. I think Leo is the greatest. He's so cool. He's my favourite, although I don't see much of him, because he's always away surfing or skydiving. He's an action man.'

Ned 'It's a great house. We're all friends. Pete and I are really good mates. We laugh about the same things. Leo's really funny, but you can't really have intelligent conversations with him. The girls, Alicia and Grace, are good fun. Alicia has lived here the longest. I think Alicia may be interested in me and secretly, she's my favourite. Pete likes Grace, but I don't think Grace feels romantic about Pete. I'm probably more Grace's type than Pete.'

Grace 'I love the house and I love the people who live in it. I've been here for nearly a year. Maybe because we're the only two girls in the house, I'm close to Alicia. I really like Leo, although he's hardly ever there. Ned and Pete are like kids. Ned thinks he's great, but the only one who agrees with that is Pete. Ned is big-headed, but Pete is so sweet. And he's generous, intelligent and sensitive. And don't tell anyone, but I think he's really good-looking. He's my real favourite.'

Leo 'I've lived in the house with the others for two years now. It's a cool house. We never fall out. I'm really happy there. Alicia is my favourite – she's like our mother.'

2 Read the article again and underline the correct words.

a) Pete and Ned have <u>similar</u> / different interests.
b) Pete thinks Ned is **confident / arrogant**, while Grace thinks Ned is **confident / arrogant**.
c) **Grace / Alicia** has lived in the house longer than anyone else.
d) Leo spends **the most / the least** time in the house.
e) Ned thinks Leo is **amusing / intelligent**.
f) Grace likes **Pete / Ned**.
g) Leo gets on best with **Grace / Alicia**.

3 ● 1.28 Listen to a conversation between Ned and Alicia. What is Ned's news?

4 Listen again. Are the statements true or false?

a) Alicia already knew about Ned's news.
b) Pete and Grace have liked each other for a long time.
c) Grace has a boyfriend called Dan.
d) Ned says he's interested in Grace.
e) Pete told Ned he was meeting Grace.
f) Alicia is interested in Ned.

Writing & Speaking

1 Read the email and match the descriptions (*a–f*) with the paragraphs (*1–6*).

a) Opening phrase
b) Signing off (+ your name)
c) Main message
d) Greeting (+ name) *Paragraph 1*
e) Extra information (often attachments)
f) Closing phrase

① Hi Leo,

② How's it going in Switzerland? Is there much snow in the mountains?

③ I've got some shocking news. Pete and Grace have got together. I didn't know about it until I saw them in town. I was walking down the High Street when I saw them in the Grand Café. They were holding hands across the table! When I asked Alicia later, she said they've liked each other for ages! I couldn't believe it. Did you know? I'm thinking of asking Alicia out. I'm sure she likes me. What do you think?

④ Anyway, see you next week.

⑤ All the best, Ned

⑥ PS I'm attaching a photo I took with my mobile of them (holding hands!).

2 In which paragraphs (*1–6*) in the email in Exercise 1 could you use the following words and phrases?

a) Best wishes, *5*
b) Dear Leo,
c) Hello!
d) How are things?
e) I can't wait to see you.
f) I hope everything's going well.
g) I'm really looking forward to hearing from you.
h) I'm sending you the latest photos.
i) Love,
j) Regards,
k) Speak to you soon.
l) Thanks for your email.

3 Imagine you are Leo. Write an email replying to Ned. Use some of the phrases from Exercise 1 and Exercise 2. Give Ned some advice about Alicia.

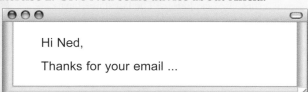

Hi Ned,

Thanks for your email ...

4 Work in pairs or small groups. Discuss the questions.

a) How often do you write emails?
b) How many emails do you send and receive in a day/week?
c) Are your emails mainly work-related or personal?
d) Do you ever receive unwanted emails?

5 Choose one of the emails below and write it.

a) Write an email to a friend.
   • You are replying to an email from your friend.
   • Thank them for their email.
   • You have some exciting news about another friend. Give details.
   • Send a photo with your email.

b) Write an email to a friend.
   • You went to dinner at your friend's house.
   • Thank your friend for the meal.
   • Make positive comments about the food.
   • Send some photos with the email.

▶ 1.29 **Song:** *You've Got a Friend.*

Party

Grammar Phrasal verbs. Future forms. Pronouns: *anybody*, *somebody*, etc.
Vocabulary Festivals. Collocations with *do* and *make*. Parties
Useful phrases Inviting; making excuses

Reading

Think of a festival you know or have heard about. How much do you know about it?

a)   What is the name of the festival?
b)   When does it take place?
c)   How long does it go on for?

d)   What do you know about its history?
e)   How do people celebrate?
f)   How does the festival end?

Read this article about a big Spanish festival and find answers to the questions above.

Las Fallas

It's March, and I'm in Valencia, Spain's third largest city, with my new friend, José. It's one o'clock in the morning. All around us, fireworks are going off and the streets are full of noisy people. 'Welcome to Las Fallas,' José smiles. 'You're going to see that Valencians really know how to put on a
5   good party!' Seven hours later, I understood what he meant.

Las Fallas, Valencia's famous festival, takes place every March and goes on for a week. It takes a whole year to organise, and everybody joins in the preparations. The city is alive and buzzing all week, but, like all good parties, it is at night when people really get down to some serious celebrating.
10   The tradition of Las Fallas began in the eighteenth century. At that time, craftsmen used wooden candelabra to light up their workshops. To celebrate the end of winter, they burnt their candelabra on bonfires, and had a party. Later they made the candelabra into lifelike statues, and then dressed them up to look like well-known but unpopular local characters.
15   Nowadays the lifelike statues are made of cardboard. Some of them are over thirty metres high and are worth 200,000 euros, but they all go up in flames before the end of the festival.

The Valencians like their guests to enjoy themselves, but after only one hour's sleep it's difficult to keep up with them. Nobody's allowed to sleep
20   during Las Fallas! A brass band passes through the streets in the morning and wakes everybody up.

For many of the locals, the highlight of the festival is the flower parade. A procession of 200,000 girls and boys, wearing traditional dress, march into the city centre, bringing flowers to decorate the statue of the Virgin Mary.
25   The festival reaches its climax on 19th March, a public holiday and St Joseph's Day. This is the night when the cardboard statues are burnt. Everybody looks forward to midnight. Firecrackers go off every second or two, and midnight passes in a shower of explosions. The last statue burns down, and the party is over. Well, almost … the bars fill up and people carry
30   on eating and drinking until the early hours of the morning. I have no idea how they keep it up! So I say goodbye to José, as he heads for the next bar. It will take me weeks to get over it, but I've had the time of my life.

Vocabulary

1 Complete this description of Las Fallas with the words in the box.

> bonfires ~~festival~~ firecrackers fireworks parade procession statues traditional dress

Las Fallas takes place in March and goes on for a week. The main feature of the (1) *festival* is the enormous lifelike (2) _____ which are burnt in huge (3) _____ on the last day. The incredibly loud (4) _____ that go off every lunchtime in the city centre make Las Fallas the noisiest festival in the world. There is also a spectacular display of (5) _____ in the park at midnight. One of the highlights of the festival is the (6) _____ of girls and boys in (7) _____ . They (8) _____ through the city centre, bringing flowers for the Virgin Mary.

2 Write a short summary of a festival you know about. Read your summary to a partner.

Vocabulary & Grammar

Phrasal verbs

Intransitive (no object)
**go off   come back
stay in**

Transitive (takes an object)
a) Separable:
put sth **on   take** sth **off
wear** sth **out**

b) Not separable:
get over sth   **head for** sth
look into sth

1 The nine phrasal verbs in the table are from the article on page 32. Find them in the text and match each one to a word or phrase in the box with the same meaning.

Intransitive	Transitive	
	Separable	**Not separable**
go off	put something on	get down to something
join in	dress something up	look forward to something
burn down	keep something up	get over something

> anticipate excitedly   continue at the same speed   destroy with fire ~~explode~~ organise   participate   put special clothes on   recover   start

go off = explode

2 Which of these sentences is grammatically incorrect? Cross it out.
a) You can **look** the word **up** in a dictionary.
b) You can **look** it **up** in a dictionary.
c) You can **look up** the word in a dictionary.
d) You can **look up** it in a dictionary.

Complete the rule with *always, sometimes* or *never*.

When the object of a separable phrasal verb is a pronoun (*me, you, it,* etc.), it _____ comes between the verb (*look*) and the particle (*up*).

3 Put the words in brackets in the correct order to make phrasal verb sentences with pronouns.
a) I hate clearing up the mess after I've had a party. (I hate / it / clearing / up)
   I hate clearing it up.
b) When my boss has a party, I look after her children. (I / after / look / them)
c) I usually try on several outfits before I go to a party. (I / try / on / them)
d) I always want to turn the music down at parties. (I / want to / down / turn / it)
e) It's difficult to come up with ideas for presents. (It's difficult to / them / with / come up)
f) I'm looking forward to my next birthday party. (I'm / to / looking forward / it)

4   **Pairwork** **Student A:** page 117 **Student B:** page 122

Listening

1   Think about last New Year's Eve. Work with a partner and ask and answer these questions.

   a) Where were you?   b) Who were you with?   c) What did you do?

2   What do you know about Chinese New Year? Decide whether you think the statements below are true or false.

   a)   New Year takes place *in early January*.
   b)   Just before New Year, people *clean their houses to sweep away bad luck*.
   c)   Some people also *put up red decorations to frighten away bad luck*.
   d)   The traditional New Year's Eve dinner is *Peking duck*.
   e)   People usually spend New Year's Eve with *their friends*.
   f)   On New Year's Eve people *stay in and watch television*.
   g)   At midnight on New Year's Eve people *set off fireworks and firecrackers*.

   🌐 1.30 Listen to Hua and check your ideas. Correct the statements that are false.

3   Work with a partner. Rewrite the statements in Exercise 2 with information about New Year's Eve celebrations in your country.

Vocabulary

1   Underline the correct verbs in the following extract from the interview about Chinese New Year.
   'I'm going to help my mother to (1) **do** / **make** the housework. We're going to sweep away all the bad luck and (2) **do** / **make** room for good luck to come in.'

2   Complete the questions with the correct form of *do* or *make*.

   a)   Do you always _____ New Year's resolutions?
   b)   Who usually _____ the cooking in your house?
   c)   Have you ever _____ a promise that you haven't kept?
   d)   Are you _____ any type of training course at the moment?
   e)   When was the last time you _____ a wish? Did it come true?
   f)   When you _____ the shopping do you usually _____ a list first?

   Ask your partner the questions.

3   Work with a partner. Decide whether the nouns in the box collocate with *do* or *make*. Use your dictionary if necessary.

   > a comment   a decision   a degree   a job   a mistake   a noise   a profit
   > a suggestion   an excuse   arrangements   money   progress   some decorating
   > some exercise   some research   some skiing   something clear   sure
   > the ironing   your homework

   Choose six collocations and write an example sentence that is true for you for each one.

   I haven't made any arrangements for New Year's Eve yet.

Grammar

Future forms

'Have you got any plans for the weekend?'

A spontaneous decision:
will
'No, I haven't. I think **I'll call** Jan and see if she's free.'

An intention:
(*be*) *going to*
'Not yet. **I'm going to call** Jan and see if she's free.'

An arrangement:
present continuous
'Yes, I have. **I'm having lunch** with Jan on Saturday.'

1 🔲 1.31 **Read and listen to Part 1 of a conversation between two flatmates. Why is Sandy unhappy?**

Zoë: Hi!
Sandy: Oh, hello.
Zoë: You don't look very happy. Has something happened at work?
Sandy: No, work's fine. David hasn't rung, and we're supposed to be going to a party tonight. What are you doing tonight? Do you fancy coming to the party with me?
Zoë: I'd love to, but (1) Steve's coming round , and (2) we're going to plan our summer holiday.
Sandy: Oh, well, what am I going to do? ... I know – (3) I'll phone James .

2 **Three different ways of talking about the future are highlighted in the conversation. Which form is used to talk about ...**

a)   a spontaneous decision (you speak at the moment you decide to do something)?
b)   an intention (you speak after you have already decided to do something)?
c)   an arrangement (you speak after you have already arranged to do something)?

3 **Read Part 2. Underline the most appropriate future form.**

James: Hello.
Sandy: Hi, James, it's Sandy. What (1) **will you do** / <u>**are you doing**</u> tonight?
James: Nothing! Well actually, (2) **I'll meet** / **I'm meeting** Alex and Suzy in town, but ...
Sandy: Do you fancy coming to a party? Alex and Suzy can come too.
James: Yes, that sounds great. (3) **I'm meeting** / **I'll meet** them at the Star Bar at 8.30.
Sandy: OK, (4) **I'll see** / **I'm going to see** you there. Bye. ... (*Puts the phone down.*)
         (5) **I'll go** / **I'm going** to the party with James.
Zoë: Good idea.
Sandy: And next time I see David (6) **I'm telling** / **I'm going to tell** him the relationship is definitely over.
Zoë: Hmm. (7) **I'll believe** / **I'm believing** that when I see it.

🔲 1.32 **Listen and check.**

▲ James

4 **Complete Part 3 by putting the verb in the most appropriate future form.**

Zoë: Hello.
David: Is Sandy there, please?
Zoë: Yes, hold on a moment – I (1 get) _____ her for you. ... It's David.
Sandy: Oh, hello, David.
David: Look, I'm really sorry I didn't call earlier, but I'm still at the office and ...
Sandy: Oh, that's all right – I forgot you were going to ring anyway.
David: Listen, I'm afraid I can't come to the party, I (2 have) _____ dinner with some important clients.
Sandy: It doesn't matter – I (3 go) _____ to the party with someone else.
David: Oh, right. OK, well I (4 call) _____ you.
Sandy: When? I mean, all right. Goodbye.
David: Bye.
Zoë: So?
Sandy: Well, he apologised – and he (5 have) _____ dinner with an important client. Anyway, I must go. See you later.

🔲 1.33 **Listen and check.**

▲ David

5 🔲 1.34 **Listen to Part 4. Is there a future for Sandy and David?**

6   Grammar *Extra* 4 page 132. Read the explanations and do the exercises.

Speaking & Reading

1 Work with a partner. Discuss when and why people have the following types of party.

- a housewarming party
- an 18th birthday party
- an office party
- a farewell/leaving party
- a surprise party
- a fancy dress party

What other types of party can you think of?

2 What do you think makes a good party? Write a list and agree on the three most important 'ingredients'.

Read the article and find out how many of your ideas are mentioned. Do you agree with the other ideas?

How to throw the best party ever (and enjoy it!)

A theme Fancy dress can be a great ice-breaker, but only if everybody dresses up. So if you want your guests to dress up, make it clear when you send invitations. Nobody wants to be the one dressed as a gorilla, if everyone else is in their most glamorous party clothes.

Create a good atmosphere If you're having the party at home, you need to push back the furniture and change a few light bulbs. Soft lighting is important to get people in the mood – and it makes them look better too. Balloons, candles and fairy lights all add to the party atmosphere.

The right people Invite more people than you want at the party, and make sure you invite some party animals to get the dancing started and some good mixers who'll mingle with the guests. Try to avoid inviting ex-partners or people who dislike each other for other reasons.

A warm welcome When your guests arrive at your door, a warm welcome will make them feel special. They'll also need somewhere to put their coats.

More than enough good food and drink There's nothing worse than running out of food or drink. And don't forget to stock up on the chopped carrots to keep the vegetarians happy.

Music First, you'll need somewhere to dance. So make sure that sofa is out of the way. Next, you'll need a good variety of music – something for everyone. You may be into old hardcore acid house techno rave music, and it's your party so you can do what you like, but you may find that nobody else is dancing.

Games Are you over twelve? So stop it.

Three golden rules

1 **Delegate!** You can't do everything. You'll need four helpers: someone to meet and greet the guests; someone to take care of the bar; someone to take care of the food; and someone to do the music.

2 **Don't worry about the mess!** It's no fun for party guests to see the host running around holding a dustpan and brush.

3 **Enjoy yourself!**

Vocabulary

1 Find words or phrases from the article above to complete the descriptions.

a) You can ask people to dress up in *fancy* dress for your party.
b) You are a g_____ when you go to a party.
c) You receive an i_____ from somebody who wants you to go to their party.
d) You try to create a good a_____ to get people in the mood for your party.
e) You m_____ so that you can talk to as many people as possible at a party.
f) You should g_____ your guests with a warm welcome when they arrive at your party.
g) You are the h_____ when you throw a party.
h) You can use a d_____ and brush to clear up the mess after a party.

2 Have you ever thrown a party? What was it like? Tell your partner.

Grammar

anybody, somebody, etc.

Somebody is coming.
I can't hear **anything**.
I've looked **everywhere**.
No one cares.

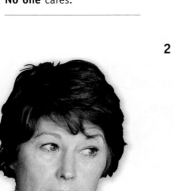

1 Complete the table.

People	everybody everyone	(1) *somebody* (2) _____	(4) _____ (5) _____	(7) _____ no one
Things	everything	something	(6) _____	(8) _____
Places	everywhere	(3) _____	anywhere	(9) _____

2 Underline the correct pronoun to complete the conversation.

Mum: Is that you, Dylan? You're late. Where have you been?
Dylan: (1) **Nowhere.** / **Anywhere.**
Mum: But you're an hour late!
Dylan: OK, I went to the park.
Mum: Who with?
Dylan: (2) **Anyone.** / **No one.** I went on my own.
Mum: Where's Sophie?
Dylan: I don't know. (3) **Somewhere** / **Nowhere** in town.
Mum: What's happened?
Dylan: (4) **Nothing!** / **Anything!** Stop asking questions.
Mum: What do you want for dinner tonight?
Dylan: (5) **Anything.** / **Everything.** I don't care.
Mum: We could try that new Chinese restaurant –
   (6) **everyone** / **someone** says it's great.
Dylan: OK.
Mum: Good. Now, what did you do at school today?

🌐 **1.35** Listen and check. Do you know anybody like Dylan?

Pronunciation

1 🌐 **1.36** Listen and repeat the lyrics from different pop songs.

a) We're gonna have a party.
b) Do you wanna dance?
c) I wanna be your man.
d) Just do what you gotta do.
e) Gotta get over you.
f) Ain't never gonna fall in love again.

2 Rewrite the pop lyrics in Exercise 1 in full sentences.

Speaking: anecdote

◀ Paul – before the party

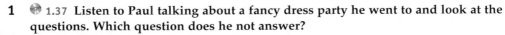

1 🌐 **1.37** Listen to Paul talking about a fancy dress party he went to and look at the questions. Which question does he not answer?

a) Whose party was it?
b) Why did she have a party?
c) What sort of party was it?
d) Was there a theme?
e) Where was the party?
f) How many people were there?
g) How many people did you know?
h) What did you eat and drink?
i) What was the music like?
j) Did you dance?
k) Did you stay until the end?

1 It was a fancy dress party.
2 At least seventy.
3 At Maggie's house.
4 Everybody dressed up as something beginning with *M*.
5 It was fantastic.
6 My friend Maggie's.
7 Not everybody.
8 Because she was moving abroad.
9 Thai food and Thai beer.
10 Yes, a lot.

Match the questions with the answers (*1–10*). Listen again and check.

2 You are going to tell your partner about a party you've been to.
• Ask yourself the questions in Exercise 1.
• Think about *what* to say and *how* to say it.
• Tell your partner about the party.

▲ Paul – in fancy dress

Useful phrases

1 🔘 **1.38 Read and listen to Rose speaking to four friends. Which friend doesn't she know very well?**

a)

Rose:	Do you fancy coming to the cinema tonight?
Ian:	Yes, good idea. What are you going to see?
Rose:	The new James Bond film.
Ian:	Oh no, I've seen it.
Rose:	Oh, what a shame. Is it any good?
Ian:	No, it's terrible.

b)

Rose:	Would you like to come to the cinema tonight?
Lucy:	I'd love to but I'm working tonight.
Rose:	Oh, what a shame.
Lucy:	I know. What are you going to see?
Rose:	The new Bond film.
Lucy:	Oh, I've heard it's really good – the best one so far.

c)

Rose:	Are you doing anything tonight?
Megan:	No, why?
Rose:	I'm going to see the new Bond film. Do you fancy coming?
Megan:	No, I'm afraid I can't. I have to get up really early tomorrow. Why don't you ask Alan?
Rose:	Alan? No, I can't. I don't know him well enough.
Megan:	Don't be silly. He'd be really pleased.

d)

Rose:	Oh, hi Alan. It's Rose.
Alan:	Hi Rose. How are you?
Rose:	Very well, thanks. I was wondering if you'd like to go to the cinema tonight.
Alan:	Yes, that sounds great. What's on?
Rose:	Well, I was thinking of seeing the new James Bond film.
Alan:	Great. What time do you want to meet?

2 Read the conversations again. Look at the highlighted useful phrases. Find:

a) three ways of inviting somebody to do something.
b) two ways of accepting an invitation.
c) two ways of refusing an invitation.
d) one way of asking somebody if they are free to go out.
e) one way of sounding disappointed.

🔘 **1.39 Listen, check and repeat the useful phrases.**

3 Work with a partner. Practise the conversations in Exercise 1.

4 Work with a partner. Write a conversation based on the situation below.

- **Student A**: You want to meet up with Student B and go somewhere. Make at least three suggestions.
- **Student B**: You don't want to go anywhere with Student A. Make excuses.

Practise your conversation. Take it in turns to be Student A and Student B.

Vocabulary *Extra*

Phrasal verbs

1 Work with a partner. Decide which particle in each list does *not* go with *take* to form a phrasal verb. Cross it out.

a) about   after   in   on   up

b) apart   at   down   off   out

c) back   over   through   to   without

Check in the dictionary entry. Tick the phrasal verbs you know.

2 Complete the table with the dictionary entry for each phrasal verb in the box.

> I don't **take after** my mum.   Sorry, I **take** it **back**.
> The plane is **taking off**.   Why did you **take** him **on**?
> He **took to** them immediately.   We've **taken** it **up**.

Intransitive	Transitive (separable)	Transitive (not separable)
		take after sb

Where does the dictionary put the object (*sb/sth*) when the phrasal verb is: a) separable; b) not separable?

3 Many phrasal verbs have both literal and idiomatic meanings. Underline the idiomatic meanings of these phrasal verbs.

a) take back: **return sth you have bought / admit that you said sth wrong**

b) take down: **write sth / dismantle a structure**

c) take in: **understand and remember sth / allow sb to stay in your house**

d) take off: **remove clothing, etc. / aircraft: start flying**

e) take out: **get sth official from a bank, etc / remove sth from a pocket, etc.**

f) take up: **fill space or time / start doing sth new**

Check your ideas in the dictionary extract.

4 Complete the sentences with phrasal verbs from Exercise 3.

a) I'm a nervous flyer: I don't mind *taking off* but I hate landing.

b) I usually _____ travel insurance when I go abroad.

c) I'm going to _____ jogging one of these days.

d) When I realise that I'm wrong about something, I always _____ it _____ .

e) I find that explanations in English are sometimes difficult to _____ .

f) If I don't _____ some notes in class, I can never remember what the lesson is about.

Are any of the sentences true for you?

5 Look at the sentences. Decide which alternative is not possible in each case. Cross it out.

a) People say I take after my **mother / father / dog**.

b) My **career / business / car** never really took off.

c) I've never taken out a **rent / mortgage / bank loan**.

d) Recently, I've taken to **wearing a suit / walking to work / having a baby**.

e) I'd like to take up **swimming / sleeping / yoga**.

6 Check your own dictionary. What example sentences does it give for the phrasal verbs in Exercise 5?

PHRASAL VERBS ,take ,after sb to look or behave like an older relative

,take sth a'part to separate an object into its pieces: *Ben was taking apart an old bicycle.*

,take sth 'back 1 to take something that you have bought back to the shop because it is broken or not suitable 2 to admit that something that you said was wrong: *I'm sorry – I take it back.*

,take sth 'down 1 to separate a large structure into its pieces 2 to write information on a piece of paper: *The police took down our addresses and phone numbers.*

,take sb 'in 1 to allow someone to stay in your house or your country 2 **be taken in** to be tricked so that you believe something that is not true

,take sth 'in 1 to understand and remember something that you hear or read: *I'm not sure how much of his explanation she took in.* 2 to make a piece of clothing more narrow or more tight, so that it fits you

,take 'off 1 if an aircraft takes off, it leaves the ground and starts to fly ≠ LAND 2 to become successful or popular very fast: *Her business has really taken off.* 3 *informal* to leave a place suddenly

,take sth 'off 1 to remove a piece of clothing from your body ≠ PUT STH ON 2 to spend a particular amount of time away from work: *I'm taking Monday off to go to London.*

,take 'on sth to develop a particular character or appearance: *Our website is taking on a new look.*

,take sb 'on 1 to start to employ someone 2 to fight or compete against someone

,take sth 'on to accept some work or responsibility

,take sb 'out to take someone to a place such as a cinema or a restaurant and pay for them: *She's taking her parents out for dinner.*

,take sth 'out 1 to remove something from a place: *Henry took out his wallet.* 2 to get something officially: *When you take out insurance, read the small print.*

,take sth 'out on sb to treat someone badly because you are angry, upset, or tired, although it is not their fault

,take (sth) 'over to begin to do something that someone else was doing: *Jane took over as director after Richard retired.*

,take sth 'over to take control of something, especially another company

,take sb 'through sth to explain something to someone in detail

'take to sth to start doing something as a habit: *Recently he's taken to wearing a cap.*

'take to sb/sth to begin to like someone or something: *I took to John immediately.*

,take 'up sth to fill a particular amount of space or time: *These files take up a lot of disk space.*

,take sth 'up to start doing something regularly as a habit, job, or interest: *Chris has taken up jogging.* ♦ *The new teacher will take up her post in May.*

,take sb 'up on sth to accept an offer or invitation that someone has made: *I've decided to take you up on that job offer.*

,take sth 'up with sb to complain to someone about a problem

---

5 Edible

Grammar Countable and uncountable nouns. Quantity expressions. *used to / would*
Vocabulary Partitives. Food. Taste and texture
Useful phrases At a restaurant: register

Reading & Speaking

1 Read through the questions below and guess how your partner would answer.

Are you a chocolate addict?

1 Do you think about chocolate several times a day?
2 Do you usually eat some chocolate before midday?
3 In a café, when your friends order coffee, do you usually order a hot chocolate?
4 Is chocolate your favourite ice cream flavour?
5 Do you have a favourite bar of chocolate, for example: Mars, Kit Kat, etc.
6 Can you name more than ten types of chocolate bar?
7 Do you find it painful to share your chocolate with other people?
8 Do you eat at least six pieces of chocolate per day?

If you answered yes to at least three of the questions, you're probably a chocoholic.

Compare your answers. Who is the bigger chocoholic?
Could you live without chocolate?

2 Decide whether the statements about chocolate are true or false.

Chocolate trivia
1 Chocolate is good for you.
2 White chocolate is not real chocolate.
3 Chocolate contains 'happy chemicals'.
4 Dark chocolate is healthier than milk chocolate.
5 A piece of chocolate is a good treat for a dog.
6 Americans are the world's biggest per capita chocolate consumers.
7 The average person will consume 10,000 chocolate bars in a lifetime.
8 A fifty gram bar of chocolate contains the same amount of caffeine as a cup of coffee.
9 American and Russian space flights have always had several bars of chocolate on board.
10 In Alfred Hitchcock's film, *Psycho*, chocolate syrup was used for blood in the famous shower scene.

🔊 2.01 Listen and check your answers.

3 Look at the first statement from *Chocolate trivia*. Replace *chocolate* with each word in the box to make new statements. Use plural forms if the words are countable.

Chocolate is good for you. → *Chips are good for you.*

chip crisp fish fruit milk salt sleep sugar travel vegetable vitamin work

Work with a partner. Discuss which statements you agree/disagree with.

Grammar

Nouns and quantity expressions

Nouns and quantity expressions

Countable nouns
Use: *none, not any, a few, several, some, many, a lot, lots, plenty*

Uncountable nouns
Use: *none, not any, a little, a bit, some, much, a lot, lots, plenty*

not enough = less than you need
too much/many = more than you need

1 **Complete the statements with either *Countable* or *Uncountable*.**

(1) _____ nouns have a singular and a plural form. You can use *a/an* and numbers with them. You use the plural form when you are talking in general.

an apple / apples ➔ *Apples are good for you.*

(2) _____ nouns have only one form. You <u>can't</u> use *a/an* or numbers with them. Most (but not all) have a singular form.

knowledge (NOT ~~a knowledge~~) ➔ *Knowledge is power.*

2 **The uncountable noun *chocolate* can also be countable (*a chocolate*). Which other nouns in the box can sometimes be countable depending on the context?**

> beer bread cake coffee meat
> money nature pasta rice salad
> whisky yoghurt

▲ chocolate

a chocolate ▶

3 **Complete the questions with *many* or *much*. Four answers are given to each question. Cross out the answer that is not possible.**

So far today …

a) how *many* friends have you texted?
   None / A couple / A little / Lots.

b) how _____ time have you spent online?
   None / Very little / Not enough / A lot of.

c) how _____ phone calls have you made?
   Very few / Two or three / Lots / So much.

d) how _____ coffees have you had?
   None / Several / Not enough / Too much.

e) how _____ money have you spent? **Not many / A bit / A lot / Far too much**.

f) how _____ work have you done? **None / Enough / Plenty / Lots of**.

Underline the answers that are true for you or write true answers of your own. Ask your partner the questions.

4 Grammar *Extra* 5 page 134. Read the explanations and do the exercises.

Vocabulary

1 **Match words from column *A* with words from column *B* to make common collocations.**

A	B
a) a bar of	1 bananas / flowers
b) a bowl of	2 chocolate / soap
c) a box of	3 cigarettes / crisps
d) a bunch of	4 honey / instant coffee
e) a jar of	5 chocolates / matches
f) a packet of	6 fruit / sugar

2 **Work with a partner. Add the words in the box to column *B* to make more collocations.**

> biscuits cereal grapes keys marmalade raspberry jam rice seeds
> soup spaghetti tea tissues tools

Tell your partner how often you buy, consume or use these items.

Speaking

1 Add the names of different people in the class. Try to make true sentences.

a) _____ is a vegetarian.
b) _____ is a good cook.
c) _____ always has a big breakfast.
d) _____ drinks a lot of coffee.

e) _____ doesn't like fish.
f) _____ always has lunch in the same place.
g) _____ often eats fast food.
h) _____ usually has wine with dinner.

2 Ask questions to check your ideas.

'Veronica, are you a vegetarian?'

Vocabulary & Pronunciation

1 Look at the photograph. How many items of food can you name?

2 Look at the lists. What types of food do the colours represent?

a) veal cod limes trout beans tuna
b) leeks plums hake figs prawns peaches
c) turkey olives mussels melons mushrooms sardines
d) garlic cherries lobster onions grapefruits courgettes
e) peppers bacon salmon spinach mangoes cauliflower
f) sausages lettuces cabbages oranges radishes potatoes
g) aubergines strawberries cucumbers celery raspberries tomatoes

🔊 2.02 **Listen, repeat and mark the stressed syllable. What is different about the last word in each row?**

3 Complete the questions with the most appropriate contrasting word from the box.

~~cooked~~ draught /drɑːft/ frozen heavy mild sweet weak white

a) Raw or *cooked* vegetables?
b) Light meals or _____ meals?
c) Red meat or _____ meat?
d) Fresh fish or _____ fish?

e) Strong coffee or _____ coffee?
f) Strong cheese or _____ cheese?
g) Bottled beer or _____ beer?
h) Dry wine or _____ wine?

Ask the questions and find out your partner's preferences.

Listening

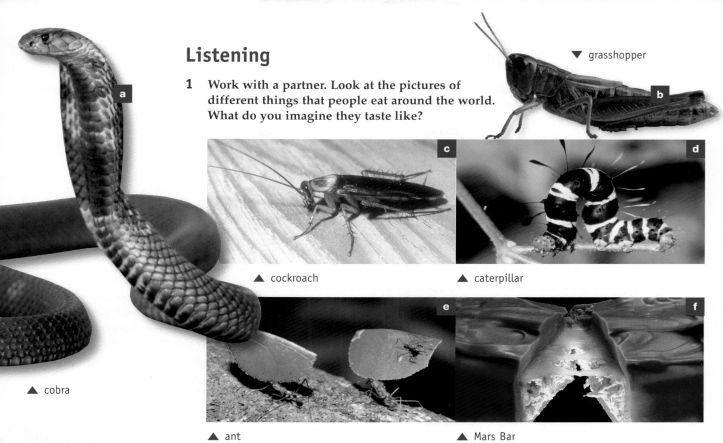

▼ grasshopper

▲ cobra

▲ cockroach

▲ caterpillar

▲ ant

▲ Mars Bar

1 Work with a partner. Look at the pictures of different things that people eat around the world. What do you imagine they taste like?

2 🌐 2.03 Listen to an interview with somebody who has tried all these things. Match each dish (*a–f*) with the adjectives (*1–6*) he uses to describe them.

a) baked cobra in China
b) fried grasshoppers in Thailand
c) roasted cockroaches in Indonesia
d) boiled and sundried caterpillars in Africa
e) roasted chocolate ants in Colombia
f) deep-fried Mars Bar in Scotland

1 dry, bland
2 crunchy, sweet, fruity
3 greasy, sweet, disgusting
4 crisp, tasty
5 meaty, tough, chewy, delicious
6 sweet, crisp

3 Have you tried any of the dishes he talks about? Would you like to? What is the most unusual thing you have ever eaten? Tell your partner.

Vocabulary & Speaking

1 Add words to the table from Listening Exercise 2.

Ways of cooking food	Ways of describing taste	Ways of describing texture
boil	bitter	creamy
grill	salty	*dry*
bake	spicy	
	bland	

2 Work with a partner. Take it in turns to describe one of the items of food in the box for your partner to guess what it is.

> apples   crème caramel   curry   dark chocolate   English food   biscuits
> fresh bread   fried eggs   meat which is over-cooked   milk chocolate   pizza
> plain white rice   raw carrots   salted peanuts   seafood   strong coffee
> tinned anchovies   your mother's cooking

'It's crunchy on the outside and chewy on the inside.' 'Fresh bread?' 'Yes, that's right.'
'They're crunchy and salty' 'Apples?' 'No, apples aren't salty.' 'Peanuts'?' 'That's right.'

3 What are the best and worst meals you've ever had? Describe them to your partner.

Reading

1 Read the article. What was Emma Bunton's favourite food as a child? What food didn't she like?

Memories of food

Both my mum and dad were great cooks when I was growing up. Well, my dad was. My mum would try, bless her. As a family, we always used to try new things and experiment with food. I remember being in Spain when I was about six, and all the kids wanted burgers and chips, and I remember digging into prawns and
5 garlic. I've always loved trying new foods. The only things I really dislike are peas. And my mum still gives them to me!

Restaurants were always a real treat when I was growing up. My brother and I would share food because we couldn't really afford to splurge, and so now when I go out to eat I treat it as a luxury and I feel lucky. My favourite food was the sort
10 of thing that I remember having a lot when I was younger – the classics that my dad used to cook: shepherd's pie, roast dinners and spaghetti bolognese. He used to make a shepherd's pie to die for, with a tiny layer of cheese and a bit of tomato.

When I was growing up, we always used to eat around a table, except for Saturday night, which was a tray dinner in front of the TV as a treat. I think that's
15 why I enjoy food, because meals were, and still are, a family event. We used to go to my nan's on Sunday – she used to make these lovely cherry pies. Now on Sundays I go to my dad's house. I think of him sitting at the table on a Sunday when I was little, and he would eat half and then leave the rest for later.

20 I think a happy childhood gives you a balanced view of food and of yourself. I eat what I fancy and I feel good about it. I feel lucky that I escaped all the size zero nonsense when I was younger. I've had times with the press, especially during the Spice Girl days, when they've
25 called me fat. Of course it does hurt, but having a great family and having normal, non-famous people around me keeps me grounded.

Emma Bunton: 'Baby Spice' ▶

Glossary
digging into: eating enthusiastically
treat noun [C]: something that gives special pleasure
splurge verb [I]: spend a lot of money
shepherd's pie noun [C or U]: English dish made from minced meat covered with mashed potato
to die for *informal*: so good that you really want it
nan's: grandmother's (house)
size zero: extremely thin. It refers to the US clothing size (a European 32-34).
keeps me grounded: helps me to remember what's important in life

2 Look at the following statements about Emma's childhood. Are they true or false?

a) Emma's mother was a better cook than her father.
b) Her family enjoyed eating new things.
c) She went to Spain when she was about six.
d) Her mother still cooks peas for her.
e) She often went to restaurants with her family.
f) In restaurants Emma and her brother always had one plate between them.
g) Her father often made shepherd's pie.
h) Her family ate around a table every night.
i) She had lunch at her grandmother's house on Sundays.
j) She eats whatever she wants these days.

3 Rewrite the sentences in Exercise 2 in the first person. Change the information so that the sentences are true for you.

a) *My mother was a better cook than my father.*

Grammar

used to / would

used to: for repeated actions or states in the past
He **used to be** very thin.
He **didn't use to eat** much.
Did he **use to go** running?
Yes, he **did**.
No, he **didn't**.

would ('d): for repeated actions in the past
I'd walk to school every morning.

1 Work with a partner. Look again at the statements (*a–j*) in Exercise 2 on page 44. Number each statement *1, 2, 3* or *4* according to the descriptions in this table.

a) 2   b) 1   c) ...

Description	Alternative verb structures
1 Describes a repeated action in the past	*used to* + verb or *would ('d)* + verb
2 Describes a state in the past	*used to* + verb
3 Describes a single action in the past	None
4 Describes an action or state in the present	None

2 Look at the sentences (*a–j*) below about childhood and answer the questions.

1 In which sentences can you replace the underlined verb with *used to* + verb?
2 In which sentences can you replace the underlined verb with *would ('d)* + verb?

When I was a child ...

a) I <u>cycled</u> to school every morning.
b) I <u>played</u> football after school every day.
c) I <u>went</u> on a school trip to Egypt.
d) I <u>was</u> afraid of the dark.
e) I <u>didn't believe</u> in ghosts.
f) My mother <u>did</u> all the cooking.
g) I <u>didn't like</u> vegetables.
h) I <u>broke</u> my leg on a skiing holiday.
i) I <u>started</u> learning the piano.
j) I <u>went</u> to church every Sunday.

Are the sentences true for you? Rewrite all the sentences so they are true for you. Use *used to* + verb or *would ('d)* + verb where possible.

3   Pairwork **Student A:** page 117   **Student B:** page 122

Speaking: anecdote

1   2.04 Listen to Julio from Brazil talking about his life when he was a child between the ages of five and ten. Which two questions does he not answer?

a) How many people were in your family?
b) Who used to do most of the cooking?
c) Did you use to help in the kitchen?
d) Were there some things you didn't use to like eating?
e) What time did you use to have lunch?
f) Where did you use to have lunch?
g) What time did you use to have dinner?
h) Which room did you use to eat dinner in?
i) Did your family use to eat in restaurants much?
j) What did you use to eat on Sundays?
k) What was your favourite dish when you were a child?

1 At seven o'clock.
2 Five.
3 In the kitchen.
4 My mother.
5 Pasta.
6 Rice and beans.
7 Yes, I used to chop the vegetables.
8 Yes, meat.
9 Yes, every Saturday.

Match the questions with the answers (*1–9*). Listen again and check.

2 You are going to tell your partner about your life when you were a child between the ages of five and ten.

• Ask yourself the questions in Exercise 1.
• Think about *what* to say and *how* to say it.
• Tell your partner about your life when you were a child.

Useful phrases

1 🔘 2.05 Listen to a conversation in a restaurant. Match the conversation to picture *a* or picture *b*.

2 🔘 2.06 Listen to another version of the conversation. What differences do you notice?

3 🔘 2.07 Listen and repeat the useful phrases from the conversation.

a) Excuse me. We're ready to order now.
b) Can we have two coffees and the bill, please?
c) Yes, a table for two in the name of Brown.
d) Yes, two gin and tonics, please.
e) I'll have the grilled salmon steak.
f) Do you have anything near the window?
g) No, I'm all right, thank you.
h) I'll have the lamb, please.
i) It was lovely, thank you.
j) Not quite. Could you give us a few more minutes?

4 Complete the restaurant conversation with the useful phrases from Exercise 3.

Waiter: Good afternoon. Do you have a reservation?
Man: (1) *Yes, a table for two in the name of Brown.*
Waiter: Oh yes. Is this table OK for you?
Man: (2) _____ .
Waiter: Yes, of course, follow me.

Waiter: Are you ready to order yet?
Woman: (3) _____ ?
Waiter: Of course. Would you like to order some drinks?
Woman: (4) _____ .

Woman: (5) _____ .
Waiter: Very good. What can I get you?
Woman: (6) _____ .
Waiter: OK. And sir?
Man: (7) _____ .

Waiter: Would you like to see the dessert menu?
Woman: (8) _____ .
Man: (9) _____ .
Waiter: Certainly. How was your meal?
Woman: (10) _____ .

Listen again to the full conversation and check your answers. Practise the conversation with a partner.

Vocabulary *Extra*

Nouns and articles

1 The table shows how articles combine with different types of noun. Complete the first column with the correct noun type from the box.

> Countable nouns   Plural nouns   Uncountable nouns

Noun type	Singular			Plural	
	no article	with *a/an*	with *the*	no article	with *the*
a) _____	book	a book	the book	books	the books
b) _____	advice	✗ ✗ ✗	the advice	✗ ✗ ✗	✗ ✗ ✗
c) _____	✗ ✗ ✗	✗ ✗ ✗	✗ ✗ ✗	jeans	the jeans

Copy the table and add the nine nouns (*behaviour – trousers*) in the dictionary extracts. There are three examples for each type of noun.

2 Check your own dictionary. How does it show you whether a noun is countable, uncountable or plural? Look up the nouns in the box. What do they all have in common?

> equipment   happiness   health   luck   luggage   money   news   weather

3 Read the dictionary entry for *the* and classify the five examples given under the following headings.

The person or thing has already been mentioned	The person or thing is known about	The person or thing is 'the only one'
	Have you locked the door?	

4 Complete this Edward Lear poem by asking yourself the questions about each noun. If you know the answer, put *the*. If you don't know the answer, put *a*.

> There was (1) *a* **young lady** from Niger   – Which young lady?
> Who smiled as she rode on (2) ___ **tiger**.   – Which tiger?
> They came back from (3) ___ **ride**   – Which ride?
> With (4) ___ **lady** inside   – Which lady?
> And (5) ___ **smile** on (6) ___ **face** of   – Which smile? Which face?
> (7) ___ **tiger**.   – Which tiger?!

5 Read the dictionary note about the use of *the* to refer to things or people in a general way. Cross out *the* if it is incorrect in these generalisations.

a) ~~The~~ men are better drivers than ~~the~~ women.
b) The life gets harder as you get older.
c) The time is more important than the money.
d) The women are more careful with money than the men.
e) The children are getting fatter: they don't do enough exercise.
f) It's impossible to live without the music.

Do you agree or disagree with the generalisations? Discuss with a partner.

---

behaviour /bɪˈheɪvjə/ noun [U] ★★★

child /tʃaɪld/ (plural **children**) noun [C] ★★★

clothes /kləʊðz/ noun [plural] ★★★

index /ˈɪndeks/ (plural indexes or indices) noun [C] ★★

knowledge /ˈnɒlɪdʒ/ noun [U] ★★★

research /rɪˈsɜːtʃ/ noun [U] ★★

scissors /ˈsɪzəz/ noun [plural]

sheep /ʃiːp/ (plural **sheep**) noun [C] ★★

trousers /ˈtraʊzəz/ noun [plural] ★★

The is used as the **definite article** before a noun.

1 talking about sb/sth when you know who or which used before a noun when that person or thing has already been mentioned or is known about, or when there is only one: *Have you locked the door?* ♦ *I have to look after the children.* ♦ *She brought me some cake and coffee, but the cake was stale.* ♦ *The sun was hidden behind a cloud.* ♦ *the best hotel in Paris*

DO NOT use **the** when you are referring to things or people in a general way: *Children need love and attention.*

6

Time

Grammar Prepositions of time. Modals of obligation and permission
Vocabulary Time expressions. Phrasal verbs. Work
Useful phrases Time idioms and expressions

Speaking & Reading

1 What do these expressions mean to you? Are there similar ones in your language?

a) 'The early bird catches the worm.'
b) 'There's no time like the present.'
c) 'Better late than never.'

2 Read and complete the questionnaire. Compare your answers with a partner.

TEST YOUR
attitude to time-keeping

1 You've arranged to meet a friend in the centre of town. How long do you wait if your friend is late?
a) Five minutes.
b) Fifteen minutes.
c) Half an hour or more.

2 You have to do a job that's difficult or unpleasant.
a) You do it straight away so that you can forget about it.
b) You do it after you've tidied your desk and organised your CDs in alphabetical order.
c) You leave it until the last minute because you need to feel the adrenalin rush produced by stress.

3 You have to catch a train or plane.
a) You arrive early and have to kill time at the station/airport.
b) You get there just in time.
c) You don't get there in time and miss the train/plane, etc.

4 Which is the time of day when you work most effectively?
a) Early in the morning.
b) Any time during the day.
c) Late at night.

5 During your holidays, ...
a) you continue to get up early – you want to make the most of every day.
b) you allow yourself to get up later and go to bed later than usual.
c) you take your watch off and try to forget what day it is.

6 Which is the best description of your ideal job?
a) A nine-to-five office job that leaves time for my hobbies.
b) A job I love, even if I have to work long or irregular hours.
c) I want to work for myself even if it means working eight days a week.

What your score means

Mostly *a*: You have a rigid attitude to time-keeping. Have you considered a career in the armed forces?

Mostly *b*: You have a healthy attitude to time-keeping. Your life is not ruled by the clock, but you manage to meet your deadlines in good time.

Mostly *c*: You have a casual attitude to time-keeping. Your stress levels are probably quite low – unlike your friends and colleagues (if you still have any!).

3 Work with your partner. Write down at least three activities that you think are a waste of time.

Grammar

Prepositions of time

at

night / the weekend
five o'clock / 2.45 p.m., etc.

on

Sunday, Monday, etc.
Friday night /
Sunday morning, etc.
1st May / 22nd June, etc.

in

the morning / afternoon /
evening
the spring / summer, etc.
January / February, etc.
the sixties

during

a whole period of time
an event or activity (eg
the war / a visit / a flight)

on time (at the right time)
in time (before it's too late)

1 Underline the correct preposition in these sentences.

a) I work best **at** / **during** night.
b) We have a big family meal **on** / **in** New Year's Eve.
c) I start work every morning **at** / **on** 9.00 a.m.
d) I usually get home **in** / **on** time to read my children a bedtime story.
e) I never have a nap **at** / **in** the afternoon.
f) My birthday is **at** / **in** March. In fact it's **in** / **on** 6th March.
g) I swim in the sea as much as possible **during** / **at** my holidays.
h) My boss never starts meetings **in** / **on** time. She's always late.
i) I did a lot of sightseeing **in** / **during** my last trip abroad.
j) My mother was born **in** / **at** the fifties.

Are the sentences true for you? Are they true for your partner? Ask questions.

'What time of day do you work best?' *'What do you do on New Year's Eve?'*

2 Grammar *Extra* 6, Part 1 page 136. Read the explanations and do the exercises.

Vocabulary

1 Look at the month of February. Imagine today is the 15th and follow the instructions.

a) Cross out: St Valentine's Day, the leap year day.

b) Underline: the day before yesterday, the weekend before last, the day after tomorrow, the Monday after next.

February						
Mon	Tue	Wed	Thu	Fri	Sat	Sun
		1	2	3	4	5
6	7	8	9	10	11	12
13	14	15	16	17	18	19
20	21	22	23	24	25	26
27	28	29				

c) Circle: tomorrow, next Saturday, a week today, a week tomorrow.

d) Put in brackets: in four days' time, a fortnight ago, the whole of last week (Mon – Fri).

Apart from the 15th which other eight dates are still free?

2 Use expressions from Exercise 1 to tell your partner about some of the things you've done recently or plan to do in the future.

'The day before yesterday I went out till 4.00 a.m.' *'The weekend after next it's my birthday.'*

Pronunciation

1 🌐 **2.08** Listen and write the order in which you hear these groups of ordinal numbers.

a) 1st 2nd 3rd 4th 5th ☐

b) 1st 4th 5th 3rd 2nd ☐

c) 4th 5th 1st 2nd 3rd [1]

d) 5th 1st 4th 3rd 2nd ☐

Dictate the ordinal numbers *1st – 5th* in any order to your partner. Check what they have written.

2 Practise saying these important dates in the British calendar.

a) 14/02   b) 01/04   c) 01/05   d) 31/10   e) 05/11   f) 25/12

🌐 **2.09** Listen, check and repeat. Why are they important?

Reading

1 How do you remember all the things you have to do each day/week/month? Tell a partner.

2 Read the article and match each of the names of the people mentioned with photos *a–d*.

TIME-SAVING TIPS
Lists

Making lists is relaxing. It makes you feel important – all those things to do. It calms you down (it's OK, it's on a list somewhere) and it makes you feel good when you cross something off.

5 The world divides into two types of list-makers. Type A makes orderly lists, prioritises and calmly sets to work on them. Type B waits until panic sets in, grabs the nearest envelope and scribbles all over it, sighs with relief and promptly loses it.

10 The more you have to do, the more you need a list, and few people with high-powered jobs get by without them.

Julie Rost, chief executive of a large chain of supermarkets, says, 'Before I go to bed, I have to write 15 down everything that's going to stop me sleeping. If I write something down, I feel I won't forget it, so my lists are a great comfort.'

Jane Levy used to write lists, but she would forget where she put them and then waste precious time 20 looking for them. Then a couple of years ago she came up with a new system. Now she writes key words on the back of her hand! 'At least I can't lose it,' she says.

True, but too many trips to the bathroom could have disastrous results.

25 Des O'Brien, a self-employed business consultant, uses another method for organising his time. He writes a list of things to do and then organises them into categories: things that have to be done straight away; other things that it would be good to do today; things that are 30 important but don't have to be done immediately; and things that he can put off but that he doesn't want to forget. 'Using categories to order the world is the way the human mind works,' he says.

It's all a question of what works best for you, whether 35 it's a tidy notebook, a forest of Post-it® notes or the back of your hand. Having tried all these, Kerry Johns, student, relies on her personal organiser. 'My personal organiser has changed my life.' she says. 'Up to now, I've always relied on my good memory, but now that I'm 40 working and studying, I find I've got too much to keep in my head.'

So what are you waiting for? There's no better time than the present to take control of your work and life. So, get out your pencil and paper and make a list.

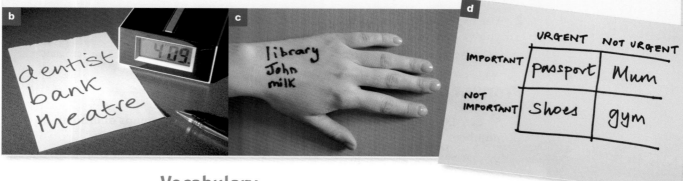

Vocabulary

1 Replace the underlined phrases with the correct form of phrasal verbs from the article in the Reading section.

  a) At the end of a stressful day, I find cooking <u>relaxes me</u>. (line 2) *calms me down*

  b) At the supermarket, I <u>delete things from</u> my list as I put them in the trolley. (line 4)

  c) I can <u>manage</u> on five hours' sleep, but I prefer at least seven hours. (line 11)

  d) I'm very good at <u>inventing</u> excuses when I'm late. (line 20)

  e) I always <u>delay</u> making difficult decisions till the last minute. (line 31)

  f) I <u>trust</u> my mother to wake me up in the morning. (line 37)

2 Are any of the sentences true for you? Compare with your partner.

Grammar

Modal verb structures

I **must** arrive on time.
I **mustn't** be late.

You **should** go to bed earlier.
You **shouldn't** stay up so late.

He **has to** take a test, but she **doesn't have to** take it.

They **can** wait in here, but they **can't** leave early.

1 Look at the table and complete the explanation with *must* or *should*.

	Urgent	Not urgent
Important	I must do it today.	I must do it soon.
Not important	I should do it today.	I should do it soon.

(1) *Must* and (2) _____ are modal verbs. You can use them to give advice. (3) _____ is much stronger than (4) _____ . (5) _____ means it is **important** or **necessary** to do something. (6) _____ means it is a **good idea** to do something.

Copy the table and write things that you need to do in each square. Use *must* and *should* to tell your partner about your priorities for today / this week / this month.

2 Des O'Brien talks about the advantages and disadvantages of working from home. Read what he says and underline the appropriate verb structures.

'I love working from home. I (1) **don't have to** / **have to** drive to work, I (2) **mustn't** / **don't have to** sit in traffic, and parking is not my problem any more.

I (3) **can't** / **don't have to** get dressed in the morning – I (4) **can** / **have to** wear my pyjamas all day. In fact, I (5) **don't have to** / **mustn't** get up in the morning at all! If I like, I (6) **must** / **can** work all night. It's up to me.

There's nobody to tell me, 'You (7) **can** / **must** be punctual. You (8) **mustn't** / **don't have to** make personal phone calls. You (9) **can't** / **don't have to** do your shopping online ...'

There are only a couple of downsides. I (10) **can** / **have to** phone somebody if I want a chat or a gossip, and I can't blame anything on anybody else – I'm the only person here!'

🔊 **2.10 Listen and check. Talk to your partner about other advantages or disadvantages of working from home.**

3 Complete the table with an appropriate heading: *It's necessary; It's permitted; It's not permitted; It's not necessary.*

A: *It's necessary*	**B:** _____	**C:** _____	**D:** _____
have to must	don't have to	can	can't mustn't

4 Complete the sentences with a modal from the table in Exercise 3. Use an appropriate tense.

a) I _____ work tomorrow. It's a national holiday.
b) I _____ renew my passport. I've got a foreign business trip coming up.
c) Yesterday I _____ put on a suit. We had an important meeting.
d) I _____ forget to buy a card for my boss. It's her birthday tomorrow.
e) I _____ park near the office any more. It's become a 'residents only' zone.
f) My parents weren't strict. I _____ watch TV whenever I wanted to.

Are any of these sentences true for you?

5 Grammar *Extra* 6, Part 2 page 136. Read the explanations and do the exercises.

Listening

1 Look at three people in their different work places. What jobs do you think they do and how do you think their working conditions compare?

🔊 2.11–2.13 Listen and check your ideas.

2 Read about the working conditions for each job. Are the sentences true or false? Listen again to check.

Job 1	Job 2	Job 3
a) You can get extra pay for working overtime. b) Women are allowed to wear trousers. c) You aren't allowed to have relationships with other people in the company.	a) You can work at home whenever you like. b) You aren't supposed to have any breaks. c) You can wear whatever you like.	a) You often have to work at weekends. b) You can't work for more than twelve hours in a week. c) You're supposed to wear a hat all the time.

3 Replace each highlighted expression in Exercise 2 with *should, shouldn't, mustn't* or *can* so that the sentences have the same meaning.

Would you like to do one of these jobs?

Vocabulary

1 Replace the underlined expressions with expressions in the box.

> open-plan office   qualifications   shifts   work to a deadline
> works flexible hours   unsociable hours

a) Have you ever done a job where you had to work <u>in the evenings and at weekends</u>?
b) What are the advantages and disadvantages of an <u>office with no dividing walls</u>?
c) Are you the sort of person who works well when they have to <u>finish a job by a certain time</u>?
d) Do you know anybody who <u>can start and finish work when they like</u>?
e) What is the job of your dreams, and what special <u>diplomas or degrees</u> do you need to do it?
f) If the salary was high, could you work twelve-hour <u>periods of time</u>, sometimes at night?

2 Work with a partner. Ask and answer the questions in Exercise 1. What are your ideal working conditions?

3 **Pairwork Student A:** page 117   **Student B:** page 122

Writing

1 Here are some examples of phrases often used in business letters. Complete them using the words in the box.

> apply   complain   confirm   enclose   grateful   hearing   pleased   response   16th May   ~~Unfortunately~~

a) *Unfortunately* I am not available on the date you suggest in your letter.
b) Thank you for your letter of _____ which I received this morning.
c) I _____ my curriculum vitae for your attention.
d) I would be _____ if you could send me some information about your school.
e) I would be _____ to attend an interview at any time convenient to you.
f) I am writing to _____ about the damage caused by your company when they delivered a sofa to my home last week.
g) We look forward to _____ from you as soon as possible.
h) We would be grateful if you could _____ your reservation in writing.
i) I am writing in _____ to your advertisement in *The Guardian*.
j) I would like to _____ for the position of IT assistant in your school.

2 Match each of the phrases (*a–j*) in Exercise 1 with one of the functions (*1–10*) below.

1 asking for information	7 complaining
2 applying for a job	8 responding to an advertisement
3 thanking someone for their letter	9 asking for confirmation
4 closing a letter	10 saying that you are sending something
5 giving bad news	with the letter
6 giving good news	

3 Antonia Clifford is interested in applying for the post of flight attendant. Do you think her letter is a suitable letter of application? Why? Why not?

world**wide**
airlines
Flight attendants

Worldwide Airlines are currently seeking friendly, service-oriented people who take pride in their performance and appearance.

• Applicants must be over twenty years of age and have at least two years' post high school education or work experience.

• Physical requirements: able to lift, push and pull heavy articles as required.

• Minimum height 1m 60. Maximum height 1m 85.

• Languages: able to read, write, speak and understand English. Other languages an advantage.

• Interested candidates can write to the following address for an application form and further information: Worldwide Airlines Inc., PO Box 2983, Chicago, Illinois, USA

156b East 49th Street
Santa Barbara
California

Worldwide Airlines Inc.
PO Box 2983
Chicago
Illinois

February 5th 2009

Dear Mr or Mrs,

Application for the post of flight attendant

I saw your advertisement in the Morning Post and I want to be a flight attendant.

I am 21 years old and I have just graduated from university. I have put my c.v. with this letter so that you can see what I've done and I'd love to come for an interview any time you like.

How about sending me an application form and some more information about the job?

I can't wait to hear from you!

Lots of love.

Toni

4 Improve Antonia's letter by using some of the phrases in Exercise 1.

Useful phrases

1   **Read and match the conversations (*a–c*) with the pictures (*1–3*).**

a)   A: (1) <u>We're ahead of schedule</u>.
B: Yes, hopefully we'll be there (2) <u>before</u> dinner.
A: Oh yes, I should think so. In fact, we may even (3) <u>be early</u>.
B: Well, that's OK. If we have some time before dinner, we can go to the gym.
A: The gym? I'd rather (4) <u>find something to do</u> in the mall!

b)   The Global Earth Party will put the environment at the top of the agenda. We've asked the same question (5) <u>repeatedly</u>: when will the government do something about global warming? (6) <u>We haven't got much time left</u> – we need to act now. Vote for the Global Earth Party today!

c)   Teacher: Come along children. Stop running. OK, (7) <u>one by one</u>. Ruben, stop pushing. Come on children, let's go back to class.
Child: But we didn't have time to finish our game, Miss.
Teacher: Yes, I know, (8) <u>time goes very quickly</u> when you're having fun. But we have work to do.

2   **Replace the underlined phrases in Exercise 1 with the time expressions below (*a–h*).**

a)   We're running out of time
b)   We're making good time
c)   have time to spare
d)   time and time again
e)   one at a time
f)   in time for
g)   time flies
h)   kill time

🔘 2.14 **Listen to the conversations and check your answers.**

3   🔘 2.15 **Listen and repeat the useful phrases from the conversations.**

4   **Work with a partner. Choose three of the expressions from Exercise 2 and include them in a short conversation.**

Practise your conversation.

Vocabulary *Extra*

Words that are sometimes confused

1 Read the information about the difference between *job* and *work*. What is the key grammatical difference between the words?

2 Complete the questions with *job/jobs* or *work*. In which sentences are both possible?

a) Have you ever had a holiday _____ ?
b) What kind of _____ does your father do?
c) Is it easy to find _____ in your country?
d) How many different part-time _____ have you had?
e) What time do most people start _____ in your country?
f) Have you ever been offered a _____ in a foreign country?

Ask your partner the questions.

3 Look at more words that are sometimes confused. Complete the dictionary examples (*a*–*g*) with the correct alternative. Use the dictionary definitions to help you.

a) actually / currently
   ♦ We've spoken on the phone but we've never _____ met.
   ♦ This is the best recording _____ available on CD.

b) travel / trip
   ♦ The whole family went on a _____ to Florida.
   ♦ Foreign _____ never really appealed to him until he retired.

c) career / course
   ♦ He has just started out on a _____ as a photographer.
   ♦ She's on a management _____ this week.

d) fun / funny
   ♦ Our day at the beach was really _____ .
   ♦ Don't laugh; it isn't _____ .

e) borrow / lend
   ♦ Could you _____ me your umbrella?
   ♦ Can I _____ your umbrella?

f) argue / discuss
   ♦ Don't _____ with me – you know I'm right.
   ♦ We're meeting to _____ the matter next week.

g) lose (lost) / miss (missed)
   ♦ I _____ the last train home again.
   ♦ I've _____ my bag. Have you seen it?

4 Complete the questions with an appropriate word from Exercise 3. You may have to change the form of the word.

When was the last time you …
a) *argued* with your parents?
b) heard a really _____ joke?
c) went on a foreign _____ ?
d) _____ some books from a library?
e) read a book about _____ ?
f) did a training _____ ?
g) _____ a bus?
h) _____ some money to a friend?
i) _____ your house keys?
j) thought about changing your _____ ?

Ask your partner the questions.

5 Check your own dictionary. What example sentences does it give for the words on this page?

• You can refer to what someone does in order to get paid as their **work** or their **job**: *Do you find your work OR your job interesting?* • *What kind of work OR job does he do?*
• **Work** is uncountable with this meaning, so it never has **a** in front of it and is never plural: *He's looking for work.* • *It's fascinating work.* • *Has he found a job?* • *She has had many different jobs.*

---

actually /ˈæktʃuəli/ adv ★★★
1 used for emphasising what is really true

argue /ˈɑːgjuː/ verb ★★★
1 [I] to discuss something that you disagree about, usually in an angry way = QUARREL

borrow /ˈbɒrəʊ/ verb ★★
1 [T] to receive and use something that belongs to someone else, and promise to give it back

career[1] /kəˈrɪə/ noun [C] ★★
1 a job or profession that you work at for some time

course[1] /kɔːs/ noun [C] ★★★
1 a series of lessons or lectures in an academic subject or a practical skill

currently /ˈkʌrəntli/ adv ★★★
at the present time

discuss /diˈskʌs/ verb [T] ★★★
1 to talk about something with someone

fun[2] /fʌn/ adj enjoyable

funny /ˈfʌni/ adj ★★★
1 someone or something that is funny makes you laugh

lend /lend/ (past tense and past participle **lent** /lent/) verb ★★★
1 [T] to give someone something for a short time, expecting that they will give it back to you later

lose /luːz/ (past tense and past participle **lost** /lɒst/) verb ★★★
2 [T] to be unable to find someone or something

miss[1] /mɪs/ verb ★★★
3 [T] to be too late for something such as a train or bus

travel[2] /ˈtrævəl/ noun [U] ★★★
the activity of travelling

trip /trɪp/ noun [C] ★★
an occasion when you go somewhere and come back again = JOURNEY

Review B

▶ **Grammar** *Extra* pages 132–137

Grammar

1 Correct the three sentences where the pronoun is in the incorrect position.

a) He had a cold but he got over **it** quickly. ✔
b) I've used these boots so much I've worn out **them**.
c) My brother was ill last week, and I had to look **him** after.
d) If you don't understand the word, look **it** up.
e) Before you buy that shirt you should try on **it**.
f) I dropped the plant on the floor and had to clear **it** up.

2 Complete the sentences. Use *will*, *going to* or the present continuous.

a) 'It's too hot.' 'OK, I (open) *'ll open* a window.'
b) I (train) _____ as an actor when I leave school.
c) She (meet) _____ Jon and Sue at eight o'clock.
d) I don't want to go out. I (stay in) _____ and read my book.
e) 'I can't get through to Dave. Oh, I know, I (try) _____ calling him on his mobile.' 'Good idea.'
f) He (arrive) _____ on the 11.15 train from York.

3 Complete with the words in the box.

anyone	anything	~~everywhere~~	no one
nothing	nowhere	someone	

Rod: Where have you been? I've been looking (1) *everywhere* for you.
Dana: Over there. I was talking to (2) _____ .
Rod: Who? Is it (3) _____ I know?
Dana: No, it's (4) _____ you know – a new person in my office. ... Hey, is there (5) _____ to eat?
Rod: No. There's (6) _____ to eat or drink – and (7) _____ to sit! ... I've had enough. Do you want to go?

4 Tick the three correct sentences. Change the incorrect sentences. Use *used to*, *didn't use to* or *would*.

When I was young ...
a) I'd have blond hair. *I used to have blond hair.*
b) I used to have a dog.
c) I wouldn't believe in ghosts.
d) I'd love everything my mother cooked.
e) I'd go swimming on Saturdays.
f) I didn't use to play a musical instrument.

Which sentences are true for you? Compare with a partner.

5 Underline the correct preposition.

We got married (1 **in / on**) a warm Saturday (2 **at / in**) spring. We had a party (3 **in / on**) the evening. (4 **During / On**) the party we danced and everyone had a lovely time. (5 **At / On**) ten o'clock (6 **at / in**) night we drove to the airport to go on my surprise honeymoon. (7 **During / In**) the flight my husband told me we were going to Cuba. We landed (8 **at / on**) four o'clock (9 **in / on**) Sunday morning. (10 **At / In**) eight o'clock (11 **during / on**) Sunday evening the island experienced a terrible hurricane. We flew out (12 **at / on**) Monday morning after the shortest honeymoon in history!

6 Make sentence *B* mean the same as sentence *A*. Use the words in the box.

can	can't	don't have to	have to	must
mustn't	~~should~~	shouldn't		

a) A It's a good idea for you to see a doctor.
   B You *should* see a doctor.
b) A It's not necessary for you to come, but you are permitted if you want.
   B You _____ come but you _____ if you want.
c) A It's not a good idea to stay up so late.
   B You _____ stay up so late.
d) A I'm sorry, but you are not permitted to see the manager.
   B I'm sorry, but you _____ see the manager.
e) A You are not permitted to tell her.
   B You _____ tell her.
f) A It is necessary for you to stop smoking immediately, Mr Smith.
   B You _____ stop smoking immediately, Mr Smith.
g) A My wife says it is necessary for me to be home by 8.00 p.m.
   B I _____ be home by 8.00 p.m.

7 Spot the mistake! Cross out the incorrect sentence.

1 a) ~~Have you got your coat? ... Put on it.~~
  b) Have you got your coat? ... Put it on.
2 a) I'm calling you tomorrow.
  b) I'll call you tomorrow.
3 a) How much time do we have?
  b) How many time do we have?
4 a) He would be very fat.
  b) He used to be very fat.
5 a) She can come anytime she likes.
  b) She can to come anytime she likes.
6 a) Sshh! You don't have to talk in here.
  b) Sshh! You mustn't talk in here.

Vocabulary

1 **Rewrite the sentences. Replace the underlined words with the phrasal verbs in the box.**

> are heading for   are putting on   go off
> go on   got over   join in

a) We can't <u>continue</u> like this, Ron.
   We can't go on like this, Ron.
b) Fortunately, the bomb didn't <u>explode</u>.
c) Saskia and Freddie <u>are organising</u> a big party.
d) He never <u>recovered from</u> his wife's death.
e) Hello? Yes, we <u>are moving towards</u> London now.
f) This is fun! Why don't you come and <u>participate</u>?

2 **Put the words in the box in the correct column.**

> a mistake   the shopping   a noise
> your homework   a suggestion   the ironing
> a promise   a wish   some exercise   money
> some research   the cooking

make	do
a mistake	

3 **Complete the sentences with the words in the box.**

> atmosphere   fancy dress   guests   host
> invitation   mingle

I once received an (1) *invitation* to a party. We had to wear (2) _____ . The theme of the party was horror films. I went as Frankenstein's Monster. When we arrived, the (3) _____ greeted us and showed us into the main room. He was dressed as Count Dracula. My wife, the Bride of Frankenstein, and I immediately started to (4) _____ , but it's not so easy introducing yourself to people dressed as monsters and mummies! Three other (5) _____ were dressed as Frankenstein's Monster. Even so, there was a really good (6) _____ , and the party was a great success.

4 **Complete the phrases with the words in the box.**

> bar   bowl   box   bunch   jar   packet

a) a *bunch* of flowers
b) a _____ of chocolate
c) a _____ of crisps
d) a _____ of matches
e) a _____ of honey
f) a _____ of cereal

5 **Complete the lists with the words in the box.**

> bake   bland   boil   creamy   crisp
> crunchy   delicious   disgusting   fry
> greasy   roast   tasty

Cook in oven: (1) *bake*, (2) _____
Cook in water: (3) _____
Cook in oil: (4) _____
Taste (positive): (5) _____ , (6) _____
Taste (negative): (7) _____ , (8) _____
Texture (hard): (9) _____ , (10) _____
Texture (soft): (11) _____ , (12) _____

6 **Write the date for each of the following.**

a) today
b) the day before yesterday
c) the day after tomorrow
d) a week today
e) the Tuesday before last
f) the Monday after next

7 **Complete the text with the words in the box.**

> calms   coming up   get   open-plan   put
> rely   shift   unsociable

My work is stressful at times, but I work with some great people. It's important to know you can (1) *rely* on your colleagues. We work in an (2) _____ office so everyone can see everyone else. We often work (3) _____ hours, and getting home at 4.00 a.m. can be hard on our families. I can (4) _____ by on very little food but I can't live without my tea. On a stressful day, a cup of tea really (5) _____ me down. I never (6) _____ off doing a job – I deal with it as soon as it arrives on my desk. I hate people who are always (7) _____ with excuses for why they didn't do their work. When my (8) _____ is over, I get on my bike and cycle home. There aren't many people on the roads at 3.30 a.m.

Pronunciation

1 **Look at some words from Units 4–6. Say the words and add them to the table.**

> arrangement   aubergine   banana   cinema
> courgettes   cucumber   decision   degree
> January   permission   relax   sardines
> sausages   suggestion   weekend

A: □■	B: □■□	C: ■□□
<u>cour</u>gettes	ar<u>range</u>ment	<u>au</u>bergine

2 **Underline the stressed syllable in each word.**

🎧 2.16 **Listen, check and repeat.**

Reading & Listening

1 **Read the descriptions of two famous festivals and answer the questions.**

   a) Which is the older festival?
   b) What special food and drink do people have at each festival?

Two festivals

Midsummer in Sweden

The winters in Sweden are long and dark, and the summers are short. Midsummer is one of the most popular festivals in Sweden, along with Christmas. The festival dates from ancient times and is a celebration of the warmth, light and life of the natural world in summer. All the plants are green. There are wild flowers everywhere, and the sun never
5 sets. Midsummer is a national holiday, and many people start their summer holidays on that day. It takes place on the third weekend of June, around 21st June, the longest day of the year. It's the one time of the year when people wear traditional clothes. On the day before Midsummer, everyone leaves town and goes to meet friends and family in the countryside. On Midsummer morning, people get together outside and dance around a tall wooden pole,
10 which is decorated with flowers and leaves. Then, in the evening, most people celebrate with a dinner, usually eaten outside near a beach or a lake. They eat fish – herring or salmon – with potatoes, followed by a dessert of strawberries and cream, and plenty of cold beer or schnapps. After dinner, there is dancing outside all night long under the midnight sun.

The Galway International Oyster Festival

15 For four days every year, Galway, one of the most beautiful regions of Ireland, holds its world-famous International Oyster Festival. This relatively new festival only started in 1954 and takes place every September. The first evening is the start of the Irish Oyster Opening Championships – a competition to see who can open thirty oysters the fastest. During the evening of the second day there's a big party, with music and a meal of seafood, pasta, salad,
20 champagne, Guinness, and – you guessed it – oysters! On the following day there is a parade through the streets of Galway. Then there's the highlight of the festival: the finals of the oyster opening competition. In the evening there's another party, with all-night dancing. On the last day there are more oysters and other treats, followed by a big dance in the evening. It's a long weekend of non-stop entertainment, cabaret, eating and dancing, and people come
25 to Galway from all over the world to be there. The Irish love oysters and they love a party!

2 **Read the descriptions again. Are the sentences true or false? Correct the false sentences.**

   a) Midsummer is a very popular festival in Sweden. *True.*
   b) Midsummer celebrates the end of summer.
   c) Most people spend Midsummer outside the city.
   d) Everyone goes to bed early on Midsummer Day.
   e) At the Oyster Festival, there's a competition to see who can open thirty oysters the fastest.
   f) At the Oyster Festival there are a lot of parties.
   g) The Oyster Festival is only for Irish people.

3 🌐 **2.17 Listen to the conversation and write what food and drink Carol's family has at Christmas.**

   a) Christmas Eve: *fish (sometimes salmon), fruit dessert*
   b) Christmas Day (breakfast)
   c) Christmas Day (lunch)
   d) Boxing Day (lunch)

4 **Listen again and underline the correct information.**

   a) Carol's **mum / dad** is having a party on Christmas Eve.
   b) Carol's **mum / dad** used to make dinner on Christmas Eve.
   c) Carol's family **get up late / go to church** on Christmas morning.
   d) Carol's dad **is single / has remarried**.
   e) On Christmas afternoon Carol's family **stay at home / go out for a walk**.
   f) Carol is travelling home on **Boxing Day / the day after Boxing Day**.

Writing & Speaking

1 Work with a partner. Match the questions (*a–f*) with the answers in note form (1–6).

   a) What's the name of the festival and where does it take place? *4*
   b) What does it celebrate?
   c) When is the festival and how long does it last?
   d) Who started the festival and when?
   e) What happens at the festival (traditions, entertainment, customs)?
   f) What do people eat and drink?

1 Parades, parties, dancing in the street; people dress up
2 Party time before Lent
3 Rich food, beer and wine, King Cake
4 Mardi Gras, New Orleans, USA
5 January and February; several weeks
6 French settlers, centuries ago

2 Match the parts of the text below with the questions (*a–f*) in Exercise 1.

Mardi Gras

☐ Mardi Gras has been celebrated for centuries since French settlers first came to the USA and built the city of New Orleans.

☐ People eat all kinds of rich food and drink beer or wine. There's a special cake called a 'King Cake', which is gold, green and purple – the colours of Mardi Gras. Inside the cake is a gold bean, which will bring good luck to the person who finds it.

a Mardi Gras takes place in February in the city of New Orleans, USA.

☐ In the two weeks just before 'Fat Tuesday' there are parades and all-night parties, with music and dancing in the streets. Everybody wears colourful clothes and fancy dress. In the parades, people throw beads and money.

☐ It's a big carnival, which celebrates the weeks of eating, drinking and parties before Ash Wednesday.

☐ Mardi Gras officially starts in January and goes on for several weeks until the midnight of 'Fat Tuesday', the last Tuesday before Lent. But it's the last two weeks of this period which are the busiest.

3 Think about a festival you have been to. You are going to tell your partner about it.
   • Interview your partner using the questions in Exercise 1.
   • Write their answers in note form.

4 Write a paragraph describing your partner's festival.

▶ ⏺ 2.18 **Song:** *It's My Party*

7 News

Grammar Verb patterns. Passive structures
Vocabulary Adjectives. Crime. Headline language
Useful phrases Personal news

Listening

1 **Look at the photo and discuss the questions with a partner.**

a) Who are the most photographed celebrities in your country?
b) Which celebrities are in the news at the moment and why?
c) How do you think celebrities feel about being photographed by the paparazzi?

2 **You are going to listen to an interview with Jack – an experienced paparazzo. What do you think his views are about the following? Underline** *OK* **or** *not OK.*

a) It's **OK / not OK** when paparazzi take photos of celebrities' glamorous lifestyles.
b) It's **OK / not OK** when paparazzi take unflattering photos of celebrities.
c) It's **OK / not OK** when paparazzi take photos of celebrities doing ordinary things.
d) It's **OK / not OK** when paparazzi take photos of celebrities' children.
e) It's **OK / not OK** when paparazzi follow celebrities everywhere.
f) It's **OK / not OK** when celebrities refuse to cooperate with the paparazzi.
g) It's **OK / not OK** when celebrities complain about the paparazzi.

🔵 **2.19 Listen and check your ideas.**

Do you agree with Jack? Discuss your own views with a partner.

Grammar

Verb patterns

I **can't stand waiting** around.

She**'s promised to come.**

We **explained that** it was hard.

He **asked me to wait.**

They **told us that** they need time.

1 Complete the following sentences about photographing celebrities. Use the verbs in the box.

agrees   asked   enjoy   explained   tell

a) 'People _____ seeing photos of celebrities doing ordinary things.'
b) 'Kate Moss _____ us not to take photos of her daughter.'
c) 'We've _____ that we don't want to upset her.'
d) 'Nicole Kidman always _____ to smile for the camera.'
e) 'Celebrities _____ us that we're invading their privacy.'

2 Use the verbs from Exercise 1 to complete the table of verb patterns.

Verb + *ing*-form	Verb + *to*-infinitive	Verb + *that*	Verb + sb + (*not*) *to*-infinitive	Verb + sb + *that*
• can't stand doing sth • don't mind doing sth • (1) _____ doing sth	• need to do sth • promise to do sth • try to do sth • want to do sth • (2) _____ to do sth	• realise that … • say that … • suggest that … • think that … • (3) _____ that …	• tell sb to do sth • warn sb not to do sth • (4) _____ sb to do sth	• warn sb that … • (5) _____ sb that …

3 In these statements two verbs are possible, and one is not. Cross out the verb that is not possible.

a) 'I **asked** / **told** / ~~said~~ him to stop, but he pushed the camera in my face and continued taking photos.'
b) 'I just **try** / **want** / **enjoy** to lead a normal life, but these people are making it impossible.'
c) 'When a celebrity gets aggressive, I **tell** / **explain** / **say** that I'm just doing my job.'
d) 'I **told** / **warned** / **suggested** him to stop taking photos of my little girl or I'd take him to court.'
e) 'If they don't enjoy the attention, I **think** / **suggest** / **tell** that they should change jobs.'
f) 'They're hypocritical. On the one hand they **need** / **agree** / **don't mind** to have their photos in the press, and on the other hand they **warn** / **tell** / **explain** us that we're invading their privacy.'

Who do you think made each statement: a paparazzo or a celebrity? Compare your ideas with a partner.

Vocabulary

1 Complete the sentences with these adjectives from the interview on page 60.

obsessed   desperate   hypocritical   insensitive   photogenic   unflattering

a) I read all the gossip about famous people. I can't stop myself. I'm _____ !
b) I like looking at _____ photos of celebrities. It shows that they're not perfect.
c) I think it's _____ to take photographs of celebrities when they are upset or ill. It's really unfair.
d) Some people say they're not interested in celebrities but then read about them in magazines. I think they're _____ .
e) I hate photos of myself because I always look terrible. I'm not very _____ .
f) I'm _____ to become rich and famous. I'd do anything to be a celebrity.

2 Are any of the views in Exercise 1 true for you? Discuss with a partner.

Reading & Vocabulary

1 Match the news stories (*1–6*) with the headlines (*a–f*). Compare with a partner.

News in brief

1

A television set was stolen from a Liverpool police station, while police officers were out fighting crime.

2

Fugitive James Sanders, who escaped from jail in 1975, was arrested in Texas after ringing the FBI to ask if he was still on its 'wanted' list.

3

An 85-year-old man was stopped and escorted off the M4 motorway by the traffic police because he was riding in a wheelchair. The wheelchair was being pushed along the slow lane by his 65-year-old son.

4

Burglar Frank Gort broke down in court and cried when he was sentenced to seven years in jail, claiming it was his unlucky number. An understanding judge in San Antonio Texas took pity and gave him eight years instead.

5

Police cars were involved in a dramatic chase after a notice was spotted in the back window of a car saying, 'Help us, we have been kidnapped'. It had been put there by four unhappy children who didn't want to go on holiday with their parents.

6

Prison authorities in New Zealand have been embarrassed by the escape of convicted thief Cass Mei, who managed to run faster than guards at the prison hospital. He was being treated for asthma and a dislocated knee.

a DON'T ASK

b POLICE THEFT

e UNFIT TO GUARD

c KIDNAPPED

d SLOW LANE

f KIND JUDGE

Which stories do you like best?

2 Complete the sentences using highlighted words from the stories in Exercise 1.

a) *Police officers* are people who fight crime and try to catch criminals.
b) _____ are people who patrol roads and motorways.
c) People on a _____ have committed crimes but haven't been arrested yet.
d) A _____ is someone who sentences criminals in court.
e) A _____ is someone who has stolen something and has been sentenced in court.
f) A _____ is someone who has escaped from jail and is hiding from the police.

3 Use these words from the stories in Exercise 1 to complete three more news stories

| arrested | burglar | chase | court | escorted | stolen | ~~thief~~ | traffic police |

ONE DRINK TOO MANY

A (1) *thief* who stole a bottle of whisky from a supermarket was (2) _____ for shoplifting when he went back for a bottle of Coke.

BOY RACER

Police cars were involved in a dramatic (3) _____ when an 18-year-old, driving his parents' new car, reached 160 kilometres per hour before he was stopped by (4) _____ and (5) _____ off the motorway.

SHOE REVENGE

During divorce proceedings, a woman told the (6) _____ that one shoe of every pair she owned had been (7) _____ from her house. She suspected that the (8) _____ was her husband, who was angry after she had sold the personalised registration number of his Ferrari.

Pronunciation

1   🔊 2.20 Listen and repeat the past participle endings for regular verbs commonly used in the passive.

ed = /t/	*ed* = /d/	*ed* = /ɪd/
asked based	believed called	arrested decided

ed is pronounced as an extra syllable only after the sounds /t/ or /d/. True or false?

2   Practise saying the past participle for the verbs in the box. Add them to the correct column in the table in Exercise 1.

> check   describe   escape   expect   force   involve   name   need   report
> stop   treat   use

🔊 2.21 Listen, check and repeat.

Grammar

Passives

be + past participle

It **had been done.**
It **was done.**
It **was being done.**
It **has been done.**
It **is done.**
It **is being done.**
It **is going to be done.**
It **will be done.**

1   Rewrite the following in the passive to recreate sentences from the news stories on page 62. Make the underlined words or phrases the subject of the passive verb.

   a)   Someone stole <u>a television set</u>. *A television set was stolen.*
   b)   Someone was treating <u>him</u> for asthma. *He …*
   c)   Someone has kidnapped <u>us</u>. *We …*
   d)   Four unhappy children had put <u>it</u> there. *It …*

   How is the passive formed? Find other examples of passive structures in the same news stories on page 62.

2   Look at your sentences (*a–d*) above. Tick the following explanations if you think they are correct.

   a)   In sentences *a, b, c* and *d* the object of the active verb has become the subject of the passive verb.
   b)   In sentences *a, b* and *c* the 'doer' of the action (= the agent) is either unknown, unimportant or obvious.
   c)   In sentence *d* the 'doer' of the action (= the agent) is mentioned after the verb using *by*.

3   Rewrite these newspaper extracts in the passive to make them sound more natural. Don't mention the agent.

   a)   The Oscar committee has announced the Oscar nominations.
        The Oscar nominations have been announced.
   b)   Doctors are treating the troubled film star for 'exhaustion' at Meadows Rehabilitation Centre in Arizona.
   c)   The record company has released the singer's long-awaited album to rave reviews.
   d)   Kidnappers released the hostages last night and they are on their way home to their relieved families.
   e)   The central bank will reduce interest rates by 1% before the end of the year according to most financial observers.
   f)   People have accused the fashion industry of encouraging young girls to go on starvation diets.

   Would you want to read more about any of the stories above? What sort of topics do you like reading about in the newspaper?

4   **Pairwork Student A:** page 118 **Student B:** page 123

5   **Grammar *Extra* 7** page 138. Read the explanations and do the exercises.

Reading & Listening

1 Match each photo (*a–f*) with an appropriate newspaper headline (*1–6*).

a) 2   b) …

What do you think each news item is about? Which story would you read first?

2 Find an underlined headline word in Exercise 1 that has the same meaning as the phrases below.

a) has severely damaged *hits*
b) is going to marry
c) has resigned
d) an argument
e) have increased significantly

f) financial
g) has excluded
h) the unemployed
i) an investigation
j) negotiations

Are there any similar stories in the news today?

3 🔘 2.22 Listen and match the radio news items (*a–f*) with the headlines (*1–6*) in Exercise 1.

a) 2   b) …

4 Work with a partner and complete the task.

- Write a radio news story based on one of the following three headlines (*a–c*).
- Invent any extra information you need.
- Broadcast your news to the rest of the class.

a) FANS BARRED FROM WORLD CUP FINAL
b) TEACHER QUITS IN EXAM ROW
c) FAMILIES HIT AS HOUSE PRICES SOAR

Reading & Writing

1 **Complete the email from Pia to her friend Ian. Use the words in the box.**

> Actually   Anyway   Apart   apparently   forward   getting   ~~great~~   heard
> let   news   pleased   sorry   touch   Well

To: Ian Arnold
Subject: Congratulations!

Hi Ian,

Thanks for your email. It was (1) *great* to hear from you. I'm (2) _____ I haven't replied sooner, but work's been really stressful. More about that in a minute. But first, I was really (3) _____ to hear about your promotion. You deserve it – you've worked so hard at that job. (4) _____ done! I wish you were still living in Berlin, so we could go out and celebrate.

Anyway, back to my stressful job! (5) _____ , it's much better since my boss retired. I think I told you about her. She was a real bully. Apparently, she was unhappy in her private life, but that's no reason to be horrible at work. The good (6) _____ is that we've got a new boss, and he's quite young and dynamic. He's already made a few changes, and the best thing is that he wants me to travel more, so I'll be able to see all my friends back home more often.

Talking of friends, have you (7) _____ about Anna and Giorgio? They've split up! I've no idea why, but (8) _____ , Giorgio's gone back to Italy, and Anna's refusing to talk to anybody about it. Please (9) _____ me know if you hear any more about it.

(10) _____ from that, everything's fine here in Berlin. It's getting quite hot, and I'm looking (11) _____ to going on holiday in August. What are your holiday plans?

(12) _____ , I'd better get on with my work now, but be in (13) _____ soon and tell me how you're (14) _____ on.

Lots of love,
Pia

---

2 **Read the email again and answer the questions.**

a) Who lives in Berlin?
b) Who used to live in Berlin?
c) Who's been promoted at work?
d) Who's got a new boss?
e) Who's split up?
f) Who's gone back to Italy?

3 **Work with a partner. Use the sentence beginnings below to invent a reply from Ian to Pia's email.**

To: Pia Hamilton
Subject: Re: Congratulations!

Dear Pia,

It was great …
I'm sorry …
I was so pleased …
By the way, Giorgio phoned me. Apparently, …
Apart from that, I'm looking forward to the holidays. I'm going …
Anyway, …

Lots of love,

PS Guess what! …

Compare your emails with other people in the class. Choose the email with the best ideas.

Useful phrases

1 Match the two pictures to two of the conversations (1–8).

1 A: How's Shirley?
  B: Actually, we've split up.
  A: **Oh, I'm sorry to hear that. / How exciting!**
  B: It's OK. Um, this is Sandra.

2 C: Hello. You're looking very pleased with yourself.
  D: I am! I've just passed my driving test!
  C: **Oh no. That's terrible! / Well done!** Was it your first time?
  D: No, my sixth.

3 E: Guess what! I've won a holiday to Florida.
  F: **I'm sorry to hear that. / You lucky thing!** Is it a holiday for two?
  E: Yes, I'm taking my mum.
  F: Oh.

4 G: You don't look very happy.
  H: No, I've just got my exam results. I've failed them all.
  G: **Well done! / Oh no, that's terrible!** What happened?
  H: I didn't do any work.

5 I: Have a glass of champagne!
  J: Thank you. What are you celebrating?
  I: My wife's just had a baby.
  J: **Oh, congratulations! / How annoying!**

6 K: You don't usually take the bus!
  L: No – my car's broken down again.
  K: **How annoying! / Well done!**
  L: I know. But it is twenty-five years old.

7 M: What did you do last night?
  N: I watched a documentary about snow leopards.
  M: **Oh, that sounds interesting. / Oh, I'm sorry to hear that.**
  N: Yes, unfortunately I fell asleep halfway through.

8 O: What are you up to today?
  P: I'm having my first sailing lesson.
  O: **How exciting! / Oh no, that's terrible!** Are you nervous?
  P: I am actually. I can't swim.

2 Work with a partner. Read the conversations (1–8) which show people responding to good and bad news. In each case, underline the appropriate response.

🔊 **2.23** Listen and check.

3 Classify the useful phrases that you heard in Exercise 2 in the table below.

Positive responses	Negative responses
	Oh, I'm sorry to hear that.

🔊 **2.24** Listen, check and repeat.

4 🔊 **2.25** Listen to some more pieces of good and bad news and respond appropriately.

Vocabulary *Extra*

Verb patterns

1 Complete the common verb patterns *a–j* with *ask, explain, say* or *tell*.

a) *explain* / **say** + (that)
b) **explain** / _____ / **say** how / what, etc.
c) _____ / **say** sth to sb
d) _____ sth on / about
e) _____ sb + (that)
f) _____ / **tell** sb why/how, etc.
g) _____ / **ask** sb sth
h) _____ / **tell** sb about sth
i) _____ sb for sth
j) _____ / **tell** sb to do sth

Check your answers in the dictionary extracts. Which verbs nearly always have a person (*sb*) as a direct object?

2 *Say* or *tell*? Underline the correct verbs in these sentences.

a) She <u>said</u> / **told** that she liked dancing.
b) Didn't he **say** / **tell** you that I wanted to see you?
c) I want to **say** / **tell** something on this subject.
d) Just **say** / **tell** me what she **said** / **told**.
e) '**Say** / **Tell** me about your day,' she **said** / **told**.
f) I haven't been **said** / **told** anything about it.

Check your answers in the dictionary extracts.

3 Complete the joke with the correct form of either *say* or *tell*.

Sherlock Holmes and Dr Watson went on a camping trip. As they lay down for the night, Holmes (1) *said*: 'Watson, look up into the sky and (2) _____ me what you see.'
Watson (3) _____ : 'I see millions and millions of stars.'
Holmes: 'And what does that (4) _____ you?'
Watson: 'Astronomically, it (5) _____ me that there are millions of galaxies and potentially billions of planets. Theologically, it (6) _____ me that God is great and that we are small and insignificant. Meteorologically it (7) _____ me that we will have a beautiful day tomorrow. What does it (8) _____ you?'
Holmes: 'Somebody has stolen our tent.'

4 Complete the questions with the most appropriate verb: *asked, explained, said* or *told*.

When was the last time you …

a) *told* your friends a joke?
b) _____ no to chocolate?
c) _____ somebody to 'cheer up'?
d) _____ what you do for a living?
e) _____ somebody for a lift?
f) _____ sorry to a friend?
g) _____ a friend to help you?
h) _____ the rules of a game to somebody?
i) _____ that you needed to do some exercise?
j) _____ somebody that you loved them?

Work with a partner. Ask and answer the questions.

5 Check your own dictionary. What example sentences does it include to illustrate the different verb patterns for *ask, explain, say* and *tell*?

---

ask /ɑːsk/ verb ★★★
1 [I/T] to speak to someone in order to get information from them: *I wondered who had given her the ring but was afraid to ask.* ♦ *The police wanted to **ask** us a few questions.* ♦ **ask (sb) why/how/whether etc** *She asked me how I knew about it.* ♦ **ask (sb) about sth** *Did you ask about the money?*
2 [I/T] to speak to someone because you want them to give you something, or do something for you: *If you need any help, just ask.* ♦ *Can I ask you a favour?* ♦ **ask (sb) for sth** *The children were asking for drinks.* ♦ **ask sb to do sth** *He asked us to move over a little.* ♦ **ask to do sth** *I asked to see the manager.* ♦ **ask (sb) if/whether** *Ask if we can go backstage.*

explain /ɪkˈspleɪn/ verb ★★★
1 [T] to tell someone something in a way that helps them to understand it better: **explain sth to sb** *The doctor explained the risks to me before the operation.* ♦ **+how/when/what etc** *I will try to explain how a car engine works.* ♦ **+(that)** *He explained that he would be moving to another city.*

say¹ /seɪ/ (3rd person singular **says** /sez/; past tense and past participle **said** /sed/) verb ★★★

1 express with words	**4** show sth
2 have opinion	**5** imagine sth
3 give information	**+ PHRASES**

1 [I/T] to express something using words: *'Pleased to meet you,' he said with a smile.* ♦ *'When's he coming back?' 'He didn't say.'* ♦ *The committee **said yes** (=gave permission), so we can go ahead.* ♦ *What an odd **thing to say**, Carrie thought.* ♦ *I then **said goodbye** and left.* ♦ *I've already **said sorry** for hurting his feelings.* ♦ **+(that)** *She said that she liked dancing.* ♦ **+how/what/who etc** *Did he say who called?* ♦ **say sth to sb** *Tell me what he said to you.* ♦ **say sth on/about** *I want to say something on this subject.*

tell /tel/ (past tense and past participle **told** /təʊld/) verb ★★★

1 sb gives information	**6** have clear effect
2 sth gives information	**7** see difference
3 talk about story	**8** fail to keep secret
4 order/advise to do sth	**+ PHRASES**
5 know sth	**+ PHRASAL VERBS**

1 [T] to give information to someone: *If you see anything suspicious, tell the police.* ♦ **tell sb (that)** *Didn't he tell you that I wanted to see you?* ♦ **tell sb who/what/why/how etc** *Just tell me what she said.* ♦ **tell sb sth** *He finally told me the reason he was so upset.* ♦ **tell sb (sth) about sth** *'Tell me about your day,' she said.* ♦ *I haven't been told anything about it.* → SAY
2 [T] if something such as a fact, event, or piece of equipment tells you something, it gives you or shows you some information: *The flashing light tells you when the battery needs recharging.* ♦ *What does this room tell you about the person who lived here?*
3 [T] if you tell a story or a joke, you give someone a spoken account of it: *Grandpa tells wonderful stories about the old days.* ♦ **tell sb sth** *Shall I tell you a joke?*
4 [T] to order or strongly advise someone to do something: *I'm not asking you – I'm telling you!* ♦ **tell sb to do sth** *I told you to be here on time this morning.* ♦ **tell sb what/how/when etc** *I told him what to do, but he wouldn't listen.*

8 Journey

Grammar Modals of deduction. Past perfect
Vocabulary Location. Describing places. Fixed expressions
Useful phrases Asking for directions

Reading

1 Have you ever travelled for any of these reasons? Discuss with a partner.

- to broaden your experience of the world
- to run away from a broken heart
- to learn a language (or something else)
- to take a break from your career
- to visit historical sites
- to get a suntan

What other reasons can you think of to go travelling?

2 Read this extract from *The Beach* by Alex Garland. Why did the author go travelling?

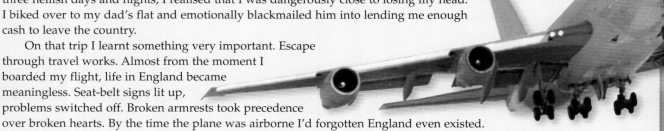

A few years ago I was going through the process of splitting up with my first serious girlfriend. She went away to Greece for the summer and when she came back she'd had a holiday romance with some Belgian guy. As if that wasn't enough, it seemed that the guy in question was going to show up in London some time over the next few weeks. After three hellish days and nights, I realised that I was dangerously close to losing my head. I biked over to my dad's flat and emotionally blackmailed him into lending me enough cash to leave the country.

On that trip I learnt something very important. Escape through travel works. Almost from the moment I boarded my flight, life in England became meaningless. Seat-belt signs lit up, problems switched off. Broken armrests took precedence over broken hearts. By the time the plane was airborne I'd forgotten England even existed.

Glossary	
split up verb [I]: end a relationship	**lose your head** verb [I] *informal*: go mad
show up verb [I] *informal*: arrive	**emotionally blackmail** verb [T]: use emotions to manipulate
	take precedence over verb [T]: become more important than

3 Are these statements true or false?

a) The author's girlfriend had a holiday romance in Belgium.
b) The author was extremely upset.
c) His father lent him money to go travelling.
d) He left England by train.
e) He missed England at first.

Do you agree that travel can help you escape from your problems?

Speaking

1 Work with your partner. Make a list of different places you've travelled to.

2 Choose five places from your list and think about how to describe where they are. Use the expressions in the box.

It's in the	north / south-west southern / north-eastern part	of (Japan). of (Peru).	It's	on the coast in the mountains in (Lombardy)	to the north of (Vigo). not far from (Bern). between (Milan) and (Turin).

Tell your partner where, when and why you travelled to these places.

Reading & Vocabulary

1 Have you ever been to a beach like the ones in the photos? Which one would you most like to visit?

Read another extract from *The Beach*. Which photo does it describe?

> Think about a lagoon, hidden from the sea and passing boats by a high, curving wall of rock. Then imagine white sands and coral gardens never damaged by dynamite fishing or trawling nets. Freshwater falls scatter the island, surrounded by jungle – not the forests of inland Thailand, but jungle.
>
> Canopies three levels deep, plants untouched for a thousand years, strangely coloured birds and monkeys in the trees. On the white sands, fishing in the coral gardens, a select community of travellers pass the months. They leave if they want to, they return, the beach never changes.

2 Read the extract again. Are these sentences true or false?

a) The lagoon is visible from the sea.
b) There's a wall of rock overlooking the beach.
c) The beach is unspoilt by fishermen.
d) Waterfalls are found in different parts of the island.
e) The island has forests all around it.
f) Large groups of people visit the island.

3 Work with a partner. Complete these descriptions using words and expressions in the box. Match the descriptions with the two other photos of beaches in Exercise 1.

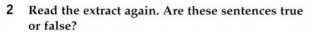

| beach community   hidden   overlooking   popular with tourists   sandy |
| southern   spectacular views   sun loungers   surrounded by   white sands |

Bondi Beach, Australia

The (1) _____ of Bondi beach stretch for roughly a kilometre between two headlands. It isn't the prettiest or largest beach in town, but it is the heart and soul of Sydney's (2) _____ .

Tourists flock to Bondi beach from all over the world – it's the place where beautiful young people go to hang out and be seen. At weekends in summer, you can hardly move for all the people.

But Bondi beach isn't only (3) _____ – local people enjoy a walk along the coastal path at the (4) _____ end of the beach. Any local will tell you that the most (5) _____ of the coast can be seen from the cliffs (6) _____ the bay.

Portinatx Beach, Ibiza

The island of Ibiza has sixty beaches, ranging from long (7) _____ stretches packed with bars and watersports, to delightful (8) _____ coves at the foot of towering cliffs. Portinatx, in the north of the island, is one of Ibiza's most attractive beaches – a horseshoe bay with fine, white sand, (9) _____ pine forests. There are bars and restaurants, a sailing school and (10) _____ for hire.

4 Work with a partner. Talk about places in your city or country ...

a) that are unspoilt.
b) where the beaches are packed with bars.
c) where the views are spectacular.
d) where young people go to hang out and be seen.
e) where you can hardly move for people at weekends in summer.
f) that are popular with foreign tourists.

Listening

1   Look at photos (*a–d*) taken on Conrad's round-the-world trip. Where do you think they were taken?

🔊 2.26 Listen to Amy and Joe discussing photographs on Conrad's web page and check your ideas. Number the photographs in the order they mention them.

2   Match the words in the box with the photos (*a–d*) in Exercise 1.

> ancient ruins   Buddhist temples   a built-up skyline   forests
> grasslands   high-rise buildings   snow-capped mountains   waterfalls

Are there any places in your country where you can see these things? Tell a partner.

Grammar

Modals of deduction

The lights aren't on:
Sam **must** be out.
(= certain)
He **can't** be in. (= certain)
He **might/may/could** be
away for the weekend or on
holiday or …
(= possible)

1 Complete these explanations of the modal structures from the discussion on page 70. Use *must* or *can't*.

a) I think it's certain = 'It _____ be Singapore … I know he stopped off there.'

b) I think it's possible = 'It might/may/could be Vietnam.'

c) I think it's impossible = 'It _____ be India, because he hasn't been there.'

2 Look at the information in the table and try and name the countries (*a–f*) from the list in the box. Discuss your ideas with a partner.

> Angola   Argentina   Brazil   Cuba   Mexico   Mozambique   Peru   Portugal
> Spain   Uruguay

Country	Population (country)	Population (biggest city)	Official language	Highest mountain	Main exports
a) _____	Over 40 million	About 4 million	Spanish	3,718m	chemicals, fruit, cars
b) _____	Nearly 11 million	Over half a million	Portuguese	2,351m	chemicals, cork, leather
c) _____	Over 186 million	Nearly 18 million	Portuguese	3,014m	animal feed, chemicals, coffee
d) _____	Over 108 million	Over 18 million	Spanish	5,700m	chemicals, coffee, cotton
e) _____	Over 40 million	Over 12 million	Spanish	6,962m	animal oils, meat
f) _____	Over 12 million	Nearly 3 million	Portuguese	2,619m	oil, diamonds

Write sentences with *must be*, *might be* or *can't be* to show how you decided.

Country 'c' must be Brazil because it's the country with the biggest population and they speak Portuguese there.

Have you ever been to any of these countries? Tell your partner.

3 Grammar *Extra* 8, Part 1 page 140. Read the explanations and do the exercises.

Pronunciation

1 🔊 2.27 Listen and repeat the words in the box. Mark the main stress.

> the Amazon   the Andes   Antarctica   Asia   the Atlantic   the Danube   Europe
> the Himalayas   the Indian Ocean   the Nile   the Pacific   the Pyrenees

2 List the words in the correct column according to size.

	Continents	Mountain ranges	Oceans	Rivers
+	Asia			
↓				
−				

🔊 2.28 Listen, check and repeat.

Reading & Listening

1   Read the article about Nick Campbell's motorbike trip across the US. What problems did he have?

Coast to coast

Nick Campbell sat at the side of the road and wondered what to do next. He looked at the second-hand Harley-Davidson he'd bought from a back-street garage in Miami at the beginning of his trip six weeks before.

5   For years he had dreamt of crossing the United States from east to west by motorbike and he'd finally decided that it was now or never. He'd given up his job, sold his car and set off for the journey of his dreams. He'd been lucky, or so he thought, to find this old Harley-Davidson
10   and had bought it for a very reasonable price – it had cost him just $600. But five kilometres from Atlanta, he had run out of luck. The motorbike had broken down.

He pushed the bike into town and found a garage. The young mechanic told him to leave the bike overnight
15   and come back the next day. The following morning, to his surprise, the man asked if the bike was for sale. 'Certainly not,' he replied, paid his bill and hit the road.

When he got to Kansas the old machine ran out of steam again. This time Nick thought about selling it and
20   buying something more reliable, but decided to carry on. When the bike was going well, he loved it.

However, in Denver, Colorado the bike broke down
25   yet again, so he decided to take it to a garage and offer it for sale. The mechanic told him to come back in the morning.

The next day, to his amazement, the man offered him $2,000. Realising the man must be soft in the head, but clearly not short of money, Nick asked for $3,000. The man agreed, and they signed the papers. Then the
30   mechanic started laughing. In fact it was several minutes before he could speak, and when he could he said, 'That's the worst deal you'll ever make, boy.' The mechanic ...

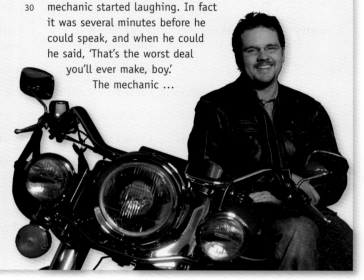

2   Work with a partner. Discuss the questions.

   a)   How much did Nick pay for the bike?
   b)   How much did the mechanic in Denver offer Nick?
   c)   How much did Nick sell it for?
   d)   Guess why the mechanic said, 'That's the worst deal you'll ever make, boy'?

🔊 **2.29**   **Listen to the story and compare the ending with your ideas. Do you think the mechanic was fair? How do you think Nick felt?**

Vocabulary

1   Look at the underlined expression from the article above. What does it mean?

'… and he'd finally decided that it was now or never.'

   a)   either now or in the future   b)   only now and not in the future

2   Work with a partner. Use words from the box to complete some more fixed expressions.

all   clean   come   give   peace   Sooner   ~~take~~

   a)   I don't particularly like watching television. I can *take* **it or leave it** .
   b)   When I go on holiday, all I want is some _____ **and quiet**.
   c)   I vacuum my car regularly because I like it to be _____ **and tidy**.
   d)   It's 200 kilometres to the coast from here, _____ **or take** a few kilometres.
   e)   My computer is getting old. _____ **or later** I'll have to buy a new one.
   f)   I don't eat chocolate for weeks. Then I'll eat three bars in one day! It's _____ **or nothing** with me.
   g)   My teenagers treat our house like a hotel. They just _____ **and go** as they please.

Are any of the sentences true for you?

Grammar

Past perfect

had + past participle

We were too late: the train **had** already **left**.
I knew I **hadn't been** there before.

1 Look at Nick Campbell's route across America and answer the questions.

a) Where was he at the beginning of the story?
b) Where had he begun his motorbike journey?
c) Where did he finish his motorbike journey?

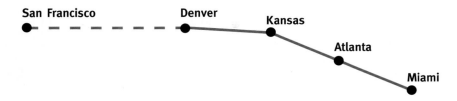

San Francisco — Denver — Kansas — Atlanta — Miami

2 Look at these extracts. Add the name of the city where these events happened.

a) Nick Campbell sat at the side of the road and wondered what to do next. *Atlanta*
b) … he had dreamt of crossing the United States …
c) … he'd given up his job, sold his car and set off …
d) … he had bought the Harley-Davidson for a very reasonable price …
e) … the old machine ran out of steam again.
f) … the bike broke down yet again …

Why are all the events that happened in Miami described in the past perfect?

3 Work with a partner. Complete each of these sentences with a verb in the past perfect to make up a story about Michael's journey to Moscow.

a) Michael was looking forward to his business trip to Moscow because …
b) He was late leaving the house because …
c) The traffic was very slow from his house to the airport because …
d) At the check-in he had to accept a seat at the back of the plane because …
e) The departure was delayed because …
f) As the plane was taking off, he suddenly remembered that …

Compare your ideas with other people in the class.

4 Pairwork **Student A:** page 118 **Student B:** page 123

5 Grammar *Extra* 8, Part 2 page 140. Read the explanations and do the exercises.

Speaking: anecdote

1 🌐 2.30 Listen to Suzi talking about a journey she has been on. Cross out the wrong information in each of her answers.

a) Where did the journey start? **The Dead Sea.**
b) Where did the journey finish? **St Christopher's Monastery.**
c) What was the reason for the journey? **I couldn't go diving.**
d) What form of transport did you use? **A big van.**
e) What was the weather like? **Hot and windy.**
f) Who did you go with? **Seven tourists, a guide and a driver.**
g) How long did it take you? **Three hours.**
h) What did you do during the journey? **I looked out of the window at the sea.**
i) Did you stop en route? What for? **Yes, to take photos and buy food.**
j) Would you go on the same journey again? Why? **Yes, but in my own car.**

Correct the information. Listen again and check.

2 You are going to tell your partner about a journey you have been on.

• Ask yourself the questions in Exercise 1.
• Think about *what* to say and *how* to say it.
• Tell your partner about your journey.

Useful phrases

1 🌐 **2.31 Read and listen to a conversation between a couple in a car. Answer the questions.**

a) Where do they want to go?
b) Which number road are they looking for?
c) How many times do they pass the supermarket?

Angie: Rick, do you know where we are?

Rick: Yes, of course. Why?

Angie: Because we've passed the same supermarket twice.

Rick: Oh dear.

Angie: You'd better stop and ask somebody.

Rick: OK. ... Excuse me, I'm trying to get to Andover. Do you know how we can get onto the A34 from here?

Man 1: Yes, first you need to turn round and then take the first turning on the left. Go to the end of the road and you'll come to a roundabout. Take the third exit and you'll come onto the A34.

Rick: Great, thanks. ... Did he say left or right?

Angie: I can't remember. Look, stop and ask that woman.

Rick: Excuse me, we're looking for the road to Andover. Could you tell me which way we need to go?

Woman: Andover? Go straight down here until you come to a petrol station. Then turn left and follow the signs.

Rick: OK, thanks. ... I haven't seen the petrol station yet.

Angie: No, neither have I, but here's that supermarket again.

Rick: Oh no. ... Excuse me, we're lost. Do you have any idea where the A34 is?

Man 2: Er, no, sorry.

2 **Read the conversation again and complete the useful phrases.**

Saying what you're looking for
a) Excuse me, I'm trying *to get to* Andover.
b) Excuse me, we're looking _____ Andover.

Asking for directions
c) Do you know how _____ the A34?
d) Could you tell me which _____ ?
e) Do you have any idea where _____ ?

Giving directions
f) You need to turn _____ and then take _____ the left.
g) Go to the end of the road and you'll _____ .
h) Take the third _____ .
i) Go straight down here until _____ .
j) Turn left and follow _____ .

🌐 **2.32 Listen, check and repeat.**

3 **Work with a partner. Rewrite the following questions in less direct language. Refer to useful phrases *c–e* in Exercise 2 and start your questions with *Do you know ...?* *Could you tell me ...?* or *Do you have any idea ...?***

a) Where's the nearest bank? *Excuse me. Do you know where the nearest bank is?*
b) How can I get to the airport from here?
c) I'm looking for the bus station. Which way do I need to go?
d) How can I get to the centre of town from here?
e) Where can I get a taxi?
f) How can I get to the cinema from here?

Ask each other the questions and give appropriate directions from where you are now.

Vocabulary *Extra*

Dictionary labels

1 Match the dictionary labels with their definitions.

a) *British*
b) *American*
c) *formal*
d) *informal*

1 Not used in everyday speech or writing.
2 Used in American English but not in British English.
3 Used commonly in speech but not in writing.
4 Used in British English but not in American English.

2 Use an appropriate label from Exercise 1 as a heading for the word lists (*1–3*).

1	2	3
candy	booze	alight
sidewalk	guy	beverage
trash can	nerd	refrain

Check your answers in the dictionary extracts.

3 Work with a partner. Decide what each notice means and where you might see it. Use the dictionary extracts to help you.

a Kindly refrain from smoking in this area

b Foot passengers please disembark via the steps at the front of the ferry

c All cyclists must dismount here

d The use of calculators is not permissible

e Do not alight from the train whilst it is still in motion

f Alcoholic beverages cannot be purchased by persons under the age of 18

Write less formal versions of each notice.

a Please don't smoke around here.

4 Rewrite these sentences in British English.

a) Last year, I took my vacation in the fall.
   Last year, I went on holiday in the autumn.
b) We keep our trash can in the yard.
c) I never eat candy or cookies between meals.
d) I get angry with truck drivers who go too fast on the freeway.
e) When I go downtown I walk or use the subway.
f) There's a mailbox on the sidewalk in front of my house.

Are any of the sentences true for you?

5 Check your own dictionary. What kinds of labels does it use?

---

alight[2] /əˈlaɪt/ verb [I] *formal* to get off a train, bus, or other vehicle

beverage /ˈbev(ə)rɪdʒ/ noun [C] *formal* a drink

booze[1] /buːz/ noun [C] *informal* alcoholic drinks

candy /ˈkændi/ noun [C/U] *American* a sweet, or sweets

cookie /ˈkʊki/ noun [C] *American* a biscuit

disembark /ˌdɪsɪmˈbɑːk/ verb [I] *formal* to get off a ship or a plane

dismount /dɪsˈmaʊnt/ verb [I] *formal* to get off a horse or a bike

downtown /ˌdaʊnˈtaʊn/ adj, adv *American* in or near the business or shopping centre of a city ≠ UPTOWN

fall[2] /fɔːl/ noun ★★★ 6 [singular] *American* autumn

freeway /ˈfriːweɪ/ [C] *American* a wide fast road in a US city that you do not pay to use

guy /gaɪ/ noun [C] ★★ *informal* a man

mailbox /ˈmeɪlˌbɒks/ noun [C] 2 *American* a postbox

nerd /nɜːd/ noun [C] *informal* someone who is boring and not fashionable

permissible /pɜːˈmɪs(ə)bl/ adj *formal* if something is permissible, you are allowed to do it

persons /ˈpɜːsənz/ noun [C] *formal* the plural of person is people, but in formal or official language the form persons is used

purchase[1] /ˈpɜːtʃəs/ noun *formal* 2 [C] something that you buy

refrain /rɪˈfreɪn/ verb [I] *formal* to stop yourself from doing something

sidewalk /ˈsaɪdˌwɔːk/ noun [C] *American* the pavement by the side of the road

subway /ˈsʌbˌweɪ/ noun [C] 2 *American* a railway that goes under the ground

trash can /ˈtræʃ kæn/ noun [C] *American* a bin for putting rubbish in

truck /trʌk/ noun [C] ★★ *American* a large road vehicle that is used for carrying goods = lorry

vacation /v(ə)ˈkeɪʃn/ noun 2 [C/U] *American* a holiday

yard /jɑːd/ noun [C] ★★ 4 *American* a GARDEN at the front, back, or side of a house

9 Opinions

Grammar Reported statements and questions
Vocabulary Books. Films. Music. *ed* and *ing* adjectives
Useful phrases Giving your opinion

Speaking & Reading

1 Work with a partner of the opposite sex, if possible. Read the comments and complete the table according to your opinion.

Things women *never* say	Things men *never* say
	a

a) 'Let's ask that woman for directions.'
b) 'I've just picked up that enormous spider in the bath.'
c) 'But I just don't need another pair of shoes.'
d) 'You drive, darling – you're so much better at it than me.'
e) 'Do you think I'd look better if I put on a few kilos?'
f) 'Let's switch off the TV, I want to talk about our relationship.'
g) 'I'd love to have dinner with your sister. The only thing on telly tonight is football.'
h) 'Shall I check the tyre pressures when I go to the petrol station?'

Work with your partner. Add one other comment to each column.

2 Do the questionnaire. Then compare your answers with your partner.

SURVEY
Men and Women

One thousand British men and women between the ages of 18 and 35 were interviewed for a survey to find out the differences between male and female attitudes to relationships. These are the questions they were asked.

Tick the answers a), b) or c).

1 **Have you done any of the following to attract somebody?**
   a) Bought new clothes.
   b) Dieted.
   c) Lied about your age.

2 **After a first date, when do you expect him/her to call you?**
   a) The next day.
   b) Within three days.
   c) Within a fortnight.

3 **If he/she doesn't arrive on time for a first date, how long will you wait?**
   a) Five minutes.
   b) Fifteen minutes.
   c) Half an hour or more.

4 **If your partner forgets your birthday, how do you feel?**
   a) I get upset.
   b) I get angry.
   c) I don't care – it's only a birthday.

5 **What is your attitude to marriage?**
   a) I'm in favour of marriage.
   b) I don't have strong feelings about marriage.
   c) I consider marriage to be unnecessary.

6 **What is your attitude to fathers staying at home to look after the children?**
   a) It's a good idea.
   b) It's not ideal but it's OK.
   c) It's not appropriate.

Reading

1 Read about some of the more interesting findings to come out of the survey. Complete the survey results with *men* or *women*, as you think appropriate.

SURVEY RESULTS
Men and Women

On attraction Three out of four women said that they had bought new clothes to attract somebody, compared with only one in five men. Similarly, while just over half of the women told us that they had dieted so that they would
5 be more attractive, only one in ten men admitted that they had done the same. However, a significant number of both men and women admitted that they had lied about their age, with the important difference that (1) _____ tended to say they were older, while (2) _____ were more likely to
10 knock a few years off their age.

On dating The majority of people said that they expected to be called within three days after a first date. However, 35% of (3) _____ insisted that they expected to be phoned the next day, while only 19% of (4) _____ gave this answer.
15 On average, men are prepared to wait longer on a first date if the woman doesn't arrive on time. 18% of women said that they would only wait for five minutes, whereas 67% of men claimed that they would wait half an hour or more.

On birthdays The results of the survey suggest that
20 (5) _____ attach greater importance to birthdays than (6) _____ . 49% of women admitted that they got angry or upset, if their partner forgot their birthday, while more than three-quarters of the men interviewed claimed that they didn't care.

25 **On marriage** The results of the survey show that (7) _____ are more in favour of marriage than (8) _____ . 41% of (9) _____ said that they considered marriage to be unnecessary, and 20% told us that they didn't mind whether they got married or not. When we asked
30 (10) _____ about marriage, four out of five told us that they definitely intended to get married one day.

On childcare 65% of (11) _____ are in favour of fathers staying at home to look after the children. However, when we asked (12) _____ for their opinion, the majority replied
35 that it was not appropriate.

2 🔊 2.33 Listen and check. Would the survey results be different in your country?

Grammar

Reported statements

'She's not there.'
➜ He **told us** that she **wasn't** there.

'I've bought some new clothes.'
➜ She **said** that she**'d bought** some new clothes.

1 Which of the reporting verbs in the box can you use to complete the statement below?

admitted	claimed	explained	insisted	replied	said	suggested	told

'*Just over half of the women _____ us that they **had dieted**.*'

Which word must you delete from the statement if you use any of the other verbs?

2 In the reported statement in Exercise 1 the verb *diet* is in the past perfect. Which sentence (*a, b, c* or *d*) did the women actually say?

a) 'Yes, I was dieting.'   b) 'Yes, I diet.'   c) 'Yes, I've dieted.'   d) 'Yes, I'll diet.'

When you report speech, you usually move the tense back (eg present perfect becomes past perfect). True or false?

3 Complete these sentences in direct speech. Use the reported statements highlighted in the survey results above to help you choose the correct form of the verb.

a) 'Yes, I (buy) *have bought* new clothes to attract somebody.'
b) 'Yes, I (lie) _____ about my age.'
c) 'Yes, I (wait) _____ half an hour or more if my date is late.'
d) 'Yes, I (get) _____ angry, if my partner (forget) _____ my birthday.'
e) 'I (not mind) _____ whether I (get) _____ married or not.'
f) 'It (not be) _____ appropriate for fathers to stay at home.'

4 **Grammar *Extra* 9** page 142. Read the explanations and do the exercises.

Speaking

Find out how many people in the class …

- are reading a novel at the moment.
- enjoy reading biographies and autobiographies.
- still listen to the same music that they did ten years ago.
- have a favourite place to read.
- buy and play CDs.
- prefer watching a film to reading a book.
- have been to a concert recently.
- have seen a film they didn't enjoy recently.

Listening & Vocabulary

1 🔊 **2.34 Listen to seven conversations. What are the people talking about in each one? Write *B* for a book, *F* for a film and *M* for music.**

1 M, 2 …

2 The table contains words and expressions relating to books, films and music from the seven conversations in Exercise 1. Complete the table with the correct heading (*Books / Films / Music*) for each column.

a) _____	b) _____	c) _____
acting photography special effects tearjerker	album lyrics performing live techno track	bestseller can't put it down chapters difficult to get into

Add these words to the table. Some words go in more than one column. Add words of your own.

band   blues   classical   dance   director   fantasy   gig   hip-hop   a hit horror   musical   novel   orchestra   paperback   plot   premier   reggae science fiction   short story   soundtrack   stereo system   storyline   subtitles

3 🔊 **2.35 Listen to these extracts from film soundtracks. What sort of film do you think they go with? Choose from the list below.**

action films   comedies   gangster films   horror films   love stories romantic comedies   science fiction films   spy films   thrillers   war films   westerns

Work in groups. Think of some films of each of the types above. Which types of films do people in your group like best?

Reading & Grammar

1 Read this web report of an interview with Tom Hanks. Why is he known as 'Mr Nice Guy'?

Mr Nice Guy

In an online interview for Contactmusic.com, Hollywood actor, Tom Hanks, has revealed that he's happy being known as 'Mr Nice Guy'.

When <u>they asked him how he felt about his 'nice guy' persona</u>, he told them that he was happy with it and that he felt confident that he lived up to his reputation.

5   They asked him where this reputation had come from, and he told them that he thought it was because he had always cooperated with the press. They asked him whether he had ever had problems with the paparazzi, and he told them that he hadn't because he respected people, even when he didn't like them.

Brisbanetimes.com asked the *Forrest Gump* star why he always played the part of
10   the nice guy in films and never the villain. He reminded them that he had played the part of an executioner in *The Green Mile*, but, because of his nice guy image, the media had reported that he was a 'nice executioner'!

Finally, Chinadaily.com asked him what his current plans were, and he said that he wanted to direct again, but that he couldn't do that at the moment, because it would take him away from his children. What a nice guy!

Reported questions

'How do you feel?'
➔ We asked him **how he felt.**
'Have you ever had problems?'
➔ We asked him **whether/ if he had ever had** problems.

2 What are the actual questions that were used in the interview?
Underline the five reported questions in the report and rewrite them in direct speech.

How do you feel about your 'nice guy' persona?

3 Look at the examples in Exercise 2 and decide if the following statements are true or false when you report questions.

a) The tense usually moves back in a reported question (present simple ➔ past simple).

b) *Whether* or *if* are used to report *yes/no* questions. (*Did you go out?* ➔ *She asked me if I'd been out.*)

c) The word order changes to **subject** + *verb* (*Who are you?* ➔ *He asked me who I was.*).

4   **Pairwork** **Student A:** page 119 **Student B:** page 124

Speaking: anecdote

1 🌐 2.36 Listen to Alice talking about a film she enjoyed. Read the questions and tick the answers that are correct.

a) What's the title of the film? *Forrest Gump.* ✓
b) When and where did you see it? **The other night at the cinema.**
c) Who's in it? **Tom Hanks, Robin Wright and Sally Field.**
d) Who directed it? **I can't remember.**
e) What is it based on? **A true story.**
f) What type of film is it? **A thriller.**
g) What's the main story? **It's about the life of Forrest Gump.**
h) What do you particularly like about it? **The bits where he meets famous people.**
i) What was the soundtrack like? **Great.**
j) What kind of ending does it have? **A happy ending.**
k) Would you recommend this film? **No, I wouldn't.**

Listen again and change the incorrect answers.

2 You are going to tell your partner about a film you enjoyed.

- Ask yourself the questions in Exercise 1.
- Think about *what* to say and *how* to say it.
- Tell your partner about a film you enjoyed.

Vocabulary & Speaking

1 Read and underline the correct alternatives in the sentences below.

BOOK

choice

We asked several people the question, 'How do you choose a book to read?' Here are their replies.

'I judge a book by its cover. If the cover looks (1) **interesting** / **interested**, I buy the book. Sometimes I'm lucky, and the book is good. And sometimes I'm (2) **disappointing** / **disappointed**.'

'I always read book reviews in newspapers and magazines, and when I read about a book that sounds (3) **interesting** / **interested**, I write it down in my diary.'

'I don't take any risks – I always read books by authors I know. I get really (4) **exciting** / **excited** when one of my favourite authors brings out a new book, and I buy it immediately. This way I'm never (5) **disappointing** / **disappointed**.

'I read the first page, and if it's (6) **boring** / **bored**, I don't buy the book – if I want to turn over the page and carry on reading, I buy the book.'

'It's easy – I never read fiction but I'm (7) **fascinating** / **fascinated** by biographies of famous people. I find strong women in history particularly (8) **inspiring** / **inspired**.'

'I tend to choose books written by women. Women have a better feeling for characters and the relationships between them, and that's what I find (9) **interesting** / **interested** in a book. Having said that, I've just finished *The Beach* by Alex Garland, and it was brilliant!'

🔘 2.37 Listen and check your answers. How do *you* choose a book?

2 Add the adjectives in Exercise 1 to the table below.

To describe how people feel	To describe the thing (or person) that causes the feeling
annoyed challenged confused exhausted relaxed tired worried	annoying challenging confusing exhausting relaxing tiring worrying

3 Tell your partner how you're feeling today. Explain why. Choose words from the table in Exercise 2 or use your own ideas.

Choose three other adjectives and say what makes you feel like this.
'On Monday evenings I feel exhausted. I work in a bar and it's very tiring.'

Pronunciation

1 Say the words in the box and add them to the table.

~~annoying~~ challenging disappointing entertaining exciting exhausting interesting overwhelming worrying

A: ☐□□	B: □☐□	C: □□☐□
	ann<u>oy</u>ing	

2 Underline the stressed syllable in each word.

🔘 2.38 Listen, check and repeat.

Reading & Vocabulary

1 Look at the photograph and read the synopsis of *Pride and Prejudice* by Jane Austen. What kind of book is it? Would you be interested in reading it? Why? / Why not?

---

http://synopsisnovels.com

Home Search Shop Bookmarks

Pride and Prejudice (Jane Austen): **synopsis**

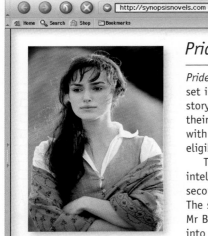

Keira Knightly as Elizabeth Bennet in the film *Pride and Prejudice* (2005)

Pride and Prejudice is a classic romantic novel set in England in the late 18th century. The story revolves around Mr and Mrs Bennet and their five daughters. Mrs Bennet is obsessed with finding wealthy husbands for her five eligible daughters.

The central female character is lively, intelligent and rebellious Elizabeth, the second of Mr and Mrs Bennet's daughters. The story begins with the news that Mr Bingley, a wealthy single man, is moving into a neighbouring estate. Mrs Bennet is determined to marry one of her daughters to Mr Bingley and is delighted when he is attracted to Jane, her eldest.

Elizabeth takes an instant dislike to Mr Darcy, Mr Bingley's rich and aristocratic friend. The handsome and mysterious Mr Darcy at first considers Elizabeth to be socially inferior to him, but he gradually grows more interested in her. She continues to despise him and instead becomes attracted to a handsome, but dishonest, military officer.

Fate causes Elizabeth and Darcy to cross paths frequently, and while they don't appear to like one another, they can't stop thinking about each other.

As the story unfolds, true love overcomes class, family, pride and prejudice, and the story ends with a double wedding.

---

2 Read these reviews of *Pride and Prejudice* from a website. In the spaces provided, write the score that you think each person gave the book.

a) I love Jane Austen's novels, and *Pride and Prejudice* is my favourite. The characters are engaging and believable, especially Elizabeth. The storyline is brilliant and I found it hard to put down. It's wonderful! *Jan, New York.* 9/10

b) I didn't particularly enjoy reading *Pride and Prejudice* but I thought it was well written and quite witty and amusing in parts. *Will, UK* __ /10

c) I don't usually read romantic novels, but I was surprised how much I enjoyed *Pride and Prejudice*. I think Jane Austen manages to describe 18th century society very well. However, I think her novels probably appeal more to women, and I don't think I'll be reading any more of her books. *Frank, Sydney* __ /10

d) I bought Jane Austen's novel because I enjoyed the film. The best thing about the book is the hilarious dialogue and even though I knew how the story ended, I was still relieved when things turned out well for the main characters. *Agnes, Scotland* __ /10

e) This is the most boring book I have ever read. I couldn't relate to the characters at all – I thought they were irritating and silly, and there isn't much of a story. *Mico, Sweden* __ /10

---

3 Replace the *italicised* words in the following sentences with the words in the box.

central   engaging   gripping   is set   storyline   thought-provoking

a) The story *takes place* in New York.
b) One of the *main* characters is a spy.
c) The characters are believable and *appealing*.
d) The *plot* is complex and full of twists.
e) It was *really exciting* from start to finish.
f) It was *stimulating and intriguing*.

Think of a book you have read or a film you have seen that fits each of the descriptions above. Tell a partner about it.

Writing

Write a review of a book. Include the following information.

- The title of the book and the author.
- The type of book.
- Where it takes place.
- The central characters.
- A summary of the plot (in the present tense).
- What you liked or didn't like about the book.

Useful phrases

1 Work in groups of three. Discuss the advantages and disadvantages of owning a car. Note down as many points as you can.

2 🌐 2.39 Listen to three friends having a discussion about owning a car. Do they mention any of the same points you noted down?

3 Work with a partner. Complete the conversation with one word in each space.

Kim: Hi Ryan. Come in.
Jess: Hi, Ryan. What happened to you? You're late!
Ryan: Yes, I'm really sorry – I had to wait ages for a bus.
Jess: What's wrong with your car?
Ryan: I've sold it! I (1) *think* there are too many cars in this town.
Jess: Well, that's true, (2) _____ a car is useful.
Ryan: I'm not so (3) _____ about that. The traffic's awful, and I can never find a parking space.
Kim: But how are you going to get to work?
Ryan: By bicycle.
Kim: (4) _____ you think bicycles are dangerous?
Ryan: Not really. They're certainly less dangerous for the environment.
Jess: Well, as far (5) _____ I'm concerned, a car is essential – I have to drive my kids to school.
Ryan: Your kids should walk to school. If you ask (6) _____ , children don't get enough exercise.
Jess: (7) _____ 's rubbish! My kids do football, swimming and tennis – and I need a car to get them there on time.
Kim: I (8) _____ with Jess – I couldn't live without my car. I sometimes work in the evening, and I don't feel safe getting a bus late at night.
Ryan: OK, I take your point, (9) _____ aren't you worried about pollution?
Jess: Do you (10) _____ what I think? It's not my problem. I can't save the planet.
Ryan: But (11) _____ 's nonsense! Everybody can do something!
Kim: OK, OK, you're (12) _____ ! Now let's change the subject. (13) _____ do you think of my new television?
Jess: It's great – but I hope it's solar-powered!

Listen again and check your answers.

4 Classify the highlighted useful phrases from the conversation in the following table.

Ask for an opinion	Give an opinion	Agree with an opinion	Disagree with an opinion
Don't you think bicycles are dangerous?	*I think there are too many cars …*	*Well, that's true, …*	*I'm not so sure about that.*

🌐 2.40 Listen and repeat the useful phrases. Copy the stress and intonation exactly.

5 Work in groups of three. Choose a topic below and note down all the advantages and disadvantages. Write a short conversation between three friends including some useful phrases from Exercise 4.

> living abroad   being a woman or a man   using public transport
> living with your parents   working from home

Practise your conversation.

Vocabulary *Extra*

Collocations

1 Work with a partner. Decide which verbs combine most naturally with the nouns to form collocations.

	action	advice	a comment	a decision	a mistake	an opinion
give	✗	✔				
make						
take						

Check your answers in the dictionary extracts for the nouns. Notice how strong collocations are in bold in the example sentences.

2 Work with a partner. Decide if you agree or disagree with the following statements.

a) Collocation means the way that particular words regularly and naturally combine with each other. So *have an opinion* is a strong collocation, but *own an opinion* is not.

b) You should try to identify, record and learn collocations that you find in English texts or in dictionary entries.

c) Learning collocations will help you: (1) sound more natural; (2) be more precise; (3) improve your writing style.

3 Underline the correct collocation in each of these dictionary examples.

a) verb + noun
  • *The students all __gave__ / provided / spoke their opinions.*

b) adjective + noun
  • *Professor Wright has a big / high / large opinion of your work.*

c) noun + noun
  • *Despite our disagreements / differences / distinctions of opinion we remained good friends.*

d) noun + preposition
  • *What is your opinion by / for / of her latest novel?*

e) adverb + adjective
  • *It now seems highly / totally / completely unlikely that the project will be finished on time.*

f) verb + adverb
  • *Everyone spoke very strongly / greatly / highly of him.*

Check your answers in the dictionary extracts for *highly* and *opinion*.

4 Use the collocation information in the dictionary extracts for *advice* and *mistake* to complete the questions.

a) Do you sometimes ask your boss or teacher *for* advice?

b) When was the last time you o_____ advice to a friend?

c) Are you more likely to a_____ advice from your parents or your friends?

d) Have you ever i_____ somebody's advice and then regretted it?

e) What's the most e_____ mistake you've ever made?

Ask your partner the questions.

5 Check your own dictionary. How does it show information about collocations?

---

action /ˈækʃən/ noun ★★★ 1 [U] the process of doing something: *Police say they will take tough action against drug dealers* ♦

advice /ədˈvaɪs/ noun [U] ★★★ an opinion that someone gives you about the best thing to do in a particular situation: *Ask your father for advice.* ♦ *We are here to give people advice about health issues.* ♦ *I took his advice* (=did what he advised) *and left.* ♦ *She's acting on her lawyer's advice.*

> **Words often used with advice**
> *Verbs often used with advice*
> ■ **give, offer, provide** + ADVICE: give someone advice
> ■ **ask for, seek** + ADVICE: ask for advice
> ■ **accept, act on, follow, take** + ADVICE: do what someone advises
> ■ **disregard, ignore, reject** + ADVICE: not do what someone advises

comment¹ /ˈkɒment/ noun [C/U] ★★★ a written or spoken remark giving an opinion: *Did she make any comment about Eddie?* ♦

decision /dɪˈsɪʒ(ə)n/ noun ★★★ 1 [C] a choice that you make after you have thought carefully about something: *The committee will make a decision by the end of the week.* ♦ *Sometimes managers need to take decisions quickly.* ♦ *Have you come to a decision yet?* ♦ *a decision to do sth Mrs Osman has announced her decision to retire.*

highly /ˈhaɪli/ adv ★★★ 1 used before some adjectives to mean 'very', or 'very well': *It now seems highly unlikely that the project will be finished on time.* ♦ *She's a highly educated young woman.* 2 used for saying that someone or something is very good or very important: *a highly valued member of staff* ♦ *Everyone we talked to spoke very highly of him.*

mistake¹ /mɪˈsteɪk/ noun [C] ★★ 1 something that you have not done correctly, or something you say or think that is not correct: *spelling/grammar mistakes* 2 something that you do that you later wish you had not done, because it causes a lot of problems: *You're making a big mistake.* ♦ *it would be a mistake to do sth It would be a mistake to think that the trouble is over.* ♦ *make the mistake of doing sth I made the mistake of inviting Jennifer to the party.* PHRASE **by mistake** if you do something by mistake, you do it accidentally =BY ACCIDENT ≠ ON PURPOSE: *I'm sorry, I opened one of your letters by mistake.*

> **Words often used with mistake**
> *Adjectives often used with mistake (noun, sense 2)*
> ■ **bad, big, costly, dreadful, expensive, fatal, serious, terrible** + MISTAKE: used about mistakes that have bad results

opinion /əˈpɪnjən/ noun [C] ★★★ the attitude that someone has towards something, especially about how good it is: *What is your opinion of her latest novel?* ♦ *Professor Wright has a high opinion of your work* (=thinks your work is good). ♦ *The students all gave their opinions.* ♦ *Despite our differences of opinion, we remained good friends.* ♦ *The book was a waste of time, in my opinion.* ♦ *Public opinion has turned against the government in recent months.*

Review C

▶ Grammar *Extra* pages 138–143

Grammar

1 **Underline the correct words.**

a) Has anyone ever <u>told you</u> / **told** that you have beautiful eyes?

b) Do you mind **having** / **to have** your picture taken?

c) Have you ever **promised to do** / **promised doing** something and then not done it?

d) Do you enjoy **spending** / **spend** time alone at the weekend?

e) Did your parents ever tell you **not do** / **not to do** something, but you did it anyway?

Work with a partner. Ask and answer the questions.

2 **Complete the text with the passive form of the verbs.**

Yesterday two men (1 arrest) *were arrested* in Lewisham, after a bank manager (2 rob) _____ at gunpoint.

It (3 believe) _____ that the thieves used a car that (4 report) _____ stolen two days earlier. The car (5 find) _____ abandoned several miles away. The two suspects (6 take) _____ to the police station for questioning. The money (7 not find) _____ yet . Anyone with information about the robbery (8 ask) _____ to call Lewisham police.

3 **Complete the story with the past simple or past perfect form of the verbs.**

You'll never guess what happened to me last night! After finishing work, I (1 go) *went* to the gym, as usual. Then I went out to a restaurant with some clients. When it was time to go, I (2 realise) _____ I (3 leave) _____ my bag at the gym – with my keys in it! Unfortunately, my wife, Kerry (4 not be) _____ at home because she (5 go) _____ to Scotland for a meeting. Anyway, I went back to the gym, but it (6 already close) _____ . So I went home. All the lights were off, so I (7 decide) _____ to try and climb through the downstairs bathroom window, which was partly open. Just as I was trying to open the window, I (8 see) _____ a light. It was two police officers. I explained that I (9 lose) _____ my key, but they wouldn't listen. They were just going to put me in the police car, when Kerry (10 open) _____ the door. She (11 get) _____ back early from her meeting, and (12 be) _____ inside the house the whole time – watching a crime thriller on TV!

4 **Underline the correct modals of deduction.**

a) Tim's plane has landed, but he's not here yet. He **can't** / **may** be stuck in Customs.

b) There are some grey clouds in the sky. It **can** / **could** rain later.

c) Everyone is leaving the office. It **may** / **must** be the end of the day.

d) The lights in their apartment are all off. They're not answering the phone. They **can't** / **might** be at home.

5 **Complete the sentences in reported speech.**

a) 'I'm innocent!' The man told the police that he *was* innocent.

b) 'I'm not a bank robber.' He said that he _____ a bank robber.

c) 'On Monday morning I was at work.' He told the police that on Monday morning he _____ at work.

d) 'I wasn't in town when the robbery happened.' He claimed that he _____ in town when the robbery happened.

e) 'I have never seen Smith and Jones before.' He added that he _____ Smith and Jones before.

f) 'I didn't rob the bank.' He insisted that he _____ the bank.

6 **Spot the mistake! Cross out the incorrect sentence.**

1 a) ~~These computers are using all over the world.~~
   b) These computers are used all over the world.

2 a) I told him not to talk to anybody.
   b) I told him to not talk to anybody.

3 a) You've worked really hard. You must be exhausted!
   b) You've worked really hard. You can't be exhausted!

4 a) When I got to the airport, the plane was already left.
   b) When I got to the airport, the plane had already left.

5 a) They said me they weren't hungry.
   b) They told me they weren't hungry.

6 a) She asked me if I needed help.
   b) She asked me did I need help?

Vocabulary

1 **Match the definitions with the words in the box.**

> desperate ~~hypocritical~~ insensitive obsessed
> photogenic unflattering

a) to describe someone pretending to be morally good but behaving in a way that shows that they are not sincere *hypocritical*

b) unable to stop thinking about something or someone

c) to describe someone who looks good in photographs

d) not noticing or caring about other people's feelings

e) making someone seem unpleasant or unattractive

f) needing or wanting something very much

2 **Complete the sentences with the words in the box. There are two extra words.**

> arrested chase convicted court escorted
> sentenced shoplifted stolen ~~thief~~

a) The police caught the *thief* stealing a frozen chicken in the supermarket.

b) Armed police _____ the gang to the police station.

c) Yesterday three priceless paintings were _____ from an art gallery in Geneva.

d) Traffic police have _____ a sixteen-year-old boy after a ten-kilometre _____ through London.

e) The witness told the _____ that she had seen the man holding the knife.

f) After a long trial the judge _____ the men to ten years in jail.

3 **Underline the correct words.**

Dear Mum and Dad,
We're having a great time here in Jamaica. We're staying in a cabin on the (1) **sandy** / **southern** part of the island, overlooking the (2) **beach** / **white sands** of the beach below. We're (3) **surrounded** / **overlooking** by beautiful forests and have (4) **spectacular** / **towering** views of the mountains. Some of the beaches are very (5) **visible** / **popular** with tourists, but our little beach is hidden from the road, so it's completely (6) **unspoilt** / **packed**. I want to stay here for ever!
Love, Helen

4 **Complete the words for features of a landscape.**

a) *a*ncient r__ __ns
b) B__ddh__st t__mpl__
c) h__gh-r__s__ b__ __ld__ng
d) b__ __lt-__p skyl__n__
e) sn__ w-c__pp__d m__ __nt__ __n
f) w__t__rf__ll

5 **Complete the fixed expressions.**

a) I either like a person, or I hate them. It's **all or** *nothing* with me.

b) _____ **or later**, I'm going to have to get a new car.

c) I never seem to get any _____ **and quiet** at home.

d) I'd like to work in an office where I can just **come and** _____ as I please.

e) I think I spent £400 on holiday, **give or** _____ a few pounds.

f) I can't work unless my desk is **clean and** _____ .

Tick the sentences that are true for you. Discuss with a partner.

6 **Put the words in the box in the correct group. Some words can go in more than one group.**

> ~~band~~ ~~chapter~~ ~~comedy~~ gig horror
> lyrics musical orchestra plot
> science fiction storyline tearjerker
> techno western

a) music: *band,* ... b) films: *comedy,* ...
c) books: *chapter,* ...

7 **Underline the correct words.**

a) I was **fascinated** / **fascinating** by her eyes.

b) This is one of the most **boring** / **bored** films I have ever seen.

c) I was **interested** / **interesting** to hear she's writing a novel.

d) The story is **confused** / **confusing**. I don't understand it.

e) I received some **worrying** / **worried** news about my dad.

f) Are you **disappointed** / **disappointing** with your results?

Pronunciation

1 **Look at some words from Units 7–9. Say the words and add them to the table.**

> ~~annoying~~ ~~celebrity~~ ~~classical~~ director dramatic
> embarrassing experience fantasy interviewed
> photography privacy suggested

A: □▢□	B: □□□	C: □▢□□
annoying	*classical*	*celebrity*

2 **Underline the stressed syllable in each word.**

🔊 2.41 **Listen, check and repeat.**

Reading & Listening

1 Read the newspaper article and decide which sentence (*a*, *b* or *c*) best summarises the story.

a) A newsreader is sent to jail for stealing some property from her TV station.

b) A newsreader refuses to read a news item because she thinks it's too trivial.

c) A female newsreader accuses her male co-presenters of making sexist comments.

Newsreader takes a stand

MSNBC newsreader Mika Brzezinski caused a sensation on live TV when she refused to read out the station's lead story. Hotel heiress Paris Hilton had just been released from jail after serving twenty-two days for a driving offence, and the TV station wanted this to be their lead story. An emotional Brzezinski explained that she didn't want to cover such a trivial topic when there were much more serious issues in the news to report on that day. She tried to burn the script but was stopped by co-host Willie Geist. She then asked Geist to burn it, which he naturally refused to do. She tore the script up and was almost immediately handed a new copy of the same script by her producer. Meanwhile, Geist and her other male co-host, Joe Scarborough, made mocking comments and interrupted her. When she finally shredded the script, Scarborough commented, 'You've changed the world, Mika Brzezinski!', to which she replied, 'Yeah, I have. At least my world. I'm not doing it. I'm not doing the story.' Almost as soon as it happened, people started calling the station to congratulate her on taking a stand.

2 Read the text again. Are the statements true or false?

a) Mika Brzezinski is a newsreader. *True.*

b) She thought the TV station was wrong in their choice of lead story.

c) She burned her script.

d) She asked her co-host to help her destroy the script.

e) Her co-hosts listened to her respectfully.

f) In the end she agreed to cover the story.

g) People phoned into the TV station with messages of support.

3 🌐 2.42 Listen to an American radio phone-in show. Do most of the callers have a positive or negative reaction towards Mika Brzezinski's actions?

4 Listen again and underline the correct option to complete each sentence.

a) Luke thinks Mika's views represent **a minority** / **most** of America's views.

b) Luke **criticises** / **congratulates** Mika's co-hosts.

c) Mika's actions **inspired** / **disappointed** Maria.

d) Jason thinks Mika was **right** / **wrong** to refuse to read out the story.

e) Jason **agrees** / **disagrees** with Mika's co-hosts.

f) Cathy **feels** / **doesn't feel** the same way as Jason.

g) Cathy **thinks** / **doesn't think** the paparazzi reflect her opinions about Paris Hilton.

5 What do you think about Mika Brzezinski's actions? Was she right to refuse, or should a newsreader always do what the producer asks him or her to do? Work in pairs. Discuss your opinion with a partner.

Writing & Speaking

1 Work with a partner. Look at a news reporter's notes for a story and compare them with her finished article.

- John Kronau (25) arrested by NY State Police.
- Frightened cashier at Troy Savings Bank.
- Handed her note: 'Don't be alarmed – this is bank deposit – please take money out of envelope, put in my account.'
- Later said: 'It was innocent joke.'
- Added: 'I've never been in trouble with police before.'

25-year-old John Kronau (1) *was* arrested by the New York State Police after he (2) _____ frightened a bank cashier at Troy Savings Bank. Kronau handed the cashier (3) _____ note that read, 'Don't be alarmed – this is (4) _____ bank deposit – please take the money out of (5) _____ envelope and put (6) _____ into my account.' He later claimed that it (7) _____ been an innocent joke and added that he had never (8) _____ in trouble with (9) _____ police before.

Complete the finished article with the words in the box.

a	a	been	had	had	it	the	the	~~was~~

2 Choose the best headline for the article.

a BANK CASHIER ARRESTED

b MAN ROBS BANK

c JOKER HELD BY POLICE

3 Look again at the notes, the finished article and the headlines. Underline the correct words in these statements (a–c).

a) When you take notes you often **include / leave out** short words such as *a*, *the*, *be* and *have*.

b) You usually use **direct / reported** speech in notes and **direct / reported** speech in finished articles.

c) In headlines you **include / leave out** short words such as *a*, *the*, *be* and *have*.

4 Work with your partner. Read the set of notes below and write up the finished article to appear in the next edition of *Internet News*. Write a headline for the story.

- £5,000 stolen from supermarket (25 May), Liverpool.
- Local newspaper ran story, claimed thief took £7,000.
- Thief called newspaper to complain and said: 'Maybe supermarket manager took extra £2,000.'
- Staff at newspaper kept him busy on phone while police traced call.
- Arrested ten minutes later while still on phone talking to newspaper!

5 Discuss the questions in small groups.

a) What amusing news stories have you heard recently?

b) Should all news be heavy and serious, or is there a place for lightweight stories about celebrities?

c) Where do you get most of your news from – newspapers, TV or the internet?

d) In your opinion, what's the most important news story of the last week?

▶ 🎵 2.43 **Song:** *Somewhere Only We Know*

10 Childhood

Grammar Defining relative clauses. Real conditionals. Indirect questions
Vocabulary Phrasal verbs. Childhood. Proverbs. *make* and *let*
Useful phrases Describing objects

Reading & Vocabulary

1 Note down the names of three children you know. Ask a partner about the three children on their list.

'Who's Alfonso?' 'He's my nephew – my sister's son. He's …'

2 Read these children's definitions of a mother and choose the one you like best.

A mum is a person who cries when you do something bad, and cries even harder when you do something good. *(Robin, age 14)*

A mum is a person who cares for you and tucks you in at night. When you've made a mistake, she says it's all right. *(Jan, age 13)*

A mum is a woman who says 'go to bed', and when she says that, you stay very quiet and she forgets about you. *(Aishling, age 9)*

A mum is someone who always knows when there is something wrong, even if you don't tell her. *(Lisa, age 14)*

Mothers are people who sit up worrying about you, and when you come home, they yell at you. *(Gary, age 13)*

Mothers are people who are angry when you're at home and sad when you're away. *(Vinay, age 12)*

My mum is the sort of person who is always tidying up. If you put anything down and go away for a minute, when you come back to it, it has been tidied away. *(John, age 9)*

Work with your partner. Write a similar definition for a father.

3 Underline the correct particle or preposition in these questions about childhood. Use a dictionary if necessary.
a) Who **brought** you **up** / **down**?
b) Who **told** you **off** / **apart** when you were naughty?
c) Who **worried for** / **about** you when you went out at night?
d) Who **cared of** / **for** you when you were sick?
e) Who **tucked** you **in** / **away** at night?
f) Who **yelled at** / **for** you when they were angry with you?
g) Who **looked through** / **after** you when your parents were out?
h) Who **tidied up** / **out** after you had played with your toys?

Think about the different people who helped to take care of you in your own childhood – parents, older brothers and sisters, babysitters, etc. Answer the questions and compare your answers with your partner.

Listening

1 🌐 **3.01 Listen to some children defining five things from the list below. Which things do they talk about and in what order?**

a) God
b) a dinosaur
c) an iceberg
d) a vet
e) a robber
f) a museum
g) autumn
h) a desert
i) a jungle

2 **Work with a partner. Imagine you are explaining other things from the list to a four-year-old child. Write down what you would say. Ask another pair of students to identify what you have defined.**

Grammar

Defining relative clauses

an adult **who looks after you**
a child **(that) you look after**
a toy **which makes a noise**
a toy **(that) you play with**

1 **Look at the children's definitions below showing the subject of the verb in the relative clauses. Answer the questions (1–3).**

a) 'A person subject that verb helps people, in heaven.'

b) 'It's something subject that verb lived a very long time ago.'

1 In which definition can you replace the relative pronoun *that* with *which*?
2 In which definition can you replace the relative pronoun *that* with *who*?
3 Is it possible to leave out the relative pronouns in these definitions? Why? / Why not?

2 **Work with your partner. Read the definitions (a–d) of words to do with childhood and follow the instructions (1–3).**

a) A *truant* is a school pupil who stays away from school without permission.
b) A *bib* is a piece of cloth that protects babies' clothes when they are eating.
c) A *dummy* is a plastic object which you put in a baby's mouth to stop the baby crying.
d) A *nanny* is a person who you employ to look after your children.

1 Underline the relative clauses in each definition.
2 Identify the subject and the verb in each relative clause.
3 Decide which relative pronouns you must keep and which ones you can leave out.

What is the translation of these relative pronouns in your language?

3 **Pairwork Student A:** page 119 **Student B:** page 124

4 **Work with a partner. Put the words in the correct order to make questions about your memories of childhood. Then discuss questions 1 and 2.**

What can you remember about …

a) to / the school / that / went / you ? *the school that you went to?*
b) played / the toys / with / you / that ?
c) that / you / to / invited / the parties / were ?
d) the books / were / in / which / interested / you ?
e) about / that / the things / you / worried / were ?
f) the things / dream / used to / of / that / you ?

1 What type of word does each question end with?
2 Can you leave out the relative pronouns *which* and *that* in these questions? Why? / Why not?

Work with your partner. Ask and answer the questions (a–f).

5 **Grammar *Extra* 10, Part 1** page 144. Read the explanations and do the exercises.

Reading

1 **Which of the following 'white lies' did you hear when you were a child? Tell a partner.**

a) If you write to Father Christmas, he'll bring you presents.
b) If you put your tooth under your pillow, the Tooth Fairy will take it.
c) If you eat your crusts, your hair will curl.
d) If you eat carrots, you'll be able to see in the dark.
e) If the wind changes, the expression on your face will stay forever.
f) If you tell a lie, your nose will grow.
g) If you sit too near the television, you'll get square eyes.

2 **Which of these two statements do you agree with?**

a) It's wrong to tell children a lie under any circumstances. They won't trust you later in life.
b) It's OK to tell children a white lie if it protects their innocence or stimulates their imagination.

Read the article and find out which statement the psychologists agree with.

Lies, white lies ... and psychologists

I lie to my four-year-old child, and not just about Father Christmas and the tooth fairy. I started when he was about two years old, and now I can't help myself. If he wants to watch television, and I think he's already watched enough
5 for one day, I tell him that he'll get square eyes. I tell him that, unless he eats his carrots, he'll have to wear glasses, and that if he eats his crusts, he'll have lovely curly hair.

Most parents tell their children lies, and they're usually the same lies that their parents told them. But is there
10 anything wrong with it?

Yes, say a group of parents who feel that unless you're 100% truthful with your children, you can't expect the same in return. They think that it's better to try to make a child understand the real reasons why it's bad for him or her to
15 watch another hour of television or eat too many sweets than to take the easy route and tell a lie.

No, say busy parents who think it's ridiculous to explain the detrimental effects of too much television or the lack of nutritious value of a sweet to a four-year-old.
20 It depends, say psychologists. White lies that protect a child's innocence or stimulate their imagination are good for them.

Psychologists believe that many of these white lies may actually benefit children by stimulating their brains,
25 helping them develop language skills and making them more creative. The story of the tooth fairy, for example, aims to make the world a more magical place for children, and to help them through a stage in their life. Father Christmas
30 comes into the same category: he's part of the magic of Christmas, and parents enjoy the fun and excitement he brings to their children.

Other white lies originate from the need to encourage children to eat properly. If a child thinks that carrots will
35 improve their eyesight, they're more likely to eat up their vegetables. Crusts may not have anything to do with the curls in their hair, but if the story helps to get a child to finish their lunch, then the white lie is worth telling.

Some myths were created to improve children's behaviour.
40 They warn them to stop pulling stupid faces or stop telling lies. Others are designed to avoid unpleasant or awkward truths, such as where babies come from and why great grandma doesn't come to lunch
45 any more.

So should parents feel guilty for not being 100% truthful with their children? In my opinion,
50 no, because most white lies are fun or educational. But make sure you know the difference between a serious lie and a
55 white lie – you don't want your nose to grow in front of your children!

3 **According to the article what are the potential benefits of telling white lies? Match a verb from box *A* with a noun from box *B* and write sentences to explain the benefits.**

A
~~avoid~~   develop   eat up
protect   stimulate

B
~~awkward truths~~   imagination   innocence
language skills   vegetables

White lies can help avoid awkward truths.

What common white lies are children told in your country? What things did your parents use to say to you? Tell your partner.

Pronunciation

1 🌐 3.02 **Listen to the words and identify the silent letter in each group.**

   a) know   knee   knife
       Silent letter = k
   b) white   hour   ghost
   c) doubt   debt   bomb

   d) <u>c</u>astle   li<u>s</u>ten   of<u>t</u>en
   e) whose   wrist   sword
   f) psy<u>ch</u>ologist   pneu<u>m</u>onia   psy<u>ch</u>iatrist

2 **Listen and repeat.**

Grammar

Real conditionals

If it**'s** fine on Sunday,
we**'ll go** for a picnic.
If you **want** to join us,
bring some food.
Jon **won't come** unless
you ask him.

unless = if … not

1 **Read this extract from the article on page 90.**

   … unless he eats his carrots, he'll have to wear glasses …

   Complete the second sentence so that it has the same meaning as the extract above.

   If he _____ his carrots, he'll have to wear glasses.

2 **Read these rules about real conditional sentences. Are they true or false?**

   a) Real conditional sentences have two clauses: an *if*-clause and a main clause.
   b) They talk about 'real' or possible situations including threats, warnings and promises.
   c) You usually use a present tense in the *if*-clause – you <u>never</u> use *will*.
   d) You usually use *will, can, might*, etc. or an imperative form in the main clause.
   e) *Unless* means the same as *if … not*.

3 **Work with a partner. Read the following sentences said by a parent to a child and discuss the meanings. Underline the correct alternatives.**

   a) If <u>**you're**</u> / **you'll be** very good, I might buy you an ice cream.
   b) If **you fall off** / **you'll fall off** that wall, don't come crying to me.
   c) If **you'll phone** / **you're phoning** your friends this evening, don't stay on the line too long.
   d) **If** / **Unless** you hurry up, you'll be late for school.
   e) If **you haven't finished** / **you've finished** your homework, you can't watch TV.
   f) If **you've finished** / **you are finishing** your dinner, you can leave the table.
   g) **If** / **Unless** you're going to stay out late, take a front door key.
   h) If **you're going to play** / **you'll play** that awful music, shut your bedroom door.

   What age (0–18) do you think the child would be if a parent was saying these things?

4   **Grammar *Extra* 10, Part 2** page 144. Read the explanations and do the exercises.

Vocabulary & Speaking

1 **Correct the statements (*a–f*).**

   a) If the boss ~~will be~~ *is* away, nobody will do any work.
   b) If you will get something easily, you won't be sorry to lose it.
   c) Unless you will consider something carefully, you might fail.
   d) Unless you will concentrate, you won't succeed.
   e) If you will fail the first time, you might not want to try again.
   f) Unless you will make an effort, you won't succeed.

   1 You snooze, you lose.
   2 No pain, no gain.
   3 Once bitten, twice shy.
   4 Easy come, easy go.
   5 Look before you leap.
   6 When the cat's away, the mice will play.

   Match each statement (*a–f*) to a common English proverb (1–6).

2 **Work with a partner. Think of other proverbs you have in your own language(s). How would you say them in English using *If …* or *Unless …* ?**

Listening & Grammar

1 🔘 **3.03 Listen to a television programme about bringing up children and choose the best definition for *pushy parents*.**

a) Parents who are very liberal and give their children lots of freedom.
b) Parents who are very ambitious for their children to be the best, whatever the cost.
c) Parents who are very strict and don't allow their children to play or have friends.

2 Listen again and underline the correct alternative.

a) George and Rachel **agree** / **disagree** about how to bring up their daughter.
b) Hayley is **four** / **five** years old.
c) Rachel wants Hayley to be a **rock** / **film** star.
d) Hayley has singing lessons and acting classes every **week** / **summer**.
e) At the weekend Hayley goes to **parties** / **auditions**.
f) George thinks his wife is **obsessed** / **reasonable**.
g) **George** / **Rachel** is the 'pushy parent'.

3 The studio audience asked George and Rachel some questions. Look at the answers. Write *G* if you think it's George's opinion and *R* if you think it's Rachel's.

a) How does Hayley feel?
'She enjoys life.' ☐   'She's too young to know.' ☐

b) What are you going to do when Hayley starts school?
'Continue doing auditions. We've invested a lot of time and money.' ☐
'Stop doing auditions. Our child isn't a business.' ☐

c) Are you depriving Hayley of a normal childhood?
'Yes.' ☐   'No.' ☐

d) Do you have any other children and how are they affected?
'Yes, our son misses his mom.' ☐   'Yes, our son is proud of his little sister.' ☐

e) How stressful is it to be a film star?
'Very stressful.' ☐   'We can cope.' ☐

🔘 **3.04 Listen and check.**

Indirect questions

How **does she feel?** ➜
Do you know how
she feels?

Is she happy? ➜
Can you tell me **if/whether
she's** happy?

4 The questions in Exercise 3 are direct questions, but the audience actually asked indirect questions. Complete their indirect questions using the question frames below.

a) Do you know … *how Hayley feels?*
b) Can you tell me …
c) Do you think …
d) Could you tell me …
e) Do you have any idea …

🔘 **3.05 Listen and check.**

5 Work with a partner. Answer these questions about the construction of indirect questions.

a) Do you use *do/does/did* in indirect questions?
b) Is the word order (subject + verb) the same as in affirmative sentences?
c) Do you use *if/whether* for *yes/no* questions?

6 Work with your partner. Put the ends of these indirect questions in the correct order.

a) Do you think … were / your parents / 'pushy parents' ?
your parents were 'pushy parents'?
b) Do you know … in the same city / if / were born / your parents ?
c) Do you have any idea … your parents / how / met ?
d) Do you think … children / enough freedom / have / these days ?
e) Can you tell me … are / what / your ambitions for your children ?

Ask your partner the questions.

Vocabulary

1 **Rewrite the sentences using *make* or *let*.**

   a) 'I'm not **forcing her to do** anything against her will.' ➔ '*I'm not …*'
   b) 'She's a kid – **allow her to play, allow her to have** friends.' ➔ '*She's a kid – …*'

Which comment did Rachel make? Which comment did George make?

Choose *1* or *2* to complete the rule.

The correct verb pattern for *make* and *let* is:
1 *make / let* + somebody + *to*-infinitive.   2 *make / let* + somebody + infinitive without *to*.

2 **Complete the sentences with two words from the box so that they make sense.**

let   made   me   us

   a) My parents *let me* wear jewellery to school.
   b) My parents _____ do the washing up after dinner.
   c) Our school teachers _____ use their first names.
   d) My sister never _____ borrow her clothes.
   e) My parents _____ keep my room tidy.
   f) My brother sometimes _____ borrow his MP3 player.
   g) My parents _____ dye my hair.
   h) Our sports teacher _____ play outside in bad weather.

**How many sentences are true for you? Change the sentences into questions.
Ask a partner.**

'Did your parents let you wear jewellery to school?' 'No, they didn't. Did yours?'

Speaking: anecdote

1 🌐 3.06 **Listen to Rafi talking about an activity he used to do when he was a child. Underline the correct information.**

Rafi, when he was nine years old ▶

   a) What was the activity? **Martial arts.** / **Art classes.**
   b) Why did you choose that activity? **I liked kung fu movies.** / **My friends did it.**
   c) Was it your idea or your parents' idea? **It was my parents' idea.** / **My idea.**
   d) Did you enjoy it? **No, I hated it.** / **Yes, I was obsessed with it.**
   e) How often did you do it? **Once a week.** / **Two or three times a week.**
   f) Where did you do it? **At a gym in the city centre.** / **At school.**
   g) How did you get there and back? **My parents drove me there.** / **I went by bicycle.**
   h) Do you still do it now? **Yes, I do.** / **No, I gave it up.**
   i) Would you encourage your own children to do the same thing? **No, absolutely not!** / **Yes, definitely.**

2 **You are going to tell your partner about an activity you did when you were a child.**

   • Ask yourself the questions in Exercise 1.
   • Think about *what* to say and *how* to say it.
   • Tell your partner about your activity.

Useful phrases

1 🌐 **3.07** **Read and listen to four people describing their favourite gadget. Match the conversations (a–d) with four of the pictures (1–6).**

a)
A: It's one of those things you use to massage your head and it feels amazing.
B: What does it look like?
A: It's made of metal and it looks like a big spider with long legs.

b)
C: It's a kind of fan that sprays water in your face.
D: What's it for?
C: It's for cooling yourself down when it's really hot.

c)
E: Have you seen this fantastic gadget?
F: What do you do with it?
E: You use it to peel a pineapple. You put it on top of the pineapple and turn it until it reaches the bottom. Then you pull it out, and you have a perfect cylinder of pineapple.

d)
G: Oh no, there's an enormous spider in the bath – go and get the spider catcher.
H: What does it look like?
G: It's round with a long handle.

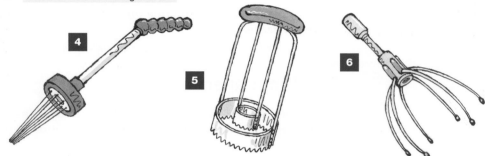

2 **Read the conversations again and complete the table with the highlighted useful phrases.**

Purpose: what it's for	Appearance: what it looks like	Material: what it's made of
a) *It's one of those things you use to massage your head.* b) It's for _____ c) You use it to _____	d) *It looks like a big spider.* e) It's _____	f) It's made of _____

🌐 **3.08** **Listen and repeat the useful phrases.**

3 **Look at the words and phrases in the box. Find three more ways to complete each of the useful phrases b, c, e and f in Exercise 2. Use your dictionary if necessary.**

> cardboard   light the gas   long and thin   plastic   rectangular
> ~~removing stains~~   small and square   stainless steel   recharge your mobile phone
> ~~storing things~~   straightening your hair   unblock toilets

b) It's for removing stains / storing things / …

4 **Work with a partner. Write conversations to describe the purpose, appearance and material of the two other objects in Exercise 1.**

Practise your conversations.

5 **Describe your own favourite gadgets to your partner.**

Vocabulary *Extra*

Word families

1 Work with a partner. Which word in each list does not exist? Cross it out.

  a) disqualify misuse overcooked undernational

  b) disused misqualify under-cooked unemployment

  c) inadvisable overnationalistic reusable unqualified

Check your ideas in the dictionary extracts. Tick the words you know.

2 Look again at the dictionary extracts. How do the prefixes in the box change the meanings of the base words?

dis   mis   over   re   un / in   under

Match each prefix with its approximate meaning (*a–f*).

  a) not = _____   c) wrongly = _____   e) again = _____

  b) too much = _____ d) no longer = _____ f) not enough = _____

3 Guess the meaning of the following words.

  a) discontinue b) misprint c) oversleep d) redo e) unaware
  f) underpay

Check your answers in your own dictionary.

4 Copy the table and complete it by putting the words from the dictionary extracts in the appropriate columns according to their word class.

Verb	Adjective	Noun	Noun (person)
advise	*advisable*	*advice*	*adviser*
cook			
employ			
	national		
qualify			
use			

Match the parts of speech (*a–d*) with the lists of typical suffixes (*1–4*).

  a) verb   1 able (ible), al, ed, ful, ic, less

  b) adjective   2 age, er, ing, ion, ism, ity, ment

  c) noun   3 ee, er (or)

  d) noun (person) 4 ify, ize (ise)

5 Choose a word from Exercise 4 to complete each sentence.

  a) I'm not a very good (cook) _____ . I don't even know how to boil an egg.

  b) I hate the (national) _____ feelings that events like the World Cup encourage.

  c) Everyone needs a financial (advise) _____ . They can save you a lot of money.

  d) I think that experience is more important than a lot of (qualify) _____ .

  e) I try to (use) _____ any water bottles that I buy instead of just throwing them away.

  f) I've never been (employ) _____ . Since I started working, I haven't stopped.

Are any of the sentences true for you?

6 Check your own dictionary. How does it present word families?

Word family: advise
Words in the same family as advise
- advice *n*
- advisable *adj*
- adviser *n*
- advisory *adj*
- inadvisable *adj*

Word family: cook
Words in the same family as cook
- cooked *adj*
- overcooked *adj*
- cookery *n*
- cooker *n*
- under-cooked *adj*
- cooking *n*

Word family: employ
Words in the same family as employ
- employed *adj*
- employment *n*
- employer *n*
- unemployed *adj*
- unemployment *n*
- employee *n*

Word family: national
Words in the same family as national
- nation *n*
- nationalize *v*
- nationalism *n*
- nationality *n*
- international *adj*
- nationalized *adj*
- nationalistic *adj*
- multinational *adj,n*

Word family: qualify
Words in the same family as qualify
- qualification *n*
- qualified *adj*
- disqualified *adj*
- qualifier *n*
- unqualified *adj*
- disqualify *v*

Word family: use
Words in the same family as use
- usage *n*
- used *adj*
- useful *adj*
- useless *adj*
- reusable *adj*
- user *n*
- disused *adj*
- misuse *n, v*
- reuse *v*

Grammar Unreal conditionals. Wishes and regrets
Vocabulary Adverbs of attitude/manner. Age
Useful phrases On the telephone

Listening & Vocabulary

1 **Work with a partner. Make a list of your favourite rock/pop bands or singers.**

- Who gives the best live performance?
- Which band or singer is the most successful?
- Do you think the age of the singer or band is important?

2 🔊 3.09 **Read and listen to Matt and Ella talking about a Rolling Stones gig. What do they think about: a) Mick Jagger; b) Keith Richards?**

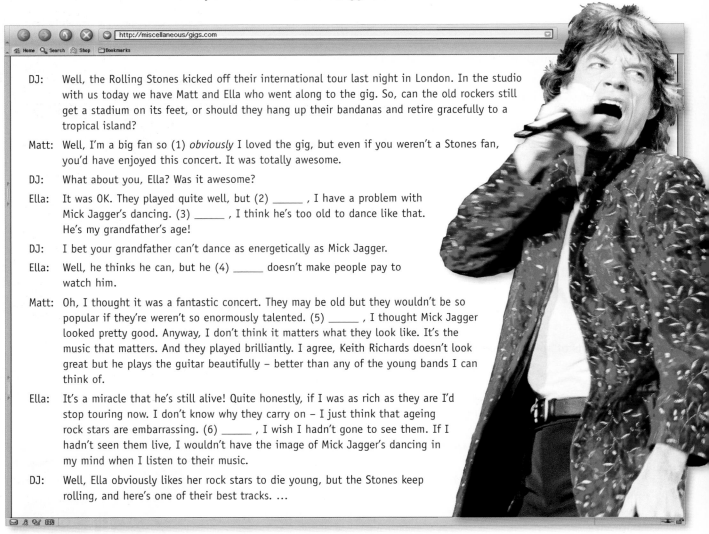

DJ: Well, the Rolling Stones kicked off their international tour last night in London. In the studio with us today we have Matt and Ella who went along to the gig. So, can the old rockers still get a stadium on its feet, or should they hang up their bandanas and retire gracefully to a tropical island?

Matt: Well, I'm a big fan so (1) *obviously* I loved the gig, but even if you weren't a Stones fan, you'd have enjoyed this concert. It was totally awesome.

DJ: What about you, Ella? Was it awesome?

Ella: It was OK. They played quite well, but (2) _____ , I have a problem with Mick Jagger's dancing. (3) _____ , I think he's too old to dance like that. He's my grandfather's age!

DJ: I bet your grandfather can't dance as energetically as Mick Jagger.

Ella: Well, he thinks he can, but he (4) _____ doesn't make people pay to watch him.

Matt: Oh, I thought it was a fantastic concert. They may be old but they wouldn't be so popular if they're weren't so enormously talented. (5) _____ , I thought Mick Jagger looked pretty good. Anyway, I don't think it matters what they look like. It's the music that matters. And they played brilliantly. I agree, Keith Richards doesn't look great but he plays the guitar beautifully – better than any of the young bands I can think of.

Ella: It's a miracle that he's still alive! Quite honestly, if I was as rich as they are I'd stop touring now. I don't know why they carry on – I just think that ageing rock stars are embarrassing. (6) _____ , I wish I hadn't gone to see them. If I hadn't seen them live, I wouldn't have the image of Mick Jagger's dancing in my mind when I listen to their music.

DJ: Well, Ella obviously likes her rock stars to die young, but the Stones keep rolling, and here's one of their best tracks. ...

3 **Complete the interview with appropriate 'attitude' adverbs from the lists below.**

1 ~~obviously~~ / surprisingly / unfortunately   4 definitely / actually / stupidly
2 hopefully / unfortunately / predictably   5 Clearly / Apparently / Personally
3 Fortunately / Basically / Unbelievably   6 Naturally / Actually / Fortunately

Listen again and check.

Which bands have you seen or would like to see live? Tell your partner.

Pronunciation

1 Practise saying the attitude adverbs in the box and then add them to the table. There are four in each column. Underline the stressed syllable.

> ~~actually~~   apparently   definitely   fortunately   incredibly   naturally
> obviously   positively   practically   predictably   regularly   surprisingly

A: ☐☐☐	B: ☐☐☐☐	C: ☐☐☐☐
_ac_tually		

2 🔊 3.10 Listen, check and repeat.

Vocabulary

1 Look at this simple sentence structure. In which position (*1–4*) is it possible to put the adverb of manner *beautifully*?

    subject   verb   object
① Keith Richards ② plays ③ the guitar ④.

2 Rewrite these sentences in the correct order.
a) I / don't know / very well / the Rolling Stones' music
b) English bands / a lot / I / like
c) I / very loud / my music / like playing
d) I / any musical instruments / very well / can't play
e) don't enjoy / I / karaoke / very much
f) the last concert I went to / very well / I / don't remember

How many of the sentences are true for you? Rewrite the sentences so that they are all true for you. Compare your sentences with a partner.

Grammar

Unreal conditionals (1)

Real situation:
I **can't** sing. I**'m not** in a band.
time (present) =
tense (present)

Unreal or imaginary situation: If I **could** sing, I**'d be** in a band.
time (present) ≠ tense (past)

if-clause: past simple
Main clause: *would/wouldn't* + infinitive

1 Work with your partner. Look at the unreal conditional sentence about the Rolling Stones. Tick the 'real situation' (*a, b* or *c*) that the sentence is based on.

'… they <u>wouldn't be</u> so popular if they <u>weren't</u> so enormously talented.'

a) They are popular. They are talented.
b) They were popular. They were talented.
c) They will be popular. They will be talented.

Underline the correct alternative.

When you want to talk about unreal or imaginary situations in the present:
use (1) **the past simple** / *would* + **infinitive** in the *if*-clause;
use (2) **the past simple** / *would* + **infinitive** in the main clause.

2 Write unreal conditional sentences based on the real situations below. Start each sentence with *If …*
a) I don't have a car. I can't drive to work.
   If I had a car, I'd be able to drive to work.
b) I can't cook. I don't invite my friends round for dinner.
c) I don't live abroad. I see my family very regularly.
d) I go out every night. I'm always tired.
e) I don't have time. I don't do my English homework.
f) I have to learn English. I can't learn another language.

Are any of these conditional sentences true for you? Discuss with your partner.

3 **Pairwork** **Student A:** page 120   **Student B:** page 125

Reading

1 **Work in groups. Look at the photo in the advertisement but don't read the poem. Invent an identity for the man in the photo.**

   a) What's his name?
   b) How old is he?
   c) Where does he live?
   d) What's his family background?
   e) What has he done in his life?
   f) Is he happy?

Compare your ideas with other people in the class.

If I had my life to live over,
I'd try to make more mistakes next time.

I would relax.

I would be sillier than I have been this trip.

I know of very few things I would take
seriously.

I would take more chances.

I would take more trips.

I would climb more mountains, swim more
rivers and watch more sunsets.

I would eat more ice cream and less beans.

I would have more actual troubles and
fewer imaginary ones.

You see, I am one of those people who live
prophylactically and sanely and sensibly,

hour after hour, day after day.

Oh, I have had my moments and, if I had to
do it over again, I'd have more of them.

In fact, I'd try to have nothing else. Just
moments, one after another.

If I had my life to live over,

I would start bare-footed earlier in the
spring and stay that way later in the fall.

I would play hooky more.

I would ride on more merry-go-rounds.

I'd pick more daisies.

Glossary

prophylactically adverb: very carefully
sanely adverb: in a normal or reasonable way
live over verb [I] *US*: live again or relive
barefooted adj: without shoes

fall noun [C] *US*: autumn
play hooky verb [I] *US*: stay away from school
without permission
daisy noun [C]: small white wild flower

---

2   3.11 **Read and listen to the poem and decide whether it fits the character you have invented. How does the man in the poem feel about his life?**

Grammar

Wishes and regrets

Facts (present/past):
I **can't swim.** I **didn't take** lessons at school.

Wishes or regrets (past / past perfect):
I wish I **could swim.**
If only I **had taken** lessons at school.

1 Look back at the poem on page 98. Complete these sentences for the man expressing his regrets. Use the words in the box.

adventurous	~~anxious~~	enjoy	fun	over	risks	sensible	seriously

a) I wish I'd been less *anxious*.
b) I wish I'd been more _____ .
c) I wish I'd taken more _____ .
d) If only I'd had more _____ .
e) I wish I hadn't been so _____ .
f) I wish I hadn't taken life so _____ .
g) If only I'd done more of the things I _____ .
h) I wish I had my life to live _____ .

2 Write the corresponding fact for each regret expressed in Exercise 1.

a) I wasn't adventurous.

Underline the correct alternative.

a) When you want to express a wish or regret about a present fact you use a **present** / **past** tense after *wish* / *if only*.

b) When you want to express a wish or regret about a past fact you use a **past** / **past perfect** tense after *wish* / *if only*.

3 Work with a partner. Write a wish or regret for each of these facts.

a) I couldn't go to the last U2 gig.
I wish / if only I'd been able to go to the last U2 gig.
b) I didn't do English at school.
c) I'm not married.
d) I don't know how to play chess.
e) I can't play the guitar.
f) I'm going on a training course next week
g) I'm studying for exams at the moment.
h) I couldn't swim when I was a child.

Are any of the facts, wishes or regrets true for you? Discuss with your partner.

4 Grammar *Extra* 11, Part 1 page 146. Read the explanations and do the exercises.

Speaking

1 Work with your partner. Think about the possible story behind each of these pictures. Write sentences beginning *I wish ...* or *If only ...*

2 Have you made any bad decisions today / this week / this year / in your life so far? Talk about them with your partner.

'I wish I hadn't gone to bed so late last night. I feel really tired today.'

Reading & Speaking

1 **Do you think there is an upper or lower age limit for these activities?**

- getting married
- having children
- learning a new language
- travelling around the world
- worrying about how you look
- leaving home

- starting a new career
- dancing to pop music in public
- learning to ski
- riding a motorbike
- wearing jeans
- playing in a rock band

Discuss your answers with a partner. Are there any other activities you think have age limits?

2 **Read the article and decide which statements are true for the writer.**

a) 'I wish I'd never met him.'
b) 'I should have been honest about my age.'
c) 'If I had told him my age at the beginning, it wouldn't have become so important.'
d) 'I shouldn't have told him about my divorce.'
e) 'If I was a man, the age difference wouldn't be a problem.'
f) 'It's all his fault: if I hadn't met him, I wouldn't have turned into an ageist and a liar.'

Ageism turned me into a liar

For most of my life, age has seemed unimportant. My friends of both sexes have been younger, older or the same age. When I was in my early thirties I went out with a man of twenty-three. One of the most attractive men I know is in his mid-fifties.

5 The first time I experienced a problem with age was on my fortieth birthday. Much to my surprise, it was a deeply traumatic event. Forty seemed to be so much older than thirty-nine. Anyway, I slowly got over the shock and tried to convince myself that life begins at forty …

I met him playing badminton. He's thirty-one and looks about nineteen – he has no idea how old I am.

10 All my life I've been totally honest. I return extra change to astonished shopkeepers, I've never travelled without a ticket and in job interviews I tell them all the reasons why they shouldn't employ me!

So, early on in the relationship I told him the truth about my rocky past – my divorce, my financial difficulties. I even admitted that I dye my hair. I told him I'm older

15 than he is, but something stopped me from telling him the whole truth about my age.

And now I'm in trouble – serious trouble. Silence has made the problem much greater. If I had told him before, it wouldn't have become such a big issue. If I had been brave enough to admit that I was eleven years older than him, I wouldn't be so worried about him finding out the truth. The other day, I even hid my passport under

20 a pile of papers.

I know that if I was a man, I would never have got into this mess. Being eleven years older is nothing for a man. But in my case, it's the other way round, the world judges older women harshly. I'm afraid he would do the same.

I have become an ageist and a liar and I have no one to blame but myself.

3 **Work with your partner. Imagine the conversation between the writer and her partner when she tells him the truth. Write down your ideas. Begin like this:**

Man: *You look worried. What's on your mind?*
Woman: *Actually, there is something I've been meaning to tell you …*

🔘 **3.12** **Listen to the conversation and compare your ideas. What would you do now if you were in the writer's position?**

4 **Work in small groups and discuss the questions.**

a) How old are your youngest and oldest friends?
b) What might the problems be for a couple who have a big age difference?
c) Under what circumstances might you lie about your age?
d) What ages do you think are particularly significant in life?
e) What is the best age to be?
f) What is the worst age to be?

Grammar

Unreal conditionals (2)

Real situation:
I **didn't have** a map.
I **got** lost.
time (past) = tense (past)

Unreal or imaginary
situation:
If I**'d had** a map, I
wouldn't have got lost.
time (past) ≠
tense (past perfect)

if-clause: past perfect
Main clause: *would/wouldn't*
+ *have* + past participle

1 Work with a partner. Look at the unreal conditional sentence from the article on page 100. Tick the real situation (*a, b* or *c*) that the sentence is based on.

*'If I had told him before,
it wouldn't have become
such a big issue.'*

a) I don't tell him. It doesn't become a big issue.
b) I didn't tell him. It became a big issue.
c) I won't tell him. It won't become a big issue.

Underline the correct alternative.

When you want to talk about 'unreal' or imaginary situations in the past:
use (1) **the past perfect** / *would + have* + **past participle** in the *if*-clause;
use (2) **the past perfect** / *would + have* + **past participle** in the main clause.

2 Write unreal conditional sentences based on the real situations below. Start each sentence with *If …*

a) I didn't see you yesterday. I didn't say hello.
    If I'd seen you yesterday, I'd have said hello.
b) I stayed up late last night. I overslept this morning.
c) I couldn't find a parking space. I arrived late for the class.
d) My sister travelled round the world. She met her future husband.
e) I didn't learn to drive when I was 18. I didn't have a car at university.
f) It rained yesterday. I didn't go for a walk.

Are any of these conditional sentences true for you? Discuss with your partner.

3 Grammar *Extra* 11, Part 2 page 146. Read the explanations and do the exercises.

Reading & Speaking

1 Work with a partner. Look at these four key words from three different stories. What do you think each story is about?

1   scruffy, begging, university, rebel
2   aisles, trolley, conveyor belt, stolen
3   dinner, oven, licked, burnt

2 Read and complete the texts by matching the words from Exercise 1 to each story. Discuss what you would have done in each situation.

a) I was in the supermarket yesterday and I saw this elderly woman shuffling up and down the _____ . She didn't have a _____ and was putting her shopping straight into her bag. Anyway, I thought nothing more about it and carried on doing my shopping, and when I went to queue up to pay, there she was in front of me. I watched her put one tin of cat food on the _____ and pay for it. Then she walked out with her bag full of _____ shopping.

b) Something awful happened to me last week. I'd invited six people round for _____ , and you know how I hate cooking. Anyway, I spent all afternoon preparing the meal and actually I was quite pleased with how it turned out. I even managed to get all the vegetables ready at the same time as the meat. So, the vegetables were on the table, and I just had to get the chicken out of the _____ . I lifted it out and I don't know how it happened, but I dropped it on the kitchen floor, and before I could pick it up, the cat had _____ it. She regretted it afterwards, because she _____ her tongue.

c) I had a very strange experience the other day. I was up in London for a meeting, and it was lunchtime. It was a lovely day, so I bought a sandwich and went for a walk. I was just on my way back to the office when I noticed a _____ , bearded man _____ in the street. I recognised him immediately – it was someone I'd been at _____ with – a brilliant rugby player. He'd always been a bit of a _____ , but a very clever man. We'd been very good friends, but I'd lost touch with him when we left university.

🌐 3.13 **Listen and find out what the people did. Do you think they did the right thing?**

Useful phrases

1 Look at the useful phrases (*1–7*) for telephoning. In each case, cross out the phrase that is unusual or incorrect.

1   Hello. / Good morning. / ~~Speak me~~.
2   Is (*name*) there? / I'd like to speak to (*name*), please. / Is there (*name*)?
3   Are you (*name*)? / Is that (*name*)? / Who's calling, please?
4   Hold on, please. I'll try to put you through. / Hang on, I'll go and get her. / One instant.
5   I am me. / It's me. / This is (*name*) here.
6   What are you up to later? / What do you do later? / Are you available later on today?
7   I'll look forward to seeing you tomorrow. / To tomorrow. / See you tomorrow then.

2 Read two phone calls made by Phil Jones: one to his friend, Maddy, and the other to his bank manager, Mr Moore. Complete each conversation with the most appropriate useful phrase from Exercise 1.

Conversation A

Janet: (1) _____
Phil: Oh, hi. (2) _____
Janet: (3) _____
Phil: Yes, hello Janet. How are you?
Janet: Fine, thanks. (4) _____
Maddy: Hello.
Phil: Hi! (5) _____
Maddy: Hello you. What have you been up to?
Phil: Oh, just working. Listen, I can't chat now. (6) _____
Maddy: I've got to work this evening but I thought we could go to the cinema tomorrow.
Phil: OK, I'll come round at about seven.
Maddy: (7) _____
Phil: Bye.

Conversation B

Receptionist: (1) _____ Northminster Bank. Can I help you?
Phil: Yes, (2) _____
Receptionist: (3) _____
Phil: My name's Philip Jones.
Receptionist: OK, (4) _____ ... Oh, Mr Jones, I'm afraid he's on the other line. Would you like to hold?
Phil: Yes, thank you. ...
Mr Moore: Anthony Moore.
Phil: Oh, hello. (5) _____
Mr Moore: Oh, yes. Mr Jones. Thank you for getting back to me so promptly. There seems to be a problem with your account.
Phil: Oh, dear. What sort of problem?
Mr Moore: Well, you've exceeded your overdraft limit by more than £500. You really need to come to the bank to discuss it. (6) _____
Phil: I'm afraid I'm rather tied up today. Would tomorrow be convenient for you?
Mr Moore: Yes, that's fine. Ten thirty?
Phil: Yes, ten thirty's fine for me.
Mr Moore: Well, thank you for ringing. (7) _____
Phil: Goodbye.

🔘 3.14–3.15 **Listen and check.**

3 🔘 3.16 **Listen and repeat the useful phrases from *Conversation A*. Then listen and repeat the useful phrases from *Conversation B*.**

4 Work with a partner. Choose one of the situations below and write a telephone conversation.

a)   Phil phones his friend Jeff and arranges to meet him this evening.
b)   Phil phones Smiths Insurance and arranges a meeting with Mrs Bella Watson.

Practise your conversation.

Vocabulary *Extra*

Idiomatic expressions

1 Look at the dictionary extracts defining some fixed idiomatic expressions – sometimes known as 'binomials'. Replace the underlined phrases in the sentences *a–e* with a suitable binomial.

a) His English is coming on <u>very quickly</u>.
b) There aren't many sandwiches left, so you won't be able to <u>make a careful selection of what you want</u>.
c) It's all there <u>in written form</u>.
d) Her clothes were lying <u>scattered in several different places</u> on the floor.
e) We see each other <u>sometimes, but not often</u>.

Check your own dictionary. Which word do you need to look up to find the expression?

2 There is one mistake in each of the underlined idiomatic expressions in sentences *a–f*. Look at the relevant dictionary extract and correct the mistake.

a) Di has a young family and runs her own business. She certainly <u>has the hands full</u>.
b) Helen is hopeless with money. She's <u>over her neck in debt</u>.
c) Petra sometimes makes mistakes but <u>her heart is in its right place</u>.
d) Sue is always wearing fantastic clothes. She <u>has one eye for fashion</u>.
e) Tim's business isn't making much money, but he <u>keeps his head above the water</u>.
f) Boris got a fantastic job straight after university. He really <u>landed on his foot</u>.

Do any of your family, friends or colleagues fit these descriptions? Tell a partner about them.

3 Use the words in the box to complete the idiomatic expressions (*a–f*) describing feelings and emotions.

arms	dumps	minds	moon	stitches	weather

a) to be in _____
b) to be in two _____
c) to be over the _____
d) to be up in _____
e) to be under the _____
f) to be down in the _____

Check your ideas in the dictionary extracts.

Think about the last time you felt any of these emotions. Ask your partner.

When was the last time you were over the moon?

4 Check your own dictionary. Look up your six favourite idiomatic expressions on this page and answer the questions.

a) Which word do you look for first?
b) How are the idiomatic expressions organised?
c) What examples are given?

PHRASE **in black and white** in a written or printed form

PHRASE **here and there** in or to several different places

PHRASE **by/in leaps and bounds** used for saying that something improves quickly or increases a lot

PHRASE **(every) now and then/again** sometimes, but not regularly or often

PHRASE **pick and choose (sth)** to choose the things you prefer, rather than simply accepting what you are given

PHRASE **sb's heart is in the right place** used for saying that someone tries to do good things even though it does not always seem like this

PHRASE **keep your head above water** *informal* to manage to live or keep a business working even though you are not earning much money

PHRASE **have your hands full** to be extremely busy

PHRASE **land on your feet** to be lucky and get into a good situation after being in a difficult one

PHRASE **have an eye for** to have a natural ability for seeing or noticing something

PHRASE **up to your neck in sth** *informal* involved or busy with something

PHRASE **up in arms** angry and complaining about something

PHRASE **(down) in the dumps** *informal* feeling unhappy

PHRASE **be in two minds (about sth)** to not be certain about something, or to have difficulty in making a decision

PHRASE **be over the moon (about sth)** *British informal* to be very happy about something.

PHRASE **in stitches** *informal* laughing a lot

PHRASE **under the weather** *informal* not feeling well

12 Style

Grammar Adjective order. *have something done*
Vocabulary Clothes. Physical description. Verb phrases
Useful phrases Small talk

Reading

1 How many of the following statements are similar to your own views about clothes and style? Compare with a partner.
a) 'I don't think that much about fashion.'
b) 'I tend to look for clothes that are comfortable to wear.'
c) 'I like putting together outfits without too much thought.'
d) 'The total head-to-toe designer look is ridiculous.'
e) 'I don't want to stand out too much.'
f) 'I don't think anyone can teach you to have style … Either you have it or you don't.'

2 Read the two articles. Find out which statements in Exercise 1 are the views of Carla Bruni (*CB*) and which are the views of Vanessa Paradis (*VP*).

How I get dressed

◀ **Carla Bruni** *Supermodel, singer, songwriter*
Through modelling I learned how to use my body. I don't think anyone can teach you to have style though. Either you have it or you don't. I've never really had it. The modelling made me realise that you can't buy style. It's something personal and private. The total head-to-toe designer look is ridiculous. It's the opposite of fashion. A matching bag and shoe and hat makes you look like a Christmas tree. And I would never wear shoulder pads. Or pointy shoes. Or skinny jeans. Or low-waisted trousers. You take away the hips and waist – the best bits!

Vanessa Paradis *Singer and actress* ▲
I don't think that much about fashion. I suppose I like putting together outfits without too much thought and seeing what the outcome is. My parents were interior designers in Paris, so I suppose it's in my genes: we spent a lot of time seeing what went with what.

When I had the hit, *Joe le Taxi*, I was fourteen, and the only bit of style I had was a big floppy vintage hat, that I wore to everything. In those days, I also loved wearing miniskirts and leather jackets. As I became more in the public eye, I became more aware of what I wore. Being asked to model for Coco Chanel also helped me develop my style, and I started working out what suited me. As a mother of two children I tend to look for clothes that are comfortable to wear on a day-to-day basis, which is why I now love the bohemian style. The red carpet scares me – it's like being an animal in a zoo. I find the whole experience quite frightening, therefore I save my more eccentric outfits for situations I feel more comfortable with – I don't want to stand out too much.

3 Underline the correct information according to the article.
a) Vanessa Paradis' style **has / hasn't** changed since she was fourteen.
b) Carla Bruni **always / never** wears a matching hat, bag and shoes.
c) Vanessa Paradis **has / hasn't** developed her own style.
d) Vanessa Paradis **always wears / doesn't always wear** comfortable clothes during the day.
e) Carla Bruni would **always / never** wear tight jeans.

Now complete the sentences with the names of people you know. Make true sentences.

4 Think of a person you know who 'has style'. Describe them to your partner.

Vocabulary & Listening

1 **Look at the items of clothing and complete the descriptions below. Use your dictionary if necessary.**

a) fabulous American snakeskin *cowboy boots*
b) a smart pinstripe _____
c) old baggy _____
d) a plain green cotton _____
e) a red low-waisted _____
f) a wide black leather _____
g) long red leather _____
h) old black skinny _____
i) a short-sleeved checked _____
j) a long-sleeved black and white striped _____
k) a beautiful long blue silk evening _____
l) a bright orange polo-neck _____

▲ belt
▲ cowboy boots
▲ boots
▲ hoody
▲ jeans
▲ jeans
▲ dress
▲ shirt
▲ miniskirt
▲ suit
▲ jumper
▲ top

2 🔊 3.17 **Listen to four people (Al, Fran, Jay and Bea) talking about clothes. Identify their favourite items from the list in Exercise 1. Which of the items of clothing in Exercise 1 do you like/dislike?**

Grammar

1 **Put the adjectives describing Al, Fran, Jay and Bea's favourite clothes in the correct columns.**

Opinion	Size / Shape	Age	Pattern / Colour	Origin	Material / Style	NOUN
1 fabulous				American	snakeskin	cowboy boots

2 **Put the adjectives in the right order to describe these clothes.**

a) a/an / linen / dark blue / elegant / jacket
   an elegant dark blue linen jacket
b) a / V-neck / black / brand-new / T-shirt
c) a/an / silk / white / expensive / blouse
d) a / beige / woolly / plain / jumper
e) a/an / fur / old / Russian / hat
f) blue / scruffy / suede / shoes

Use three adjectives to describe the most interesting item of clothing in your wardrobe.

3 **Pairwork** **Student A:** page 120   **Student B:** page 125

Reading & Writing

1   Read the extract from the novel, *Come Together*. Are the following statements true or false?

a) The writer is an artist.   b) He's short and skinny.   c) He's rich.   d) He's single.

Say you're a girl. Say you're a girl and you're at a party, or in a pub, or in a club. Say you're a girl and you're at a party, or in a pub, or in a club, and I come up to you.

Say you've never set eyes on me before.

Some things you'll know immediately. You'll see that I'm just under six feet tall and of average build. If we shake hands, you'll notice that my grip is strong and my fingernails clean. You'll see that I have brown eyes which match my brown hair. And you'll see that I have a scar across the centre of my left eyebrow. You'll guess that I'm somewhere between twenty-five and thirty years old.

You'll ask me what I do for a living, and I'll tell you that I'm an artist, which is true, and that I make a living from it, which isn't. I won't tell you that I work in a small art gallery in Mayfair three days a week to make ends meet. You'll look at my clothes, which will probably be my friend's clothes, and wrongly assume that I'm rich. As I won't mention a girlfriend, you'll probably assume correctly that I'm single. I won't ask you if you have a boyfriend, but I will check your finger to see if you're engaged or married.

2   Complete these sentences with information about yourself.

a)   Say we meet at a party, and we've never met before, you'll see that I'm _____ tall.
b)   You'll see that I've got _____ hair and _____ eyes.
c)   You'll guess that I'm somewhere between _____ and _____ years old.
d)   You'll look at my clothes and assume that I'm _____ .
e)   If we speak, I'll tell you that I _____ , which is true, and that I _____ , which isn't.

3   Work with a partner. Discuss the questions.

a)   What sort of things do you notice about a person when you meet for the first time?
b)   What can you tell about a person from a first meeting?
c)   Are your first impressions of people usually right?

Pronunciation

1   Look at these words with different vowel combinations. Link the words with the same vowel sounds.

a)   /iː/ ——————— medium   bald   author
b)   /uː/   plain   beige   fur
c)   /ɜː/   short   blue   hair
d)   /ɔː/   third   green ——————— jeans
e)   /eɪ/   two   their   suede
f)   /eə/   wear   worse   suits

2   🌐 3.18 Listen, check and repeat.

Vocabulary

1 Complete the information about the man in the extract from *Come Together* on page 106.

Age: *between 25 and 30*	Height: _____	Build: _____
Eyes: _____	Hair: _____	Distinguishing features: _____

2 Match the words and phrases in the box to the categories in Exercise 1. Use your dictionary if necessary and find at least one other suitable word for each category.

bald   blond streaks   deep-set   freckles   a goatee   ginger   hazel
in her early thirties   in her mid-twenties   in his late teens
just over 1 metre 80   medium   messy   a mole   overweight   receding
sideburns   shoulder-length   slim   stocky   a tattoo   well-built

▲ *(photograph of man)*

3 Read descriptions (*a–c*) of different roles the film star Johnny Depp has played. Match the descriptions to the films.

a) He has a moustache and a goatee and messy black shoulder-length hair. His eyes are dark brown and he wears black eyeliner. He has a tattoo on one of his arms.

b) He's tall and skinny with large deep-set eyes and a sad expression on his thin face. His hair is messy, and there are scars on his cheeks.

c) He has wavy black hair with a grey streak at the front and long bushy sideburns. He has dark shadows under his eyes and lines on his forehead.

▲ *Edward Scissorhands*   ▲ *Sweeney Todd*   ▲ *Pirates of the Caribbean 1*

Now match each of the films to the year of its release: *1990, 2003, 2007*.

4 Write a description of a film character. Read it out. Your partner guesses who it is.

Speaking: anecdote

▲ Martin

1 🌐 3.19 Listen to Martin talking about a person he met for the first time recently. Put a cross by the answers that are wrong.

a) Where were you when you met this person? **At a friend's engagement party.**
b) Was the person a man or a woman? **It was a woman.**
c) Who introduced you? **She introduced herself.**
d) What was your first impression? **I thought she was funny and very confident.**
e) What did she look like? **She was tall with long curly black hair.**
f) Did you notice anything special about her? **She was wearing a turquoise ring.**
g) What did you talk about? **We talked about Egypt.**
h) Did you find anything in common? **We'd both been to the same place on holiday.**
i) Have you seen the person again? **Yes, I have.**

Correct the wrong answers. Listen again if necessary.

2 You are going to tell your partner about somebody you met for the first time recently.

• Ask yourself the questions in Exercise 1.
• Think about *what* to say and *how* to say it.
• Tell your partner about the person.

Listening

1 **Look at the photos of Tony Goodwin and Marilyn Cook who took part in a TV programme called *Ten Years Younger*. Discuss these questions with a partner.**

a) How old do you think Tony and Marilyn are?
b) What differences can you see between the *Before* and *After* photos?

2 🌐 **3.20 Listen to two friends, Annie and Betty, discussing the TV programme and check whether your ideas in Exercise 1 were right.**

After

After

3 **Make sentences with these words and phrases to describe what Tony and Marilyn had done.**

Tony had his Marilyn had her	clothes	cut and coloured.
	eyelids	chosen by a stylist.
	hair	done by an expert.
	make-up	lifted.
	teeth	whitened.

Listen again and check. Do you know people who look young for their age? Tell your partner about them.

Grammar

1 **Work with your partner. In each of these sentences, who cut Tony's hair?**

a) Tony cut his hair.
b) Tony had his hair cut.

have something done

She**'s had** her hair **cut**.
She **hasn't had** it **coloured**.
Has she **had** it **styled**?
Yes, she has.
No, she hasn't.

2 **Work with your partner. Complete the table below with the correct verb forms.**

Do it yourself	Have it done
a) I like washing my hair.	I like (1) *having my hair* washed.
b) I never colour my hair.	I never (2) _____ coloured.
c) I'm testing my eyes next week.	I (3) _____ next week.
d) I (4) _____ last month.	I had my teeth cleaned last month.
e) I've pierced my ears.	(5) _____ .
f) (6) _____ .	I want to have my bedroom repainted.

Cross out unlikely or unusual sentences. Tick any sentences that are true for you.

3 **Have it done or do it yourself? Complete the questions as in the example.**

a) If your car was dirty, would you (wash) _____ ?
   ... would you have it washed or would you wash it yourself?
b) If your winter coat was dirty, would you (clean) _____ ?
c) If your bicycle had a flat tyre, would you (repair) _____ ?
d) If your house needed redecorating, would you (do) _____ ?
e) If your kitchen knives were blunt, would you (sharpen) _____ ?
f) If your new trousers were too long, would you (take up) _____ ?

Work with your partner. Ask and answer the questions.

4 Grammar *Extra* 12 page 148. Read the explanations and do the exercises.

Vocabulary & Speaking

1 Match the verbs in box *A* with the noun phrases in box *B* to describe the sort of things people do before they leave the house in the morning.

A
do   get
have   make
put   read

B
the bed   breakfast   the children ready   some coffee
the computer on   a cup of tea   dressed   my exercises
my homework   the mail   my make-up on   the paper
the radio on   a shower   the TV on   the washing-up

2 Think about your own morning routine from the moment you get out of bed to the moment you leave the house.

a)   What do you do? What order do you do things in?
b)   How long does each activity usually take you?

Now compare with a partner. What are the differences?

Reading & Vocabulary

1 Read through these two morning routines. Underline the correct alternatives.

Person A

My alarm goes off early, and it takes me ten minutes to eat my breakfast, drink two cups of coffee, have a shower, pack my bag and read the post and thirty minutes to (1) **get dressed / wear**. I start thinking about what I'm going to (2) **get dressed / wear** while I have my breakfast. After a shower, I (3) **put on / wear** my underwear and then I look in my wardrobe and choose a pair of trousers. If they still (4) **fit / look** me, I put them on. If they feel a bit tight around the waist, I (5) **try them on / take them off** and spend a few minutes feeling guilty about all those chocolates I had last night. Then, I choose a looser pair of trousers and think about a top that (6) **goes with / fits** it. I usually (7) **have on / try on** two or three tops before I find one that (8) **looks / wears** right and (9) **feels / fits** comfortable. Finding a pair of socks usually takes about five minutes – I can find two dozen odd pairs, but none that (10) **look / match**. By now, I'm late.

Person B

I get up as late as I possibly can and jump in and out of the shower. I (1) **put on / fit** the trousers I (2) **had on / got dressed** yesterday and take a shirt out of the wardrobe – it doesn't matter which one as long as it's ironed. I find the jacket that (3) **fits / goes with** the trousers, look down and check that my socks (4) **match / feel**, and that's it. Nearly all my clothes are either green or brown, because I've been told that they are the only colours that (5) **suit / match** me. So I never really have to worry about what I (6) **look like / go with**. The important thing is to make sure I have enough time to enjoy my favourite drink of the day: that first cup of coffee …

🌐 **3.21–3.22** Do you think these are descriptions of a man or a woman? Listen and check.

2 Complete the questions with the verbs in the box. Change the verb form as necessary.

fit   get dressed   match   suit   try on   wear

a)   What colours _____ you?
b)   How long does it take you to _____ ?
c)   Do you like _____ lots of different clothes in shops?
d)   Do you usually _____ a watch?
e)   Do your brother or sister's clothes _____ you?
f)   Do you try to wear tops that _____ your eye colour?

Work with your partner. Ask and answer the questions.

3 Work with your partner. How would you get ready for some of these occasions?

- a job interview
- a first date
- an evening at the theatre
- a day on the beach
- a wedding
- a long flight
- a Saturday night out with your friends
- a Sunday afternoon stroll around town

A job interview: I'd have a shower. I'd put on a clean shirt and a smart suit. I'd …

Useful phrases

1 Work with a partner. Which of the things in the box do you think people are most likely to talk about at a wedding?

> a) politics b) the weather c) the bride and groom d) one another's clothes
> e) world peace f) the enjoyable occasion g) current divorce rates h) the food

2 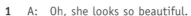 3.23 Read and listen to five conversations at a wedding. Match each conversation with a topic from Exercise 1.

1 A: Oh, she looks so beautiful.
    B: She does, doesn't she? He's a lucky, lucky man.
    A: He is.

2 C: What a lovely day!
    D: It is. So sunny. And quite warm for this time of year.
    C: I know. I don't think I need my coat.

3 E: What a lovely dress.
    F: Oh, this – I've had it for ages.
    E: Well, blue really suits you – it brings out the colour of your eyes.
    F: Do you think so? Thank you. And that's a very nice hat.
    E: Oh, I'm glad you like it. I got it in the sales – it was a bargain.
    F: Was it? Well, it looks a million dollars.

4 G: This dessert is delicious.
    H: It is, isn't it?
    G: Don't you want your strawberry?
    H: Yes, I do – I was just saving it. Get off!

5 I: Thank you so much for a lovely day. We've had a wonderful time.
    J: You're welcome. I'm glad you could make it.
    I: Oh, we wouldn't have missed it for the world. Would we, Arthur?
    K: Hm? Oh, no, we wouldn't. Absolutely. Thank you for inviting us.
    J: Oh, don't mention it. Well, have a safe journey home.
    I: We will. Goodbye.

3 Complete the tables with the useful phrases from the conversations in Exercise 2.

> **Making positive comments**
> a) 'Oh, she looks *so beautiful*.'
> b) ' _____ day!'
> c) 'This dessert _____ .'

> **Giving and receiving compliments**
> d) 'What a lovely dress!' 'Oh this – I've had it for ages.'
> e) 'Blue _____ .' ' _____ think so? Thank you.'
> f) ' _____ nice hat.' 'I'm _____ .'

> **Thanking and accepting thanks**
> g) 'Thank you so much for a lovely day.' 'You're welcome.'
> h) ' _____ inviting us.' 'Don't _____ .'

3.24 Listen, check and repeat.

4 Work with your partner. Write a conversation between two people at a wedding. Choose from the following options.

- the bride's mother and the groom's mother
- the bride's grandmother and a bridesmaid
- the groom and his best man

Practise your conversation.

Vocabulary *Extra*

Exploring meanings

1 Work with a partner. Look at the dictionary extract for *suspect* and discuss the questions.

a) How many dictionary entries are there for the word *suspect*?

b) Is *suspect* more commonly used as a noun, a verb or an adjective?

c) What is the difference in pronunciation between *suspect* as a verb, and *suspect* as a noun or adjective?

d) How many meanings are explained for the verb *suspect*?

e) Which is the most common meaning of the verb *suspect*?

2 Look at the sentences *a–e*. Identify the correct dictionary entry and the correct meaning of *suspect*.

a) Do you really *suspect* him of taking your money? = *entry 1 (verb), meaning 2*

b) Rhys is a *suspect* in the case of the missing money.

c) The officer *suspected* that Burns had been involved all along.

d) A *suspect* object has been disposed of at Heathrow airport.

e) His motives were *suspect*. He seemed too good to be true.

3 Homographs are words that are spelt the same but which have a different meaning and sometimes a different pronunciation. Match the example sentences with the correct pronunciation. Use the dictionary extracts to help you.

1 a) Just a **minute**, I'm on the phone.   1 /maɪˈnjuːt/
   b) The cake she gave me was **minute**!   2 /ˈmɪnɪt/

2 a) Do you shake hands in China, or **bow**?   1 /baʊ/
   b) I love that pink **bow** in her hair.   2 /bəʊ/

3 a) I've seen 'The Killers' **live** in concert twice. 1 /lɪv/
   b) Where do you **live**?   2 /laɪv/

Use your own dictionary and look up the different meanings and pronunciation for six more homographs in the box.

> close   lead   refuse   row   tear   refuse

4 Look at the dictionary entry for the adjective *soft*. It shows seven different meanings. Match sentences *a–g* with meanings 1–7.

a) I love the **soft** purring noise of a sleeping cat.

b) People who seem scary are actually often really **soft**.

c) Pasta should be eaten 'al dente' – not overcooked and **soft**!

d) In a bedroom, **soft** pastel shades are better than bright, primary colours.

e) It's better to wash your clothes in **soft** water rather than hard water.

f) Cashmere is a **soft** material. In fact it's the softest material for clothes.

g) Most parents are too **soft** with their children. Bring back discipline!

Which of the above statements do you agree with? Discuss with your partner.

5 Check your own dictionary. How does it show the information for words that belong to more than one word class and/or have more than one meaning?

---

suspect¹ /səˈspekt/ verb [T] ★★
1 to believe that something is true: +**(that)** *Police suspected that she had some connection with the robbery.*
2 to think that someone might have done something bad: *He wrote a letter naming the people whom he suspected.* ♦ **suspect sb of sth** *men suspected of involvement in the bombing*
3 to think that something might be bad: *Carl seemed very kind, but she suspected his motives.*

suspect² /ˈsʌspekt/ noun [C] **1** someone who might have committed a crime: *a murder suspect* **2** something that might have caused something bad

suspect³ /ˈsʌspekt/ adj **1** something that is suspect might not be good, honest, or reliable: *suspect motives* **2** a suspect object might be dangerous or illegal: *a suspect package*

---

bow¹ /baʊ/ verb **1** [I] to bend your body forwards from the waist in order to show respect for someone **2** [I/T] to bend your head

bow³ /bəʊ/ noun [C] **1** a weapon made from a curved piece of wood. It is used for shooting ARROWS. **2** a knot that has two circular parts and two loose ends: *The ribbon was tied in a bow.* **3** an object that you use for playing

---

live¹ /lɪv/ verb ★★★
1 [I] to have your home in a particular place: *Paris is a nice place to live.* ♦ *They lived in*

live³ /laɪv/ adv **1** if something is broadcast live, it is happening at the same time as you are watching it or listening to it **2** if something is performed live, it is performed in front of an audience

---

minute¹ /ˈmɪnɪt/ noun [C] ★★★
1 a period of 60 seconds. There are 60 minutes in one hour: *I'll meet you downstairs in ten minutes.* ♦ *The train leaves at six minutes past ten.*

minute² /maɪˈnjuːt/ adj **1** very small: *The soil contained minute quantities of uranium.* **2** very careful and detailed: *a minute examination of the evidence*

---

soft /sɒft/ adj ★★★

1 not hard/firm	5 not strict enough
2 not rough/stiff	6 kind/sympathetic
3 quiet/nice	7 about water
4 pale/gentle	+ PHRASE

1 a soft substance is easy to press or shape and is not hard or firm: *soft cheese* ♦ *The soil is fairly soft after the rain.*
2 a soft material or surface is nice to touch and not rough or stiff: *I want to get a nice soft carpet for the bedroom.* ♦ *Her skin felt soft to his touch.*
3 a soft sound is quiet and nice to listen to: *The engine noise was no more than a soft hum.*
4 a soft light or colour is pale, gentle, and nice to look at: *Her bedroom was decorated in soft shades of pink and blue.*
5 not strict enough with other people and allowing them to do things they should not do: *You're too soft – I wouldn't let them behave like that.* ♦ *They accused the minister of being soft on crime.*
6 kind and sympathetic: *He must have a soft heart beneath that stern exterior.*
7 soft water does not contain many MINERALS (=natural substances) and is easy to use with soap

---

Review D

► Grammar *Extra* pages 144–149

Grammar

1 Cross out *who/which/that* when it can be left out.

a) *India* is the country **which** I'd most like to visit.

b) There are only a few *sports* **that** really interest me.

c) I still have the first *CD* **that** I ever bought.

d) I don't like people **who** *don't tell the truth*.

e) The person **who** I spend most time with is *my friend Ben*.

Change the words in *italics* to make true sentences. Compare with a partner.

2 Complete each sentence so that it means the same as the sentence before it.

a) If you don't wear a coat, you'll catch a cold.
= Unless you *wear a coat, you'll catch a cold*.

b) We'll have to go unless they arrive in the next five minutes. = If they _____

c) If they don't work, they'll fail the exam.
= Unless they _____

d) He won't come to the party unless you ask him.
= If you _____

e) You won't be able to buy that car if you don't save your money. = Unless you _____

3 Write the words in the correct order to make questions. Change to contracted forms where possible.

a) know / you / what / doing / Do / are / next weekend / you ?
Do you know what you're doing next weekend?

b) you / Can / you / your shoes / me / bought / tell / where ?

c) think / you / politics / interesting / topic / is / an / Do ?

d) you / born / me / you / where / were / Could / tell ?

Work with your partner. Ask and answer the questions.

4 Complete the unreal conditional sentences.

a) If I (be) *were* you, I (drive) *'d drive* more carefully.

b) If I (study) _____ harder for yesterday's exam, I (pass) _____ .

c) We (learn) _____ a lot from animals if they (can) _____ talk.

d) If I (not fall) _____ asleep, I (see) _____ the rest of the film.

e) I (can) _____ call Cleo now if I (have) _____ my mobile.

f) I (not buy) _____ this car if I (know) _____ it was so unreliable.

5 Underline the correct alternative.

a) I wish I <u>could have done</u> / **can do** more with my life.

b) If only I **am** / **was** more interested in money.

c) I wish I **were** / **had been** ten years younger.

d) If only I **didn't start** / **hadn't started** smoking.

e) I wish I **have** / **had** more free time.

f) If only I **was** / **had been** born in the USA.

Which statements are true for you? Discuss with your partner.

6 Look at the pictures and underline the correct verb forms.

a) He's **had his hair cut** / **cut his hair**.

b) He's **had his hair cut** / **cut his hair**.

c) She's **fixing her car** / **having her car fixed**.

d) She's **fixing her car** / **having her car fixed**.

7 Spot the mistake! Cross out the incorrect sentence.

1 a) A blog is a diary that you write on the internet.
   b) ~~A blog is a diary that you write it on the internet.~~

2 a) We'll go out on Sunday if it will be fine.
   b) We'll go out on Sunday if it's fine.

3 a) If I didn't eat so much I won't be so fat.
   b) If I didn't eat so much I wouldn't be so fat.

4 a) I wish I hadn't bought that shirt – I hate it now.
   b) I wish I didn't buy that shirt – I hate it now.

5 a) Sean always wears the same leather black old jacket.
   b) Sean always wears the same old black leather jacket.

6 a) She is having her house decorated at the moment.
   b) She has her house decorated at the moment.

Vocabulary

1 **Correct the story with the words in the box.**

> about me   after me   at me   ~~for me~~
> me in   me off   me up

Sadly, my mum and dad died when I was very young, and I went to live with my grandparents. They cared (1) *for me* and looked (2) _____ . I always felt really loved. At night, my grandma always used to tuck (3) _____ . When I was older, if I stayed out late, they would worry (4) _____ , and then, when I got home, they would tell (5) _____ but they never yelled (6) _____ . I think they brought (7) _____ well and made me the man I am today.

2 **Complete the text with the correct form of** *make* **or** *let*.

I went to boarding school. The teachers were really nice. They (1) *let* us wear any style of clothing we wanted and they (2) _____ us use their first names, too. Of course, there were still rules. They (3) _____ us keep our rooms tidy and they (4) _____ us do our homework every evening. Overall, though, I would say they were very liberal. They even (5) _____ one girl dye her hair pink!

3 **Complete the sentences with the adverbs.**

> ~~Apparently~~   Basically   definitely   Hopefully
> incredibly   very much   very well

a) *Apparently*, Jane is having an affair with Tom.
b) Fay is _____ clever. She knows everything!
c) Ruth can play the saxophone _____ .
d) _____ , I'll pass my exams and get a good job.
e) I'm _____ going out tonight. I need some fun!
f) I don't really enjoy academic work _____ .
g) _____ , I think I'm brilliant!

4 **Put the words in the box in the correct group.**

> ~~baggy~~   ~~blouse~~   boots   checked   ~~cotton~~
> leather   linen   long-sleeved   plain   silk
> striped   suede   suit   sweater   top

a) material: *cotton*, …
b) shape/design/pattern: *baggy*, …
c) clothes: *blouse*, …

5 **Complete the descriptions with the words in the box.**

> bald   deep-set   freckles   goatee   mid-forties
> short   shoulder-length   sideburns   skinny
> ~~slim~~   tattoo   twenties

a) Arnie is a (1) *slim* man in his (2) _____ with (3) _____ grey hair and (4) _____ eyes.
b) Bobbi is a young woman with (5) _____ blonde hair. She's quite (6) _____ , with (7) _____ all over her face and a (8) _____ on her shoulder.
c) Carl is a stocky man in his (9) _____ with a (10) _____ head, long (11) _____ and a (12) _____ .

6 **Underline the correct words.**

a) How many times a week do you **do** / **have** the washing up?
b) How long does it usually take you to **get** / **put** dressed?
c) Do you **do** / **have** breakfast every day?
d) Do you **do** / **put** the TV on in the morning?
e) How many times a week do you **do** / **read** the paper?

Work with a partner. Ask and answer the questions.

Pronunciation

1 **Look at some words from Units 10–12. Say the words and add them to the table.**

> ~~adventurous~~   apparently   ~~Christmas~~
> ~~comfortable~~   ~~develop~~   dinosaur   expensive
> language   museum   naughty   psychiatrist
> pyjamas   ridiculous   talented   vegetables

A: ☐☐☐	B: ☐☐	C: ☐☐☐	D: ☐☐☐☐
comfortable	*Christmas*	*develop*	*adventurous*

2 **Underline the stressed syllable in each word.**

🔘 **3.25** **Listen, check and repeat.**

Reading & Listening

1 Read what Anna, Brad and Colin say about their lives. Complete the sentences with the correct name.

a) _____ wants a dog.   b) _____ enjoys the garden.   c) _____ owes a lot of money.

The best years of your life?

Anna Everyone keeps telling me that these are the best days of my life, but it doesn't always feel like that to me! I had quite a difficult time as a teenager – all the boyfriend dramas, friendship problems, fights with Mum and Dad – so I'm really glad all that's behind me. But I thought my life would be sorted out when I got to my thirties, and it's not that simple. I love my job – I'm a doctor – but I haven't got a social life because I'm working all the time. And I'm still paying off my student loan – I owe more than £30,000! Unless I manage to pay it off I won't be able to pay for my own children's education!

Colin Some people think that they're going to be happy when they get a boyfriend or girlfriend, or move house, or get more money. But if you think like that, you'll never be happy. I think the best years of your life are where you are now. You can't always be waiting to be happy. In some ways, I feel happier now than I did when I was young. I wish I hadn't wasted so much time worrying about things that don't matter. If I've learnt anything it's that very few things are actually that important – only your family and your health. Of course, I can't do all the things I used to do when I was younger – my legs are pretty bad these days, but I still manage to get out for a walk. What makes me happy nowadays is just sitting in the garden on a sunny day, or spending time with my grandchildren. I've got seven, you know.

Brad My life's brilliant. I'm in a band with my friends Zac and Sanjay. I play the guitar and sing. We want to be famous one day. School's OK but it's a bit boring. I'd rather be out with my friends, playing football, or playing computer games. If I was Prime Minister, I wouldn't make kids go to school all day. I'd make them go to school for just three days a week, with four days for the weekend. That would be good. One thing that's bad at the moment is that I want a dog, but my mum says we can't get one because they smell. She says I can get one when I leave home. But that won't be for ages! Sanjay's got a dog, and Zac's got two. Why can't I get one? It's not fair.

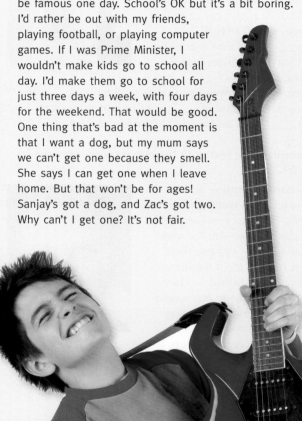

2 Read the texts again. Are the sentences true or false?

a) Anna has happy memories of her teenage years. *False*

b) Anna is too busy to go out much because of her work.

c) Brad would like to have more free time.

d) Brad's mum is going to get a dog when Brad leaves home.

e) The best years of Colin's life were when he was young.

f) Colin wishes he had spent less time worrying about his family and his health.

3 3.26 Listen to Colin talking about his life. What does he regret about his past?

4 Listen again and number the events of Colin's life in order, 1–7.

1 e, 2 ...

a) He got married.

b) He worked in a factory.

c) He became a taxi driver.

d) He started his own business.

e) He went to live with Flo and Isaac.

f) He played by the canal.

g) He had two children.

Writing & Speaking

1 **Read Karen's email to an old school friend. Complete the text with the linking words in the box.**

> After   although   and   but   so   unfortunately   When   While   who

To: anitamanning@heatmail.com
From: kwilson@greenparkschool.org

Hi Anita
It was great to get your email through schoolfriends.com. How many years is it since we last saw each other? I don't want to think about it!

Ⓐ Life's had its ups and downs, (1) *but* generally things have turned out OK for me.

Ⓑ (2) _____ school I went to college in Cheltenham, and studied drama. (3) _____ I left college I got a job with a small theatre group which worked with children in schools all over the country. I travelled a lot, and loved it.

Ⓒ (4) _____ I was working at a school in Stroud, I met and married Simon, (5) _____ was an English teacher. I left my job, and we had two children, Guy and Max, who are 13 and 15. But (6) _____ , Simon and I split up six years ago. Guy and Max live with me now, and (7) _____ we are divorced, Simon and I have stayed friends.

Ⓓ I didn't have a lot of money as a single parent, and life was tough for a while. But a few years ago I wanted to start work again, (8) _____ I retrained as a drama teacher. I love my job (9) _____ guess where I'm working now? That's right, Green Park, our old school!

Ⓔ I'm getting married in June to a man called Frank. He's retiring in a few years, and we're planning to go travelling in Australia and the USA when the boys leave home.

It would be great to meet up sometime. I wish I'd kept in touch with more friends from school. Do you ever see Michelle or Rachel? I'd love to know what they're doing now.

All the best,
Karen

2 **Match the questions (1–5) to the paragraphs (A–E) in the email.**

1 What has happened in your personal life?   C
2 What has happened in your school or professional life?
3 What are your hopes for the future?
4 How has your life been up to now?
5 What are you doing now?

3 **Think about your own answers to the questions in Exercise 2. Make notes.**

> Personal life
> • After school, went to live in France with my dad.
> • Marseilles.
> • Met Angélique.

4 **Tell your partner about your life up to now, what you're doing now and your hopes for the future. Use the notes you made in Exercise 3.**

'After I left school, I moved to France to live with my dad. We were living in Marseilles. One evening I met this girl in a bar. ...'

5 **Write an email to an old childhood friend about your life up to now, what you're doing now and your hopes for the future.**

▶ 🔊 **3.27 Song:** *Dedicated Follower of Fashion*

Pairwork: Student A

Unit 1 How similar are you?

You are going to ask Student B questions to find out how similar or different you are.

- Use the question beginnings and topics in the table below, or your own ideas.
- Take it in turns to ask and answer questions.

| How often do you … | buy a newspaper? cook? drink beer? eat Thai food? get up before 6.00 a.m.? |
| Do you ever … | go abroad? go to the theatre? go swimming? stay up all night? lose your keys? |

Write down what you have in common.
We both buy a newspaper every day. I never cook, and neither does Student B.

Unit 2 What do you know about Shakira?

Complete the text.

- Student B has the same text as you but with different information missing.
- Write down the questions you need to ask Student B in order to find out the missing information.
- Take it in turns to ask and answer questions and write the missing information in the text.
- When you have finished, check with Student B that your texts are identical.

Shakira, singer, songwriter and dancer, was born in (1) _____ in 1977. Her mother is Colombian, and her father is of Lebanese origin. She has (2) _____ brothers and sisters.

When she was only four years old, she started belly dancing. It was at this early age that she decided she wanted to be a (3) _____ .

She is still a young woman, but she has already sold fifty million albums worldwide. She has performed many times at the MTV video music award ceremonies, and in (4) _____ she won five awards at the first Latin American MTV music awards.

In 2006, her single, *Hips Don't Lie*, reached number one in the US charts.

(5) _____ is a big fan of Shakira. He personally asked her to write and perform some songs for the soundtrack of the film *Love in the Time of Cholera*.

Shakira now lives in the Bahamas, and she has just started work on (6) _____ . Her fiancé is Antonio de la Rúa – son of the ex-president of Argentina.

Shakira is hugely talented. In addition to her gifts as a singer, dancer and songwriter, she speaks five languages, and in (7) _____ she established a charity organisation to help poor children in Colombia.

Unit 3 How well do you know each other?

How well do you know Student B?

- Write Student B's name in the space provided below.
- Complete sentences *a–f* according to what you think.
- Ask Student B questions beginning, *How many …?* or *How long …?* to find out if you were right or wrong.

I think _____ (Student B's name) …	Question	✓ = I'm more or less right. ✗ = I'm completely wrong.
a) has been wearing the same watch for _____ .	How many …?	_____
b) has visited _____ continents.	How long …?	_____
c) has been living in the same house for _____ .		_____
d) has known his/her oldest friend since _____ .		_____
e) has read _____ books in the past three months.		_____
f) has been using the same mobile phone for _____ .		_____

Unit 4 Phrasal verbs

You are going to rewrite sentences using common phrasal verbs.

- Replace the highlighted verbs in sentences 1–6 with phrasal verbs. In each case choose a verb and a particle from the boxes. Use appropriate forms of the verb.
- Read out your sentences to Student B who will check that you have used the correct phrasal verb.
- Similarly, check that Student B has used the correct phrasal verbs in his/her sentences (7–12).
- Choose at least three of your sentences that describe you best, and tell Student B. Add more information.

Verbs: break come find go set take	**Particles:** for off out out up up

1 When I have to catch a plane or train, I like to begin the journey early so that I have time to spare.
2 I'd like to start doing ballroom dancing one day.
3 When I eat out in a restaurant, I always choose something I never eat at home.
4 If I end a relationship with someone, I always stay friends with them.
5 I'm very interested in discovering more about my family history.
6 I'll definitely buy the new Coldplay album as soon as it becomes available.
7 I get on with most people – I'm pretty easy-going.
8 When I arrange to meet someone, I never turn up late.
9 In an argument, I'm always the first to give in.
10 One day I intend to set up a business and run it myself.
11 I always feel much happier as soon as the sun comes out.
12 My car is very reliable; it has never broken down.

Unit 5 Childhood

Were you and Student B the same or different when you were children?

- Write six sentences about your life when you were a child, beginning *I used to …*
- Choose from the topics below or use your own ideas.

clothes and appearance food hobbies holidays home pets

I used to have curly hair. I used to hate vegetables. I used to …

- Ask Student B questions to find out how similar or different you were.

Student A: Did you use to have curly hair?
Student B: No, I didn't. My hair has always been straight.

Unit 6 Working conditions

Can you guess which job is being described?

- Choose three of the jobs from the box and write sentences about the working conditions for each one.
- Read out your sentences. Student B guesses which job you are describing.

'This person has to get up early, doesn't have to work in an office, doesn't have to wear a suit or a uniform, often has to work at weekends, often has to work with animals, should know what the weather forecast is, can spend a lot of time outside, and probably has to drive a tractor.' (Student B: 'A farmer.')

farmer flight attendant novelist shop assistant waiter nanny dentist hairdresser plumber supermodel police officer teacher racing driver chef artist bus driver DJ fire fighter gardener vet

Unit 7 Experiences

What experiences has Student B had?

- Write Student B's name in the space below.
- Write statements using phrases *a–f* that you think are true.
- Write questions to check your statements.
- Ask Student B the questions.

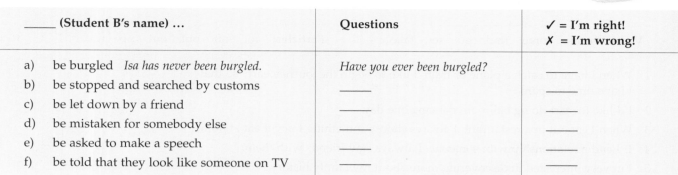

_____ (Student B's name) …	Questions	✓ = I'm right! ✗ = I'm wrong!
a) be burgled *Isa has never been burgled.*	*Have you ever been burgled?*	_____
b) be stopped and searched by customs	_____	_____
c) be let down by a friend	_____	_____
d) be mistaken for somebody else	_____	_____
e) be asked to make a speech	_____	_____
f) be told that they look like someone on TV	_____	_____

Unit 8 Automatic pilot

You are going to complete a text with Student B's help.

- Student B has the same text as you but with different verbs missing.
- Complete the text with the most appropriate forms of the verbs in brackets.
- Then take it in turns to read out your completed text and check your answers.

a) Two pilots (**fly**) *were flying* a passenger airline from London to Nairobi,

b) when one of the pilots **came out** of the cockpit to make some coffee.

c) He (**have**) _____ problems with the coffee machine,

d) so he **asked** his co-pilot to help him.

e) As the co-pilot (**leave**) _____ the cockpit,

f) he accidentally **closed** the door behind him

g) and then immediately (**realise**) _____

h) that he**'d locked** them both out of the cockpit.

i) The door (**be**) _____ fitted with an anti-terrorist lock

j) which **was** impossible to open – even for the pilots.

k) Fortunately, one of the pilots (**put**) _____ his Swiss army knife in his hand luggage

l) which he **had stored** in a locker above one of the passenger seats.

m) When he finally (**locate**) _____ the knife,

n) the two pilots **managed** to break the lock.

o) By the time the pilots (**break**) _____ into the cockpit,

p) the plane **was cruising** eastwards over the Indian Ocean.

Unit 9 A funny story

You are going to complete a funny story with Student B's help.
You have parts of the story already completed, and Student B
has other parts.

- Dictate alternate lines of the story to Student B, and write
  down the sentences that Student B dictates to you.

- Compare your completed stories, which should be identical.

A woman was playing golf when she hit the ball into the
woods. She went to look for it and found a frog in a trap.

a) The frog asked her if she could release him from the trap.

b) _____

c) So the woman freed the frog. Then the frog admitted that
   there was something he hadn't told her.

d) _____

e) The woman replied that that was fine.

f) _____

g) The frog warned her that her husband would be the most
   handsome man in the world and all the women would
   chase him.

h) _____

i) The woman said that for her second wish she wanted to
   be the richest woman in the world.

j) _____

k) The woman insisted that she didn't mind.

l) _____

m) The woman replied that she wanted to have a mild heart
   attack.

Unit 10 Call my bluff

You are going to read out three definitions of some common English words. The definitions with
crosses are false, and the one with a tick is true. Student B has to guess which definition (1, 2 or 3) is
the correct one.

- Complete one false definition for each word. Use your imagination!
- Read out your definitions and see if Student B can guess which ones are correct.
- Then listen to Student B's definitions and guess which ones are correct.

a) A 'wimp' is …
   1   a person who _____ . ✗
   2   a person who is helpful and sympathetic. ✗
   3   a person who isn't brave. ✓

b) A 'clog' is …
   1   a shoe that has a wooden sole. ✓
   2   an animal that _____ . ✗
   3   a person who is not very clever. ✗

c) A 'doodle' is …
   1   a picture you draw when you're bored or
       thinking about other things. ✓
   2   a small dog with curly hair. ✗
   3   something that _____ . ✗

d) A 'jingle' is …
   1   a place where _____ . ✗
   2   an illness that is most common in children. ✗
   3   a short piece of music that is used in advertisements. ✓

e) A 'bob' is …
   1   a woman's hairstyle. ✓
   2   an informal name for a policeman. ✗
   3   a person who _____ . ✗

Unit 11 Dilemmas

You are going to guess what Student B would do in different situations.

- Read the dilemmas below, and guess whether Student B would answer (*1, 2* or *3*) in each case.
- Ask Student B questions to find out whether you guessed correctly.

   a) If you were in a non-smoking café, and the person on the next table started smoking, what would you do?
   1   I'd go over and ask him to put his cigarette out.
   2   I'd just look at him angrily.
   3   I'd do nothing – it's up to the café management to enforce the non-smoking rule.

   b) If you needed to borrow a small sum of money, who would you ask?
   1   I'd ask my parents.
   2   I'd ask a friend.
   3   I'd ask the bank.

   c) If you wanted some advice about your career, who would you ask?
   1   I'd ask my parents.
   2   I'd ask my teacher.
   3   I'd ask people in an internet chat room.

   d) If you wanted someone to go shopping with you to help you choose an outfit for a special occasion, who would you ask?
   1   I'd ask my mother.
   2   I'd ask a friend.
   3   I wouldn't ask anybody – I'd prefer to go on my own.

   e) If a friend left their personal diary at your house by mistake, would you be tempted to read it?
   1   Absolutely not.
   2   Yes, I would be tempted, but I wouldn't do it.
   3   Yes, I'd read it.

Unit 12 Spot the differences

Student B has a similar picture to yours.

- Do not show your picture to Student B.
- Ask and answer questions to find twelve differences between your picture and Student B's picture.

Student A: In your picture is the man wearing baggy jeans?
Student B: No, he's wearing tight jeans.

Pairwork: Student B

Unit 1 How similar are you?

You are going to ask Student A questions to find out how similar or different you are.

- Use the question beginnings and topics in the table below, or your own ideas.
- Take it in turns to ask and answer questions.

How often do you …	buy something online? dance? drink tea? get bad headaches? go camping?
Do you ever …	go for a run? make new friends? ride a bicycle? take photos? watch the sunset?

Write down what you have in common.
We both buy CDs online. I never dance, and neither does Student A.

Unit 2 What do you know about Shakira?

Complete the text.

- Student A has the same text as you but with different information missing.
- Write down the questions you need to ask Student A in order to find out the missing information.
- Take it in turns to ask and answer questions and write the missing information in the text.
- When you have finished, check with Student A that your texts are identical.

Shakira, singer, songwriter and dancer, was born in Colombia in (1) _____ . Her mother is Colombian, and her father is of Lebanese origin. She has eight brothers and sisters.

When she was only (2) _____ years old, she started belly dancing. It was at this early age that she decided she wanted to be a performer.

She is still a young woman, but she has already sold (3) _____ albums worldwide. She has performed many times at the MTV video music award ceremonies, and in 2002 she won five awards at the first Latin American MTV music awards.

In 2006, her single, *Hips Don't Lie*, reached number (4) _____ in the US charts.

Gabriel Garcia Márquez is a big fan of Shakira. He personally asked her to write and perform some songs for the soundtrack of the film *Love in the Time of Cholera*.

Shakira now lives in (5) _____ , and she has just started work on her new album. Her fiancé is (6) _____ – son of the ex-president of Argentina.

Shakira is hugely talented. In addition to her gifts as a singer, dancer and songwriter, she speaks (7) _____ languages, and in 1997 she established a charity organisation to help poor children in Colombia.

Unit 3 How well do you know each other?

How well do you know Student A?

- Write Student A's name in the space provided below.
- Complete sentences *a–f* according to what you think.
- Ask Student A questions beginning, *How many …?* or *How long …?* to find out if you were right or wrong.

I think _____ (Student A's name) …	Question	✓ = I'm more or less right. ✗ = I'm completely wrong.
a) has visited _____ capital cities.	How many …?	_____
b) has been using the same computer for _____ .	How long …?	_____
c) has watched _____ hours of TV this week.		_____
d) has had _____ cups of coffee so far today.		_____
e) has been doing his/her favourite sport since _____ .		_____
f) has been listening to his/her favourite band for _____ .		_____

Unit 4 Phrasal verbs

You are going to rewrite sentences using common phrasal verbs.

- Replace the highlighted verbs in sentences *7–12* with phrasal verbs. In each case choose a verb and a particle from the boxes. Use appropriate forms of the verb.

- Read out your sentences to Student A who will check that you have used the correct phrasal verb.

- Similarly, check that Student A has used the correct phrasal verbs in his/her sentences (*1–6*).

- Choose at least three of your sentences that describe you best, and tell Student A. Add more information.

Verbs: break come get give set turn	**Particles:** down in on out up up

1 When I have to catch a plane or train, I like to <u>set off</u> early so that I have time to spare.

2 I'd like to <u>take up</u> ballroom dancing one day.

3 When I eat out in a restaurant, I always <u>go for</u> something I never eat at home.

4 If I <u>break up</u> with someone, I always stay friends with them.

5 I'm very interested in <u>finding out</u> more about my family history.

6 I'll definitely buy the new Coldplay album as soon as it <u>comes out</u>.

7 I have a friendly relationship with most people – I'm pretty easy-going.

8 When I arrange to meet someone, I never arrive late.

9 In an argument, I'm always the first to stop arguing.

10 One day I intend to start a business and run it myself.

11 I always feel much happier as soon as the sun appears.

12 My car is very reliable; it has never stopped working.

Unit 5 Childhood

Were you and Student A the same or different when you were children?

- Write six sentences about your life when you were a child, beginning *I used to …*

- Choose from the topics below or use your own ideas.

family music school sport television toys

I used to fight with my sister.   I used to like Nirvana.   I used to …

- Ask Student A questions to find out how similar or different you were.

Student B: Did you use to fight with your sister?
Student A: No, I didn't. I used to fight with my brother.

Unit 6 Working conditions

Can you guess which job is being described?

- Choose three of the jobs from the box and write sentences about the working conditions for each one.

- Read out your sentences. Student A guesses which job you are describing.

'This person has to get up early, doesn't have to work in an office, doesn't have to wear a suit or a uniform, often has to work at weekends, often has to work with animals, should know what the weather forecast is, can spend a lot of time outside, and probably has to drive a tractor.' (Student A: *'A farmer.'*)

farmer flight attendant
novelist shop assistant
waiter nanny dentist
hairdresser plumber
supermodel police officer
teacher racing driver chef
artist bus driver DJ
fire fighter gardener vet

Unit 7 Experiences

What experiences has Student A had?

- Write Student A's name in the space below.
- Write statements using phrases *a–f* that you think are true.
- Write questions to check your statements.
- Ask Student A the questions.

_____ (Student A's name) …	Questions	✓ = I'm right! ✗ = I'm wrong!
a) be injured playing sport *Karl has been injured playing sport.*	*Have you ever been injured playing sport?*	_____
b) be bitten by a snake	_____	_____
c) be given a present they didn't like	_____	_____
d) be invited to a fancy dress party	_____	_____
e) be interviewed on radio or TV	_____	_____
f) be given too much change in a shop	_____	_____

Unit 8 Automatic pilot

You are going to complete a text with Student A's help.

- Student A has the same text as you but with different verbs missing.
- Complete the text with the most appropriate forms of the verbs in brackets.
- Then take it in turns to read out your completed text and check your answers.

a) Two pilots **were flying** a passenger airline from London to Nairobi,

b) when one of the pilots (**come out**) *came out* of the cockpit to make some coffee.

c) He **was having** problems with the coffee machine,

d) so he (**ask**) _____ his co-pilot to help him.

e) As the co-pilot **was leaving** the cockpit,

f) he accidentally (**close**) _____ the door behind him

g) and then immediately **realised**

h) that he (**lock**) _____ them both out of the cockpit.

i) The door **had been** fitted with an anti-terrorist lock

j) which (**be**) _____ impossible to open – even for the pilots.

k) Fortunately, one of the pilots **had put** his Swiss army knife in his hand luggage

l) which he (**store**) _____ in a locker above one of the passenger seats.

m) When he finally **located** the knife,

n) the two pilots (**manage**) _____ to break the lock.

o) By the time the pilots **had broken** into the cockpit,

p) the plane (**cruise**) _____ eastwards over the Indian Ocean.

Unit 9 A funny story

You are going to complete a funny story with Student A's help. You have parts of the story already completed, and Student A has other parts.

- Dictate alternate lines of the story to Student A, and write down the sentences that Student A dictates to you.

- Compare your completed stories, which should be identical.

  A woman was playing golf when she hit the ball into the woods. She went to look for it and found a frog in a trap.

a) _____

b) The frog told her that he would grant her three wishes.

c) _____

d) He explained that she could have three wishes, but whatever she wished for, her husband would have ten times more.

e) _____

f) The woman said that for her first wish she wanted to be the most beautiful woman in the world.

g) _____

h) The woman insisted that that was fine, because she would be the most beautiful woman in the world, and he would only have eyes for her.

i) _____

j) The frog warned her that her husband would be ten times richer than her.

k) _____

l) The frog then asked her what she wanted her third wish to be.

m) _____

Unit 10 Call my bluff

You are going to read out three definitions of some common English words. The definitions with crosses are false, and the one with a tick is true. Student A has to guess which definition (1, 2 or 3) is the correct one.

- Complete one false definition for each word. Use your imagination!
- Listen to Student A's definitions and guess which ones are correct.
- Then read out your definitions and see if Student A can guess which ones are correct.

a) A **'bargain'** is …

  1 something you buy that costs much less than normal. ✓

  2 something you take when you have a headache. ✗

  3 something you _____ . ✗

b) The **'dole'** is …

  1 money that people get from the government when they don't have a job. ✓

  2 money that people get from _____ . ✗

  3 money that people get from their employers when they work overtime. ✗

c) A **'plug'** is …

  1 a round piece of plastic that blocks a hole. ✓

  2 something that _____ . ✗

  3 a small carpet that you put in front of a door. ✗

d) A **'stickleback'** is …

  1 a type of glue used to stick things back together. ✗

  2 a small river fish that has spikes along its back. ✓

  3 a gadget that you use to _____ . ✗

e) A **'nettle'** is …

  1 a place where _____ . ✗

  2 a plant that stings if you touch it. ✓

  3 a person who uses the internet a lot. ✗

Unit 11 Dilemmas

You are going to guess what Student A would do in different situations.

- Read the dilemmas below, and guess whether Student A would answer (*1, 2* or *3*) in each case.

- Ask Student A questions to find out whether you guessed correctly.

a) If you won two tickets to go on holiday to New York for a week, who would you take?
   1 I'd take a friend.
   2 I'd take my partner.
   3 I'd take a member of my family.

b) If you saw your favourite actor in a restaurant, what would you do?
   1 I'd stare at him/her from a distance.
   2 I'd go up and ask for his/her autograph.
   3 I'd pretend I hadn't seen him/her.

c) If you wanted to impress someone at a party, would you tell a few white lies about yourself?
   1 Never.
   2 Maybe.
   3 Definitely.

d) If a lazy friend wanted to copy your homework, what would you do?
   1 I'd say yes.
   2 I'd say no.
   3 I'd say yes, but I'd ask them for a favour in return.

e) If you were late for a meeting but you saw an elderly woman trying to carry a heavy bag, what would you do?
   1 I'd offer to help her.
   2 I'd feel sorry for her, but decide that I was in too much of a hurry to help her.
   3 I'd decide not to help her – I can't help everyone.

Unit 12 Spot the differences

Student A has a similar picture to yours.

- Do not show your picture to Student A.

- Ask and answer questions to find twelve differences between your picture and Student A's picture.

Student A: In your picture, is the man wearing baggy jeans?

Student B: No, he's wearing tight jeans.

Grammar *Extra*

Unit 1 **Tense review. Question forms**

Tense review

TENSES		ASPECT			
		simple	continuous	perfect simple	perfect continuous
Present	+ – ?	He **works**. He **doesn't work**. **Does** he **work**?	He **is working**. He **isn't working**. **Is** he **working**?	He **has worked**. He **hasn't worked**. **Has** he **worked**?	He **has been working**. He **hasn't been working**. **Has** he **been working**?
Past	+ – ?	She **worked**. She **didn't work**. **Did** she **work**?	She **was working**. She **wasn't working**. **Was** she **working**?	She **had worked**. She **hadn't worked**. **Had** she **worked**?	She **had been working**. She **hadn't been working**. **Had** she **been working**?

Question forms

Word order

The usual word order for questions is as follows.

Question word	(Auxiliary) verb	Subject	
—	Was	she	tired?
—	Have	they	arrived?
What	does	'collocation'	mean?
Who	are	you	meeting?
When	did	he	arrive?

Wh questions ending with prepositions

When verbs are followed by a preposition, you usually put the preposition at the end of the question.
'Where does she come **from**?' 'What are you interested **in**?' 'Who was she talking **about**?'

Common verb + preposition combinations:
complain about, talk about, think about, worry about; look at; be for, care for, hope for, pay for; suffer from;
believe in, confide in, be interested in, invest in; consist of; depend on, insist on, rely on, spend on;
belong to, listen to, refer to, relate to.

Subject/Object questions

Q *Who talked to you?* **A** *Dan talked to me.* (*Who* is the subject.)

Q *Who did you talk to?* **A** *I talked to Dan.* (*Who* is the object.)

When the question word is the subject of the verb in the question, you don't use *do, does* or *did*.
You put the verb in the third person.
Who **wants** *to come?* (NOT ~~Who does want to come?~~)
Which company **makes** *the most money?* (NOT ~~Which company does make the most money?~~)
What **happened**? (NOT ~~What did happen?~~)

Unit 1 Exercises

1 **Complete the sentences by putting the verb in the tense suggested.**

a) I (not study) *didn't study* English at primary school. (Past simple)
b) I (go) _____ to the USA but I (never go) _____ to the UK. (Present perfect simple)
c) This time last year I (do) _____ an intensive English course in Ireland. (Past continuous)
d) I (not use) _____ an English–English dictionary before I came to this class. (Past perfect simple)
e) I (enjoy) _____ watching foreign films in the original version. (Present simple)
f) I (read) _____ a really good English novel at the moment. (Present continuous)
g) I'm very busy at work so I (not do) _____ my English homework recently. (Present perfect continuous)

Are any of the sentences true for you?

2 **The following questions and answers come from real conversations in a law court. Complete each one with a suitable question word from the box.**

How long	how many	How old	~~What~~	What	Where	Which	why

a) Q: (1) *What* is your date of birth?
   A: July the fifteenth.
   Q: (2) _____ year?
   A: Every year.

b) Q: (3) _____ is your son – the one living with you?
   A: Thirty-eight or thirty-five, I can't remember which.
   Q: (4) _____ has he lived with you?
   A: Forty-five years.

c) Q: Doctor, (5) _____ autopsies have you performed on dead people?
   A: All my autopsies are performed on dead people.

d) Q: (6) _____ was the first thing your husband said to you when he woke that morning?
   A: He said, '(7) _____ am I, Cathy?'
   Q: And (8) _____ did that upset you?
   A: My name is Susan.

Work with a partner. Which exchange do you think is the funniest?

3 **Underline the possible response to each statement.**

a) 'My best friend likes talking.' '**What about?** / What with?'
b) 'I sent a text before the lesson.' '**Who to?** / Who from?'
c) 'I'm saving all my money.' '**What about?** / What for?'
d) 'I'm going out this evening.' '**Who for?** / Who with?'
e) 'I've just bought a fabulous present.' '**Who for?** / Who about?'
f) 'I got a very funny email yesterday.' '**Who from?** / Who with?'

Now write complete questions with the question word and preposition.

a) *What does he/she like talking about?*

4 **Complete the sentences to make them true for you.**

a) I watched _____ on TV last night.
b) _____ usually gets up the earliest in my house.
c) I normally have _____ for breakfast.
d) _____ texts me the most.
e) _____ people remembered my last birthday.
f) The number _____ bus stops near my house.
g) I had dinner with _____ last night.
h) _____ people phoned me yesterday.

Write appropriate subject or object questions to find out the same information from your partner.

a) *What did you watch on TV last night?*

Ask your partner the questions.

Unit 2 Present perfect simple. Past simple. Past continuous. Comparative and superlative structures

Part 1: Present perfect simple. Past simple. Past continuous

Present perfect and past simple

You can use the present perfect or the past simple to talk about the same completed actions.
You use the present perfect when your context is time 'up to now' – ie you **don't** say *when*.
You use the past simple when your context is 'finished' time – ie you **do** say *when* (or *when* is known).

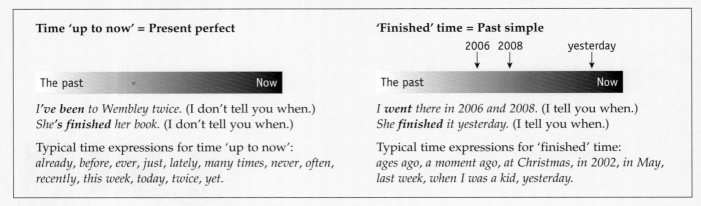

Time 'up to now' = Present perfect

The past — Now

I've been to Wembley twice. (I don't tell you when.)
She's finished her book. (I don't tell you when.)

Typical time expressions for time 'up to now':
already, before, ever, just, lately, many times, never, often, recently, this week, today, twice, yet.

'Finished' time = Past simple

2006 2008 yesterday

The past — Now

I went there in 2006 and 2008. (I tell you when.)
She finished it yesterday. (I tell you when.)

Typical time expressions for 'finished' time:
ages ago, a moment ago, at Christmas, in 2002, in May, last week, when I was a kid, yesterday.

Past continuous

You use the past continuous to describe a 'longer' activity that was in progress when other past events happened. You usually use it in contrast with the past simple.
*I **saw** them when I **was jogging** in the park.   They **were playing** golf when it **started** snowing.*

Part 2: Comparative and superlative structures

With short adjectives you add *er* to form comparatives and *est* to form superlatives. Sometimes you need to make some small spelling changes to the ending.
nice – nicer – the nicest; fit – fitter – the fittest; healthy – healthier – the healthiest

With longer adjectives you add *more* to form comparatives and *the most* to form superlatives.
exciting – more exciting – the most exciting; extreme – more extreme – the most extreme

⚠ **Special cases**

Irregular adjectives
bad – worse – the worst; good – better – the best; far – further – the furthest
Some two-syllable adjectives can end in *er* and *est*.
*My sister is much **cleverer** than me. She's **the cleverest** person I know.*
Common examples: *clever, gentle, narrow, quiet, simple.*

For some compound adjectives you change the first part of the compound.
*He's very **good-looking** – far **better-looking** than his photo. In fact, he's **the best-looking** man in the class.*
Common examples: *badly-dressed, good-looking, highly-paid, long-lasting, long-running, well-dressed, well-paid.*

Comparative adjectives

You use comparative adjectives to compare people/things with other people/things. You can use *far, much, a bit, a lot* or *slightly* to modify comparisons.
*Motor racing is **far more exciting than** golf.   A rugby pitch is **slightly bigger than** a football pitch.*

You use *not as … as* to make negative comparisons. You can use *nearly* or *quite* to modify negative comparisons.
*Golf isn't **nearly as exciting as** motor racing.   A football pitch isn't **quite as big as** a rugby pitch.*

Superlative adjectives

You use superlative adjectives to compare people/things with all the other people/things in their group.
*Manchester United is **the most successful** team in England.*

Unit 2 Exercises

Part 1

1 Complete the sentences with the present perfect or the past simple.

a) I (not go) *haven't been* to the gym recently.
b) I (never break) _____ a bone.
c) My mum (call) _____ me a few hours ago.
d) I (not see) _____ my friends much lately.
e) I (already book) _____ next year's holiday.
f) I (hate) _____ PE when I was a kid.
g) My great-grandfather (do) _____ military service.
h) I (not finish) _____ this exercise yet.

Tick the sentences that are true for you. Rewrite the sentences as questions. Ask your partner.

a) *Have you been to the gym recently?*

2 What time is it now? Complete the sentences to say what you were doing at these times in the past.

a) This time yesterday …
b) This time last Sunday …
c) This time last week …
d) This time last year …
e) This time ten years ago …
f) This time twenty years ago …

3 Read the story. The verbs (*1–12*) are all in the past continuous. Change them to the past simple if necessary.

The most exciting experience I've ever had was at Disney World in Florida. I was on holiday with my family, and we (1) **were celebrating** my parents' 25th wedding anniversary. It was a typical Florida day – the sky was blue, the sun (2) **was shining**, and everybody (3) **was having** a great time.

As I watched the roller coaster, I thought to myself, 'Those people must be mad'. Just then, my brother (4) **was coming** up to me. He (5) **was holding** two tickets. 'I'm going on the roller coaster,' he said, 'and you're coming too.' I've never done anything dangerous or exciting in my life. So I don't know why I (6) **was agreeing** to go on the roller coaster, but five minutes later I (7) **was holding** onto my seat, 35 metres in the air, sure that I was about to die. The ride (8) **was seeming** to go on forever. But finally it (9) **was stopping**, and we got off. My head was spinning, but I felt really happy. Maybe I was just glad to be alive!

Later, we looked at the photos of the day. The roller coaster photos were hilarious. Everybody (10) **was laughing** and waving their arms in the air. That is, everybody except me! I was holding on, and (11) **was screaming**. I've never been so terrified in my life, but I'm glad I (12) **was doing** it.

Part 2

1 Write the comparative and superlative forms of the adjectives in the box.

~~badly-dressed~~ big extreme fit gentle good-looking healthy intelligent popular well-paid

badly-dressed – worse-dressed – the worst-dressed

2 Write comparative sentences using the words in brackets.

a) Skydiving / extreme / table tennis (much)
   Skydiving is much more extreme than table tennis.
b) Football players / well-paid / squash players (far)
c) A basketball / big / a volleyball (a bit)
d) Judo / popular / rugby (slightly)
e) Cyclists / fit / golfers (much)
f) Surfers / good-looking / boxers (a lot)

Rewrite the sentences (*a–f*) with *nearly* or *quite* so they have the same meaning.

a) *Table tennis isn't nearly as extreme as skydiving.*

3 Choose six different superlative adjectives from Exercise 1 to describe people you know.

My Uncle David is by far the fittest person I know.

Read your sentences to a partner. Tell your partner more about each person you describe.

Unit 3 Present perfect simple and continuous

The present perfect always shows a connection between the past and the present.
It can describe the following.

1   A *finished* action (or actions) that happened in time 'up-to-now'. You don't say *when*
it happened. (Usually present perfect simple.)
*I've **bought** him a nice jacket.*
*She's **run** several marathons.*
***Have** you ever **swum** in the ocean?*

2   An *unfinished* action (or actions) that started in the past and continues now.
(Usually present perfect continuous.)
*It's **been raining** all day.*
*I've **been learning** English since 2008.*
***Have** you **been waiting** long?*

3   An *unfinished* state that started in the past and continues now. (Usually present perfect
simple.)
*I've **known** Tim for ages.*
*She's **been** here since yesterday.*
*How long **have** you **had** that car?*

⚠ **Dynamic and stative meanings: 'actions' and 'states'**
Most verbs have dynamic meanings. They describe actions: something 'happens'. When you
want to describe an unfinished action – ie one that started in the past and continues now
– you usually use the present perfect continuous.
*I've **been staying** with friends.*
*What **have** you **been doing** all day?*

Note: You can sometimes use the simple form to indicate unchanging, 'permanent' situations.
Compare:
*I've **been working** here for a few weeks.* (temporary)
*I've **worked** here since I left school.* (permanent)

Some verbs connected with knowledge, emotion or possession have stative meanings. They
describe states: nothing 'happens'. When you want to describe an unfinished state – ie one
that started in the past and continues now – you can't use the present perfect continuous.
You must use the present perfect simple.
*I've **had** flu for a few days.* (NOT ~~I've been having …~~)
*She's **known** him a long time.* (NOT ~~She's been knowing …~~)

Common verbs that often have stative meanings:
*admire, adore, appear, be, believe, belong, concern, consist, contain, deserve, detest, dislike, doubt,
envy, exist, fit, hate, have, hear, know, like, love, matter, mean, owe, own, possess, prefer, realise,
recognise, remember, resemble, see, seem, sound, smell, surprise, understand, want, wish.*

⚠ Some verbs can have both stative and dynamic meanings.
*Bob **has had** that car since it was new.* (*have* = stative meaning)
*He's **been having** some problems with it recently.* (*have* = dynamic meaning)

⚠ *for* **and** *since*
for (+ 'a period of time') and *since* (+ 'a point in time') are two ways of saying the same thing.
You often use them with the present perfect when talking about unfinished actions or states.

You use *for* when you give the **length** of the time: *for a few hours / for three months / for ages.*
You use *since* when you give the **beginning** of the time: *since Sunday / since I left university /
since 2005.*

⚠ *been* is the past participle of *be*, but you can also use it as a past participle of *go*.
Compare:
*He's **been** to the gym.* = He went and came back.
*He's **gone** to the gym.* = He went and is at the gym now.

Unit 3 Exercises

1 Complete the table with the words in the box.

> ~~three years~~   ~~I was ten~~   ages   2002   I was born   Monday   a while
> three o'clock   nearly six months   my birthday   last week   several hours   March

for	since
three years	*I was ten*

2 Put the verbs into the present perfect simple or continuous and complete the sentences to make them true for you.

a) I (go) *'ve been going* to the same hairdresser's for …
b) I (go) _____ to the same dentist since …
c) I (have) _____ my TV for …
d) I (study) _____ English since …
e) I (do) _____ the same job for …
f) I (know) _____ my oldest friend since …
g) I (use) _____ the same English dictionary for …
h) I (sit) _____ in this chair for …

Write questions for the sentences *a–h* with *How long / you …?*

a) How long have you been going to the same hairdresser's?

Ask a partner the questions.

3 Complete the sentences with *gone* or *been*.

a) It's *been* really hot today.
b) I've _____ to the gym. I feel really tired.
c) I had a headache earlier, but it's _____ now.
d) The teacher will be back soon.
    She's _____ to get some books.
e) My parents are away. They've _____ abroad.
f) I haven't _____ on holiday for ages!
g) I've never _____ to Africa.
h) I haven't _____ very busy recently.

In which sentences is *been* the past participle of *go*?

Tick any sentences that are true for you.

4 Complete the questions with the past simple, present perfect simple or present perfect continuous.

a) How many times / go to the UK?
    How many times have you been to the UK?
b) How long / live at the same address?
c) Which primary school / go to?
d) When / learn to ride a bike?
e) How many *Harry Potter* books / read?
f) How long / go to the same doctor?
g) What time / get up?
h) Where / have lunch?

Ask your partner the questions.

5 Read these sentence pairs and choose the correct ending in each case. Discuss your choices with a partner.

1 a) I've known my teacher **for a long time** / **very well**.
   b) I know my teacher **for a long time** / **very well**.

2 a) I've been going to a yoga class **for years** / **this evening**.
   b) I'm going to a yoga class **for years** / **this evening**.

3 a) I've lived in an apartment **since I was a child** / **at the moment**.
   b) I live in an apartment **since I was a child** / **at the moment**.

Are any of the sentences true for you?

Unit 4 Future forms

Will ('ll), (be) going to and the present continuous are three common forms used to talk about the future. Each one tells you something different about what happened at, or before, the moment of speaking.

will ('ll)

You can use *will ('ll)* to show that the future event is the result of a spontaneous decision made at the moment of speaking.

I'll talk to the head teacher tomorrow. (The head teacher doesn't know about this. I have made my decision to talk to him while I have been speaking.)

What will you do after university? (My assumption is that you haven't thought about this much before or that you haven't made any plans.)

will/shall has several different functional uses.

- Offers: ***Shall** I give you a lift?*
- Promises: *Don't worry. I **won't** tell anyone.*
- Suggestions: ***Shall** we sit by the window?*

will can also be used to make predictions.
I think we'll arrive at about 10.00 p.m.

(be) going to

You can use *(be) going to* to talk about your future plans or intentions. You have made a decision about a future event and you are talking about that decision.

I'm going to talk to the head teacher tomorrow. (The head teacher does not necessarily know about this yet. But I have thought about it and I intend to talk to him.)
What are you going to do after university? (My assumption is that you have thought about it and may have some plans.)

(be) going to is also used to make predictions based on present evidence.
It's going to rain. (There are lots of black clouds in the sky.)
She's going to win. (She is 100 metres ahead of all the other runners.)

Present continuous

You can use the present continuous to talk about future arrangements. You have arranged a future event and you are talking about that arrangement.

I'm talking to the head teacher tomorrow. (The head teacher knows about this because I phoned him to make an appointment.)

What are you doing after university? (My assumption is that you know what you are doing and you have already made some arrangements.)

Unit 4 **Exercises**

1 **Match each sentence *a–h* to the best explanation *1–3* according to the future form used.**

a) We**'re having** a big family party on Friday.   *3*

b) My cousins **are coming** from London.

c) Ben**'s bringing** his girlfriend.

d) I**'m going to invite** the neighbours as well.

e) Oh no! I forgot to tell Sid and Doris – I**'ll call** them.

f) Mum**'s doing** all the food.

g) I**'m going to do** all the shopping tomorrow.

h) I**'ll make** a list of what we need.

1 The speaker is making a decision as he/she speaks.

2 The speaker is talking about a decision he/she has made.

3 The speaker is talking about an arrangement.

2 **Help your friend to prepare for a party. Write offers using the verbs in brackets.**

a) 'I've got so much to do!' (give a hand?)
   'Shall I give you a hand?'

b) 'I've washed the glasses.' (dry?)

c) 'It's far too hot in here.' (open / window?)

d) 'I can't move this table.' (help?)

e) 'The phone's ringing.' (answer?)

f) 'There's someone at the door.' (get it?)

3 **Read the conversations and underline the most appropriate future form.**

a) A: Ben, your room's still a mess, and Grandma (1) <u>**'s arriving**</u> / **'ll arrive** tomorrow.

   B: OK, I told you this morning – I 'm (2) **going to tidy** / **tidying** it today.

   A: I want you to do it now!

   B: OK, OK, I (3) **'ll do** / **'m doing** it in five minutes.

b) A: Not again! That phone never stops ringing!

   B: I (4) **'m going to get** / **'ll get** it. Hello? Hold on – Andy, it's for you.

   A: OK, I (5) **'m taking** / **'ll take** it in my office.

c) A: You've been late four times this week and you haven't done your homework for two weeks. I 'm (6) **going to phone** / **phoning** your parents to discuss the matter with them.

   B: No, please don't. I (7) **'m buying** / **'ll buy** a new alarm clock today and I (8) **'ll do** / **'m going to do** my homework every night from now on, I promise.

d) A: What (9) **will you do** / **are you doing** this afternoon?

   B: Oh, I (10) **'m having** / **'ll have** lunch with Scarlett Johansson, then I (11) **'ll probably play** / **'m probably going to play** a few rounds of golf, followed by a massage, a jacuzzi and champagne cocktails at the Ritz.

   A: What?

   B: Well what do you think I (12) **'ll do!** / **'m doing!** I'm at work of course!

Who is speaking? Match the people with the conversations.

1 Two work colleagues.   3 A mother and son.

2 A teacher and pupil.   4 Two friends.

4 **Choose an appropriate future form to complete these sentences.**

a) When I'm older I (travel) *'m going to travel* around the world.

b) I (play) _____ football this weekend. It's an important game.

c) My friend (get married) _____ in July. It (probably be) _____ really hot.

d) I've got no plans this evening. I think I (just stay in) _____ .

e) I (do) _____ some shopping after the lesson. I need to get some food.

f) I (not pass) _____ my exam because I haven't studied enough.

Are any of these statements true for you?

Unit 5 Nouns and quantity expressions

Nouns

Countable nouns

Most nouns in English are countable. They have a singular and a plural form. You can use *a/an* and numbers with them.

Regular forms	*an apple / apples a box / boxes a university / universities a leaf / leaves*
Irregular forms	*a child / children a foot / feet a man / men a person / people a tooth / teeth a woman / women*

You use the plural form when you are talking in general.
Children love sweets and chocolate.   Universities need more funding.

 a or an?
You use *a* before a consonant sound: *a dollar, a euro, a hotel, a useful knife, a one-way street.*
You use *an* before a vowel sound: *an umbrella, an egg, an omelette, an MBA, an hour.*

Uncountable nouns

Some nouns in English are uncountable. Most only have a singular form. You can't use *a/an* or put a number in front of them.
He played wonderful music. (NOT ~~He played a wonderful music.~~)
We had fantastic weather. (NOT ~~We had a fantastic weather.~~)

⚠ Common uncountable nouns that are countable in other languages:
advice, architecture, baggage, food, furniture, hair, homework, information, knowledge, love, luggage, machinery, money, music, news, progress, research, traffic, transport, travel, weather, work.

Plural nouns

Some nouns are always plural and don't have a singular form. You can't use *a/an* or put a number in front of them.
I have some pink jeans. (NOT ~~I have a pink jeans.~~)

Common plural nouns:
clothes, glasses, jeans, knickers, pants, pyjamas, scissors, shorts, sunglasses, tights, trousers.

Uncountable nouns that can be countable

Some uncountable nouns can be countable depending on the meaning in context.
Glass is a useful material. (Uncountable: glass as a material.)
Can I have a clean glass? (Countable: an individual object.)

Quantity expressions

These are ways you can talk about quantity if you can't or don't want to use an exact number.

With countable nouns: *(only) a few / not many / a couple of / several / How many …?*

Only a few people came.
How many text messages do you get every day?

With uncountable nouns: *(only) a little / not much / a bit of / How much …?*

There's a little tea left but no milk.
How much information have you got?

With countable and uncountable nouns: *none / not any / some / a lot of / lots of / plenty of*

She has a lot of friends.
He didn't give me any advice.

too much/many and not enough

too + much/many (+ noun) = more than you need. *not enough* (+ noun) = less than you need.
I have too much work and not enough time.
There are too many cars and not enough buses.

Unit 5 Exercises

1 **Complete the noun phrases with:**

- *a/an* and *C* for singular countable nouns
- nothing (–) and *P* for plural countable nouns
- nothing (–) and *U* for uncountable nouns.

Use a dictionary if necessary.

a)	advice *U*	i)	justice	q)	suggestion
b)	*an* aubergine *C*	j)	knowledge	r)	traffic
c)	baggage	k)	luck	s)	travel
d)	furniture	l)	machinery	t)	trousers
e)	hair	m)	orange	u)	underpants
f)	homework	n)	progress	v)	user
g)	information	o)	rice	w)	veal
h)	jeans	p)	spaghetti	x)	weather

2 **Translate the nouns in Exercise 1. Put a cross next to any nouns that are countable in your language and uncountable in English.**

a) – advice U ➔ *un consejo C* ✗

Write an example sentence in your own language for the nouns with a cross. Translate your sentences into English.

Me dio un buen consejo. ➔ *He gave me some good advice.*

3 **Underline the only possible noun to complete each sentence.**

a) I usually wear a **jeans** / **glasses** / <u>**watch**</u> / **black socks**.
b) Today I'm wearing a **cords** / **jacket** / **black boots** / **contact lenses**.
c) I always carry a **scissors** / **sunglasses** / **comb** / **money** in my bag.
d) I've transported a **furniture** / **fridge** / **luggage** / **sports equipment** in my car.
e) I had a good **food** / **luck** / **idea** / **advice** at work today.
f) My best friend has a very nice **manners** / **clothes** / **house** / **hair**.
g) Last week I finished a difficult **work** / **research** / **training** / **book**.
h) I heard a good **interview** / **music** / **news** / **information** on the radio this morning.

Are any of the sentences true for you?

Use some of the other nouns to write eight more sentences that are true for you. Change the grammar where necessary.

I usually wear jeans.   I always carry a pair of scissors …   I had some good food …

4 **Tick the nouns in the box that you can use to complete both question *a* and question *b*.**

> beer ✔ bread coffee Coke flour honey
> meat pasta rice tea whisky yoghurt

a) Have we got any _____ ?
b) Would you like a _____ ?

5 **Read the problems that Sally and Jimmy had when they went out for dinner. Cross out the incorrect word in each sentence.**

a) There wasn't **enough** / ~~**some**~~ / **any** salt in her omelette.
b) There was **some** / **a slice of** / **a few** ham in her vegetarian salad.
c) **A few** / **Several** / **A little** of his chips were burnt.
d) There were **hardly any** / **much** / **not many** desserts they liked on the menu.
e) It was really noisy because there were **so much** / **so many** / **lots of** people.
f) He didn't have **any** / **enough** / **some** cash to pay for the meal.
g) There were **no** / **very few** / **any** taxis outside when they left.
h) He had never had **some** / **any** / **so many** problems in this restaurant before.

Unit 6 Prepositions of time. Modals of obligation and permission

Part 1: Prepositions of time

Prepositions	Examples
AT + a specific time of day	*at* five o'clock, *at* 3.45 p.m., *at* lunchtime ⚠ Some other expressions: *at* night, *at* Christmas, *at* the weekend
ON + a day, part of a day or date	*on* Tuesday, *on* Friday evening, *on* 1st January, *on* Valentine's Day
IN + a period of time	*in* the evening, *in* December, *in* the summer, *in* the sixties

in, during and *for*

You use *in* or *during* to talk about **when** something happens inside a particular period of time.
You use *for* to talk about **how long** something lasts.
Eva went to Paris *in / during* the summer.   Eva went to Paris *for* two weeks. (NOT … ~~during two weeks~~)

⚠ If the 'period of time' is expressed as an event, activity or experience, you use *during*.
She phoned me *during* the meeting. (NOT … ~~in the meeting~~)
He told me the story *during* the flight. (NOT … ~~in the flight~~)

Part 2: Modals of obligation and permission

It's necessary	It's not necessary	It's permitted	It's not permitted
have to (have got to) must need to should	don't have to (haven't got to) don't need to (needn't)	can	can't mustn't shouldn't

must and *have to*: similar meanings

Must suggests personal obligation – it's necessary, because the speaker thinks it is.
Have to suggests external obligation – it's necessary because of a rule or an arrangement.
I've got terrible toothache. **I must go** to the dentist.
I can't come to the lesson tomorrow. I **have to go** to the dentist.

When you are not sure, use *have to*: it's always correct.

must and *should*: similar meanings

Must and *should* suggest personal obligation – it's necessary because the speaker thinks it is.
You can use them to give advice. *Must* is much stronger than *should*.
You **must try** and finish this report today. (It's more than two weeks late!)
You **should try** and finish this report today. (You'll feel better if you do.)

mustn't and *don't have to*: different meanings

Mustn't means you are not permitted to do something. *Don't have to* means it is not necessary for you to do something.
You **mustn't park** here. (It's a no-parking zone.)
You **don't have to park** here. (But you can if you want.)

can and *can't*: opposite meanings

Can means something is permitted (or possible).
You **can park** here. There's no restriction.
Can't is similar to *mustn't*. It means you are not permitted to do something.
You **can't park** here. It's a no-parking zone.

Unit 6 Exercises

Part 1

1 Complete the sentences with *in*, *on* or *at*.

a) I started my job *in* 2007.
b) I usually get to work _____ about 8.15.
c) I'm never late for work. I'm always _____ time.
d) I work best _____ the morning.
e) I don't like working _____ the weekend.
f) Occasionally, I have to work _____ Saturdays.
g) _____ the summer, I sometimes cycle to work.
h) I get paid _____ 28th of each month.
i) We have a pay review _____ April.
j) We have a big office party _____ Christmas.

If necessary, change the verb (negative to positive, or positive to negative) or change the information to make all the sentences true for you.

2 Underline the correct alternative.

a) I like to learn new skills **during** / **for** the holidays.
b) I did a language course **during** / **for** August.
c) I went to Ireland **during** / **for** three weeks.
d) I hadn't been abroad **during** / **for** a long time.
e) I met an interesting couple **during** / **in** the flight.
f) His father was a pilot **during** / **for** the war.
g) He was a prisoner **during** / **for** four years.
h) I saw him once more **during** / **in** my visit.

Part 2

1 Complete the table with the correct modal verb forms. Use *he* as the subject and *go* as the main verb.

	can	must	should	have to	need to
Affirmative	*He can go.*				
Negative	*He can't go.*				
Question	*Can he go?*				

2 Underline the most appropriate alternatives to complete the text.

Five ways to get your boss to like you

1 Flatter them You (1) **don't have to** / **mustn't** tell your boss that he or she is the best boss you've ever had, or go into hysterics every time they tell a joke. But you (2) **should** / **shouldn't** find subtle ways to make them feel good: for example, you (3) **should** / **have to** ask their advice when you have a difficult job to do.

2 Agree with them You (4) **don't have to** / **mustn't** contradict your boss in front of other people, even if they're wrong.

3 Don't criticise You (5) **don't have to** / **mustn't** criticise your boss behind their back. If you have something to say, say it to their face.

4 Be honest When you're ill, you (6) **can't** / **don't have to** send a hospital report, but you (7) **should** / **can** phone your boss directly. You (8) **mustn't** / **don't have to** send a text message or email – this will make it look as if you're lying.

5 Remember how they take their coffee You (9) **should** / **can** remember how they take their coffee, so that next time they ask you to pop out to your local coffee shop, you (10) **shouldn't** / **don't have to** ask.

Which is the best piece of advice? Compare your ideas with a partner.

3 Work with a partner. Look at these things to do after the lesson and decide whether *must* or *have to* is the most appropriate way to complete each sentence.

a) I *have to* go to the bank. I've got an appointment with the manager.
b) I _____ go to the bank. I haven't got any cash.
c) I _____ remember to get my mother a birthday present.
d) I _____ go straight back to work. I have an important meeting.
e) I _____ pick up my children from school. It's the end of term.
f) I _____ post these letters. They've been in my bag since Monday!

Do you have any of these things to do after the lesson?

Unit 7 Passives

Passive = *be* (*am, was, have been*, etc.) + past participle (*used, built*, etc.)

TENSES		ASPECT			MODALS
		simple	continuous	perfect simple	*will (would, must …)*
Present	+ − ?	It's used. It isn't used. Is it used?	It's being used. It isn't being used. Is it being used?	It has been used. It hasn't been used. Has it been used?	It will be used. It won't be used. Will it be used?
Past	+ − ?	It was used. It wasn't used. Was it used?	It was being used. It wasn't being used. Was it being used?	It had been used. It hadn't been used. Had it been used?	

⚠ The continuous forms *be being* and *been being* are very rare. Avoid using them.

In passive sentences the object of the active verb becomes the subject of the passive verb. In other words, the 'receiver' of the action becomes the subject and comes at the beginning of the sentence.

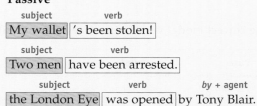

Active

subject | verb | object
Somebody | 's stolen | my wallet!

subject | verb | object
Detectives | have arrested | two men.

subject | verb | object
Tony Blair | opened | the London Eye.

Passive

subject | verb
My wallet | 's been stolen!

subject | verb
Two men | have been arrested.

subject | verb | *by* + agent
the London Eye | was opened | by Tony Blair.

In passive sentences the 'doer' of the action – known as the 'agent' – is either not mentioned at all, or mentioned at the end of the sentence in a *by*-phrase.

There are several reasons why you might want to use passive verb structures.

1   The 'doer' of the action is unknown.
*Their house **was built** in the 1980s.* (They don't know who built it.)

2   The 'doer' of the action is not important in the context.
*'When **was the Sydney Opera House built**?' 'In 1957.'* (I want to know <u>when</u> it was built not who built it.)

3   The 'doer' of the action is obvious.
*Demonstrators **were arrested** and **charged** with disturbing the peace.* (It is obvious that the police arrested and charged them.)

4   The 'receiver' of the action is what we are talking about, and the 'doer' is the new information. Generally, you tend to put 'known' information at the beginning of a sentence and 'new' information at the end. Compare the following:
*The London Eye is the most popular tourist attraction in London. **Tony Blair opened it**.*
*The London Eye is the most popular tourist attraction in London. **It was opened by Tony Blair**.*
The second version is easier to process because it follows the order of 'known' to 'new'.

The passive is much more common in written language than in spoken language.

⚠ Verbs with two objects have two possible passive structures:
*I **was given** this watch by my parents on my 18th birthday.* (The subject of the sentence is 'me/I'.)
*This watch **was given** to me by my parents on my 18th birthday.* (The subject of the sentence is 'the watch'.)

Unit 7 Exercises

1 Write the past participle forms for these verbs which are often used in the passive. What are the spelling rules for each group? Use your dictionary if necessary.

a) arrest, invent, jail, murder
arrested, … Rule: add ed
b) accuse, create, produce, prosecute
c) classify, identify, try, copy
d) acquit, ban, kidnap, mug
e) build, grow, make, steal

Rearrange the past participles into two groups according to their meaning. Use your dictionary if necessary.

Verbs used to describe crime	Verbs used to describe processes
arrested	*invented*

2 Look at the following notices and announcements. Use your dictionary if necessary. Underline the passive structures and name the tenses.

a) The film <u>was written</u>, <u>directed</u> and <u>produced</u> by Stephen Spielberg.   *Past simple*
b) Passengers are requested to remain in their seats until the plane has come to a complete standstill and the engines have been switched off.
c) Lunch is now being served.
d) Feeding the penguins is strictly prohibited.
e) Applications must be submitted by 31st December.
f) The management cannot be held responsible for any loss of property.
g) Tablets to be taken three times daily.

Where would you expect to see these notices or hear these announcements? Discuss with a partner.

3 Write affirmative and negative passive sentences. Use the verb in brackets and an appropriate tense.

a) My mother (be born) _____ in the 1950s.
My mother was born in the 1950s. / My mother wasn't born in the 1950s.
b) She (bring up) _____ in a small village.
c) She (educate) _____ at a private school.
d) She (teach) _____ English from the age of eleven.
e) She (award) _____ a scholarship to study at university.
f) She (marry) _____ in the local church.
g) She (employ) _____ by the same company for the last twenty years.

Tick the sentences which are true for you. Write three (true) passive sentences about your mother (or someone else in your family).

4 Look at these general knowledge facts. Cross out *by* + the agent if it is not necessary.

a) Chess was invented in India ~~by Indians~~.
b) Snakes are not found in Ireland by anybody.
c) 20% of the body's energy is used by the brain.
d) The Statue of Liberty was built in France by French people.
e) Fourteen muscles are used by people to smile.
f) Forty-three muscles are used by people to frown.
g) The first disposable safety razor was patented by King Camp Gillette.

How many of the facts did you know?

5 Rewrite these sentences in the passive. Start each sentence with *I*.

a) People gave me money for my last birthday.
I was given money for my last birthday.
b) My friend is showing me around her new flat this evening.
c) My employers don't pay me very much.
d) People have sent me over twenty text messages so far today.
e) Teachers taught me how to swim before I was seven.
f) People tell me that I look like my father.

Are any of the sentences true for you?

Unit 8 Modals of deduction. Past perfect

Part 1: Modals of deduction

There are many ways of expressing how certain or uncertain you are about something.

Degree of certainty	Modal auxiliaries	Other phrases
99% certain it IS ✓	It must be …	I'm sure it's …
	It may be … It could be … It might be …	Perhaps it's … Maybe it's …
99% certain it ISN'T ✗	It can't be …	I'm sure it isn't …

*They **must** be home by now. They set off over an hour ago.*
*I **might** arrive late. I've got to finish this report first.*
*Who's at the door? It **can't** be Jill – she's on holiday in France.*

⚠ The opposite of *must be* is *can't be*.
*The keys **can't be** in my coat because I wasn't wearing it. They **must be** in my bag.*

Part 2: Past perfect

Affirmative	Negative	Question	Short answer *Yes*	Short answer *No*
I/You/He, etc. **'d (had) worked.**	I/You/He, etc. **hadn't (had not) worked.**	**Had** I/you/he, etc. **worked?**	Yes, I/you/he, etc. **had.**	No, I/you/he, etc. **hadn't.**

You use the past perfect when you are talking about the past and you want to refer to an earlier past time. The past perfect clearly shows that one past event happened earlier than other past events.

*When we **arrived**, the concert **had already started**.*

| Earlier past | Past | Now |

Conjunctions such as *after, because, by the time* and *when* are often used to combine a past simple clause with a past perfect one.

The film started. I arrived. → *The film had started **when** I arrived.*
The train left. He reached the platform. → ***By the time** he reached the platform, the train had left.*
He didn't check his tyres. He had a puncture. → *He had a puncture on the motorway **because** he hadn't checked his tyres.*
We had lunch. We went for a walk. We took the bus home. → *We had lunch and then took the bus home **after** we had been for a walk.*

Unit 8 Exercises

Part 1

1 Match the sentences so that they make sense.

a) I'm going to set up my computer myself.

b) You've been driving all day.

c) Oh, dear. I must be getting old.

d) A new car? On my salary?!

e) You must be Sarah's husband.

f) Congratulations on your engagement.

1 She's told me such a lot about you.

2 You can't be serious! It's quite impossible.

3 I'm sure it can't be that difficult!

4 You must be delighted.

5 I'm afraid I can't remember your name!

6 You must be absolutely exhausted.

2 Rewrite these observations with the modal verb in brackets so that the meaning is the same.

a) I'm sure you're really cold! (must)
You must be really cold!

b) I'm sure you're joking. (must)

c) I'm sure your keys aren't far away. (can't)

d) Perhaps you won't enjoy the film. (might not)

e) I'm sure you know who she is. (must)

f) I'm sure it's not far from here. (can't)

g) Perhaps you'll meet the love of your life. (might)

h) I'm sure she isn't that old. (can't)

Think about situations when you have made observations like these. Tell a partner.

Part 2

1 Test your irregular verbs. Use the verbs in the box to complete the three lists in the table with the infinitive, past simple and past participle forms. There are eight verbs in each list.

~~bet~~ burst cost ~~dig~~ ~~drink~~ feed fight fly hurt let mean ring rise shine shrink shut sing sink slide split spread stick swim win

1 All forms the same	2 Two forms the same	3 All forms different
bet – bet – bet	*dig – dug – dug*	*drink – drank – drunk*

Check your answers on page 159. Underline any verbs you weren't sure about.

2 Work with a partner. In each case, write a second sentence changing the verb in bold into the past perfect.

a) I **had** breakfast when I got to work this morning.
I'd had breakfast when I got to work this morning.

b) I **read** *Harry Potter* when I saw the film.

c) I **travelled** a lot when I started my job.

d) I **did** the shopping when I got home yesterday evening.

e) I **passed** my driving test when I went to university.

f) This lesson **started** when I arrived.

In what way does the use of the past perfect change the meaning of the sentences?

Are any of the sentences true for you?

3 Complete the sentences to make them true for you.

a) By the time I was [age?] I had learnt how to … (swim? ski? drive? etc.)

b) By the age of [age?] I had been to more than [number?] … (countries? schools? concerts? etc.)

c) By the time I was sixteen I'd been learning [subject?] for [number?] years.

d) By the age of [age?] I had moved house [number?] times.

e) By the age of [age?] I had realised that …

f) By the time I was [age?] I had decided that …

Compare your sentences with your partner.

Unit 9 Reported statements and questions

Reporting speech means using your own words to report what somebody has said (or thought).

Direct speech	Reported speech
Ana said, 'I don't believe you.'	➔ Ana **said she didn't believe me**.
I said, 'We can talk about it tomorrow,'	➔ I **told her we could talk about it the next day**.
She said, 'Who do you think you are?'	➔ She **asked me who I thought I was**.

When you report statements 'using your own words', you need to decide which tenses, which pronouns, which time expressions and which reporting verbs to use. When you report questions you also need to change the word order.

Tenses

There is usually a logical 'back-shift' of tense. This is because what the person said is now in the past. Present becomes past; present perfect or past simple become past perfect; *can* becomes *could*, etc.

Direct speech	Reported speech
'I**'m** really tired.'	➔ She said she **was** really tired.
'I**'ve had** a great day.'	➔ He said he**'d had** a great day.
'I **cut** my finger.'	➔ She said she**'d cut** her finger.
'I**'m going to have** a shower.'	➔ He said he **was going to have** a shower.
'I **was trying** to open a tin of beans.'	➔ She said she **had been trying** to open a tin of beans.
'I **can't be** bothered to cook.'	➔ He said he **couldn't be** bothered to cook.
'I **don't want** to go out.'	➔ She said she **didn't want** to go out.
'I**'ll order** a Chinese take-away.'	➔ He said he **would order** a Chinese take-away.

Pronouns

Pronouns (*I*, *she*, *we*, etc.) and possessive adjectives (*my*, *your*, *his*, etc.) may change depending on who is reporting and who/what they are reporting.

Direct speech: '**I** understand **your** ideas but **I** don't agree with **them**.'
Report 1: *My mother told **me** that **she** understood **my** ideas but that **she** didn't agree with **them**.*
Report 2: *Ted's mother told **him** that **she** understood **his** ideas but that **she** didn't agree with **them**.*

Expressions of time or place

'Here-and-now' expressions in direct speech may change to 'there-and-then' expressions in reported speech.
'Can you **come here tomorrow**?' ➔ *He asked if I could **go there the next/following day**.*

Reporting verbs

The most common reporting verbs are *say* (*that*) and *tell somebody* (*that*). Other verbs such as *admit*, *claim*, *explain*, *insist*, *reply* or *suggest* can also be used. If you're not sure, use your dictionary to check on the correct verb pattern.
*She **said** it was her fault.* (NOT ~~She said me it was her fault.~~)
*She **told me** she hadn't been thinking.* (NOT ~~She told that she hadn't been thinking.~~)
*She **explained that** she had been very tired.* (NOT ~~She explained me that she had been very tired.~~)

Reported questions

In reported questions the word order changes to subject + verb. You don't use *do/does/did*.
For *yes/no* questions you use *if* or *whether*.
'How **are you**?' ➔ *He asked me how **I was**.*
'Have you been here long?' ➔ *He asked me **if/whether** I had been there long.*
'Where **do you come from**?' ➔ *He asked me where **I came from**.*

Imperatives

You can report an imperative with *tell somebody to do something* or *ask somebody to do something*.
'Don't worry!' ➔ *She told him not to worry.*
'Hurry up!' ➔ *He asked them to hurry up.*

Unit 9 Exercises

1 Match the beginnings and the ends of these famously 'wrong' predictions and opinions.

a) In 1898, the Munich Technical Institute said that
b) In 1899, the Commissioner of US Patents, said that
c) In 1907, Lord Haldane, British Minister of War, said
d) In 1927, Harry Warner of Warner Brothers, asked
e) In 1943, Thomas Watson, IBM chairman, said
f) In 1962, the producers of *Doctor No*, said that

1 Sean Connery couldn't play the sophisticated James Bond because he looked like a bricklayer.
2 who the hell wanted to hear actors talk.
3 Albert Einstein showed no promise.
4 there was a world market for maybe five computers.
5 everything that could be invented had been invented.
6 the aeroplane would never fly.

Rewrite the predictions and opinions as quotes.

a) 'Albert Einstein shows no promise.'

2 Read the newspaper article about a great-grandmother's lucky escape. Complete the article by changing the direct speech into reported speech.

Lucky escape

A great-grandmother told this newspaper how she escaped death by inches after being hit by a meteorite travelling at 300 mph. Margaret Smithers said (1 'It just missed my head and hit my arm.') *it had just missed her head and (had) hit her arm.*

76-year-old Margaret was hanging out washing in her garden when the brown metallic stone hit her. She said, (2 'I felt a nasty pain on my arm which started bleeding heavily.') _____ . Her husband found the three-centimetre rock on the grass. She added that (3 'I'm glad it didn't hit me on the head!') _____ ! Experts are analysing the walnut-sized rock.

A spokesman from the British Astronomical Society said, (4 'There's a good chance it is a meteorite.') _____ . But he added that (5 'The chances of being hit by one are incredibly small.') _____ . He explained that (6 'Most meteorites disintegrate as they enter the atmosphere.') _____ . However, on average, one falls to earth every week.

3 Complete the sentences with *asked, said* or *told*.

a) She *said* she didn't believe me.
b) I _____ her it was true.
c) She _____ me why I hadn't told her.
d) I _____ I'd wanted to.
e) She _____ she'd been really upset.
f) I _____ her I was sorry.
g) She _____ me if I'd go with her.
h) I _____ her I couldn't.

What do you think the conversation was about? Discuss with a partner.

4 Report the direct speech using the verb in brackets. Use *He/She* and *him/her* according to whether you think it is a man speaking to a woman or a woman speaking to a man.

a) 'I hate spending money on new clothes.' (said)
   He said that he hated spending money on new clothes.
b) 'I'm not wearing this outfit again!' (told)
c) 'Do you think I look fat in these trousers?' (ask)
d) 'I must go on a diet.' (said)
e) 'I've checked the oil and put some air in the tyres.' (told)
f) 'Don't forget that it's our anniversary tomorrow.' (asked)
g) 'I don't want to get married until I'm forty.' (said)
h) 'What time does your salsa class finish?' (asked)

Compare your ideas with a partner.

Unit 10 Defining relative clauses. Real conditionals.

Part 1: Defining relative clauses

A relative clause can define the thing or person introduced in the main clause. It comes immediately after the person or thing it is describing. You use *that* (or *who*) for people and *that* (or *which*) for things.
The <u>man</u> that/who cuts my hair is called Jo.   *A frog is an <u>animal</u> that/which lives on land and in water.*

The relative pronoun (*that, which, who*) can be the subject of the verb in the relative clause.

      subject verb   subject verb
*People **who come from** Paris are called Parisians.*   *A florist's is a shop **that sells** flowers.*

⚠ When the relative pronoun is the subject of the verb, it can never be omitted.

The relative pronoun (*that, which, who*) can be the object of the verb in the relative clause.

      object   verb   object   verb
*The work **that** you do is very interesting.*   *The man **who** I **met** yesterday is a famous artist.*

⚠ When the relative pronoun is the object of the verb, it can be omitted.
The work ~~that~~ you do is very interesting.   *The man ~~who~~ I met yesterday is a famous artist.*

Part 2: Real conditionals

Real conditional sentences – sometimes called 'first conditional' sentences – consist of an *if*-clause and a main clause. They are used to talk about present or future situations that are real or possible. These include promises, warnings and threats.
If the weather improves, we'll go for a walk.   *If you give up smoking, I'll be very happy.*
If you touch that, you'll burn your finger.   *If you don't go now, we'll call the police.*

if-clause
In most real conditional sentences, you use a present tense (simple, continuous or perfect) in the *if*-clause, even when you are talking about the future.

	if-clause	**Main clause**
Present simple	If you **arrive** early,	wait for me in the station café.
Present continuous	If you**'re spending** any time in London,	I can recommend a great hotel.
Present perfect	If you **haven't finished** by ten,	you'll miss the post.
going to	If you**'re going to** talk to me like that,	I'm leaving!
Modal auxiliary	If you **can't** do it,	ask Tom for help.

Unless means the same as *if … not*. ***Unless** you agree … = **If** you **don't** agree …*

if-clause	**Main clause**
Unless you start studying now / **If** you do**n't** start studying now,	you'll never pass your exams.

Main clause
You usually use the present simple, modal auxiliaries (especially *will/won't, can, must* and *may*), or the imperative in the main clause

if-clause	**Main clause**
If he finds out the truth,	it**'s** all over for you and me. we**'ll** be in big trouble. you **can forget** about our holiday in Rome. **deny** everything!

The *if*-clause and the main clause can often go in either order.
If I feel like going out, I'll give you a call. OR *I'll give you a call if I feel like going out.*
Use a comma after the *if*-clause when the *if*-clause comes before the main clause.

Unit 10 Exercises

Part 1

1 Make one-sentence definitions, using the relative pronouns *who/which/that*.

a) A babushka is a headscarf. Women tie it under their chin.
  *A babushka is a headscarf **which/that** women tie under their chin.*

b) A pestle is a tool. You use it to crush nuts and seeds.

c) A woodlouse is a small insect. It eats dead wood.

d) A farrier is a person. He/She makes and fits horseshoes.

e) A fandango is a dance. It originated in Spain.

f) A burglar is a person. He/She breaks into your house and steals things.

g) A rolling pin is a kitchen utensil. You use it to flatten pastry.

Tick the sentences in which the relative pronoun can be omitted.

2 Insert a relative pronoun *who/which/that* where necessary.

a) The school I went to was near my house.

b) My mum is the only person really understands me.

c) The issue worries me most is global warming.

d) The biggest party I've had was for my 21st birthday.

e) I've got a lot of friends live in the United States.

f) I think it's better to do a job you enjoy than to do a well-paid job you hate.

g) The people live next door to me are really friendly.

Which sentences are true for you? Discuss with a partner.

Part 2

1 Match the two halves of the sentences.

a) They're not going skiing tomorrow	1 if you leave now.
b) I'm not going to go for a walk	2 unless they get fresh snow.
c) You'll miss your flight	3 if they want me to.
d) You can still catch your train	4 unless you help me with my French.
e) I won't help you with your German	5 if it's raining.
f) I'll look after their children	6 unless he studies hard.
g) He won't pass his exams	7 if she really concentrates.
h) She'll be top of her class	8 unless you take a taxi to the airport.

2 Look at the advice given by children to children and underline an appropriate alternative.

a) **Unless / If** you get a bad grade at school, don't show it to your mum, **unless / if** she's on the phone.

b) Don't make an enemy of the school bully **unless / if** he's smaller than you.

c) **Unless / If** your mum is angry with your dad, don't let her brush your hair.

d) **Unless / If** you like being hit, don't tell your mum her diet's not working.

e) Don't hit your sister **unless / if** your parents are out.

f) **Unless / If** your dad asks 'Do I look stupid?', don't answer him.

g) **Unless / If** you want a kitten, start off by asking for a horse.

Which do you think is the best/funniest piece of advice? Discuss with your partner.

3 Write real conditional sentences.

a) If the weather (be) _____ good next weekend, I (go) _____ for a long run.
  If the weather is good next weekend, I'll go for a long run.

b) If it (rain) _____ tomorrow, I (not go) _____ out.

c) My friends and I (go) _____ to the beach tomorrow if it (be) _____ sunny.

d) If I (earn) _____ enough money this year, I (visit) _____ the USA.

e) I (go) _____ snowboarding this winter, if there (be) _____ enough snow.

f) I think I (see) _____ my family this weekend, unless I (have to) _____ work.

Which sentences are true for you?

Unit 11 Wishes and regrets. Unreal conditionals.

Part 1: Wishes and regrets

I wish / If only are two ways of talking about unreal situations. You can use them to express wishes or regrets about the present or the past. After *I wish / If only* the tense backshifts to show that the situation described is/was unreal (see below).

Tense changes		
Fact		**Wish/Regret**
I**'m** a teacher. Present simple	➔	If only / I wish I **wasn't**/**weren't** a teacher. Past simple
I**'m going** to the concert with Adam. Present continuous	➔	I wish / If only I **was going** with Carl. Past continuous
I **haven't studied** any other languages. Present perfect	➔	I wish / If only I **had studied** another language. Past perfect
I **left** school early Past simple	➔	If only / I wish I **hadn't left** school early. Past perfect

Other (non-tense) changes	
Fact	**Wish/Regret**
I do**n't** have **enough**/**much** time.	If only / I wish I had **more** time.
I**'m not** very **good at** maths.	If only / I wish I was/were **better at** maths.

Part 2: Unreal conditionals

Unreal conditional sentences consist of an *if*-clause and a main clause. When forming unreal conditional sentences, the tense backshifts in the *if*-clause to show that the situation described is/was imaginary.

if-clause
To show that a present (or future) situation is imaginary, you use a past tense.
To show that a past situation is imaginary, you use the past perfect.

Fact		Imaginary situation
I**'m not** a teenager.	➔	If I **was**/**were** a teenager, ...
I **didn't tell** him.	➔	If I **had told** him, ...

⚠️ *If I/he/she/it **were** is more formal than If I/he/she/it **was**. You always use were in the fixed expression If I were you ...*

Main clause
For a present or future situation you usually use *would/wouldn't* + infinitive in the main clause.
For a past situation you usually use *would/wouldn't* + *have* + the past participle in the main clause.

if-clause	Main clause
If I **could** sing,	I**'d be** in a band.
If I**'d had** a map,	I **wouldn't have got** lost.

Note: Unreal conditional sentences which refer to imaginary situations *in the present* (or future) are sometimes called 'second conditional' sentences. Unreal conditional sentences which refer to imaginary situations *in the past* are sometimes called 'third conditional' sentences.

Unit 11 Exercises

Part 1

1 Make sentences, using *I wish* or *If only*.

a) I can't play the piano.
   I wish I could play the piano.
b) I don't live near a beach.
c) I don't like my job.
d) I'm getting old.
e) I don't have enough free time.
f) I'm not good at English.
g) I have such a stressful life.
h) I don't earn a lot of money.

Which are true for you?

2 Complete the second sentence so that it means the same as the first.

a) I regret I wasn't born in another country.
   I wish … *I had been born in another country.*
b) I regret that I didn't study English more at school.
   If only …
c) I regret that I didn't go to a better school.
   I wish …
d) I regret that I didn't travel much when I had the chance.
   If only …
e) I regret that I got married so young.
   I wish …
f) I regret that I didn't work hard at university.
   If only …

Work with your partner. Discuss each regret and say if you share it.

Part 2

1 Write complete questions.

a) What / you / do / if / you / find / £100 / in the street?
   What would you do if you found £100 in the street?
b) If / you / be / able to / change your nationality, / what / you / be?
c) If / you / can / have dinner with a famous person, / who / you / choose?
d) If / you / have to / change one part of your body, / what / it / be?
e) What / you / do / if / you / see / someone stealing something in a shop?
f) If / you / can / meet / one person from history, / who / you / like it to be?

Now answer each question so that it's true for you. Write full answers to each question.

a) *If I found £100 in the street, I'd keep it.*

2 Make conditional sentences about these past situations, starting with *If …*

a) I wasn't paying attention. I walked into a lamppost.
   If I'd been paying attention, I wouldn't have walked into a lamppost.
b) I studied hard. I passed my exams.
c) I didn't study hard. I failed my exams.
d) I forgot to set my alarm clock. I overslept.
e) I missed the bus. I was late for work.
f) I bought a lottery ticket. I won some money.
g) I didn't have a map. I got lost.
h) The weather wasn't good. We didn't go camping.

Have any of these situations happened to you in the last year? Discuss with a partner.

3 Complete these sentences so that they are true for you.

a) If I had time …
b) I'd have been really happy if …
c) If I were very rich …
d) If I had been born a member of the opposite sex, …
e) If I were president of my country, …
f) I'd have been furious if …

Work with a partner. Compare your sentences. Are any the same?

Unit 12 *have something done*

You can use *have something done* (*I'm going to **have my house painted**.*) when someone does something for you – often because you have paid them to do it. As a slightly more informal alternative to *have something done* you can also use *get something done*.

Form: *have/get* + something (object) + past participle
*I'll probably **get my hair cut** next week.*
*Have you **had your ears pierced**?*
*You really should **get your eyes tested**.*

Compare the two sentences
* *Mandy cut her hair last week.*
* *Mandy had her hair cut last week.*

In the first sentence Mandy cut her own hair. In the second sentence someone else cut her hair and was probably paid for it.

Sometimes *have something done* can mean you have a (usually) negative experience.
We had our house broken into yesterday. This doesn't mean that you arranged for somebody to break into your house, but that something unfortunate happened to you.
I had my bike stolen last week.
He tried to cheat the mafia and ended up having his legs broken.

Unit 12 **Exercises**

1 **Read the sentences and underline the most appropriate verb form in each case.**

a) We're **redecorating our house** / <u>**having our house redecorated**</u> at the moment. I'll be glad when the painters have finally finished and left.

b) I'm going to **clean my car** / **have my car cleaned** later, so I've bought a new pressure washer.

c) Do you really think Angelina Jolie is ugly? I think you need to **test your eyes** / **have your eyes tested**.

d) We're going to **fix the roof** / **have the roof fixed** soon. We have to wait until the builders and can do it.

e) I'm **cooking dinner** / **having dinner cooked** for some friends this evening. We get together once a week, and tonight it's my turn to be the host.

f) My wife has just **repaired her car** / **had her car repaired**. It's great that she's such a practical person – and it saves us a lot of money!

2 **Complete the sentences with *have / get* + something + past participle, using the verb in brackets.**

a) We (deliver) _____ a takeaway _____ to our house every week.

b) I always (service) _____ my car _____ at the same garage.

c) I (cut) _____ my hair _____ once a month.

d) I usually (check) _____ my teeth _____ every six months. I've got a really good dentist.

e) We (do) _____ odd jobs _____ in our house by professionals.

f) I (take) _____ my passport _____ photos in a professional studio. They look much better.

Work with a partner. Discuss which sentences are true for you.

3 **Using the prompts, make questions with *have/get* + something + past participle.**

a) You / ever / appearance / change
   Have you ever had your appearance changed?
b) How often / you / eyes / test
c) You / ever / anything / steal
d) You / ever / ears / pierce
e) You / ever / your car / vandalise
f) How often / you / hair / cut

Work with a partner. Take it in turns to ask and answer the questions.

Unit 12 **Test yourself!**

Underline the correct option in each sentence.

Units 1–3

1 Where (a) **is** (b) **does** (c) **was** he come from?

2 (a) **Has** (b) **Is** (c) **Does** she been here long?

3 (a) **I'm online always** (b) **Always I'm online** (c) **I'm always online**.

4 (a) **I'm on the phone all the time** (b) **All the time I'm on the phone** (c) **I'm all the time on the phone**.

5 We (a) **'ve** (b) **'s** (c) **'re** swum with dolphins.

6 She (a) **haven't** (b) **hasn't** (c) **isn't** been to America.

7 He (a) **'s** (b) **was** (c) **been** playing football when he twisted his ankle.

8 It's (a) **as** (b) **by** (c) **than** far the biggest fish I've ever seen.

9 She (a) **'s liking** (b) **like** (c) **likes** taking photos.

10 I've (a) **knowing** (b) **been knowing** (c) **known** her for a long time.

Score: __ /10

Units 4–6

11 If you don't know the word, (a) **look up it** (b) **look it up** (c) **it look up**!

12 I think (a) **I'm calling** (b) **I call** (c) **I'll call** Jan and see if she's free.

13 What's happened? It's all gone dark! I can't see (a) **something** (b) **everything** (c) **anything**.

14 Is there (a) **many** (b) **much** (c) **a lot** cake left?

15 Were there (a) **many** (b) **much** (c) **a lot** people at the party?

16 I (a) **would** (b) **used to** (c) **could** be very thin when I was younger.

17 (a) **Would** (b) **Are** (c) **Did** you use to smoke?

18 I'm seeing Mr Jones (a) **at** (b) **in** (c) **on** ten o'clock.

19 I'm always late for everything. I never get to work (a) **in** (b) **on** (c) **at** time.

20 She (a) **doesn't have** (b) **have** (c) **should** to see to the doctor after all.

Score: __ /10

Units 7–9

21 I can't stand (a) **wait** (b) **to wait** (c) **waiting** around.

22 He asked me (a) **help** (b) **to help** (c) **help** him.

23 She promised (a) **come** (b) **coming** (c) **to come** at 10.00 a.m.

24 Our office is (a) **cleaning** (b) **being cleaned** (c) **cleaned** at the moment.

25 The nominations (a) **have** (b) **has** (c) **having** been announced.

26 The lights aren't on: Sam must (a) **be** (b) **was** (c) **have been** out.

27 We (a) **are** (b) **have been** (c) **were** too late: the train had already left.

28 I knew I (a) **haven't** (b) **hasn't** (c) **hadn't** been there before.

29 She said that she (a) **'ll** (b) **'d** (c) **'ve** bought some new clothes.

30 We asked him (a) **whether** (b) **when** (c) **how** he had ever had problems.

Score: __ /10

Units 10–12

31 A truant is a pupil (a) **who** (b) **he** (c) **which** stays away from school without permission.

32 If you (a) **wanted** (b) **will want** (c) **want** to join us, bring some food.

33 Jon won't come (a) **unless** (b) **if** (c) **if not** you ask him.

34 They wouldn't be so popular if they (a) **weren't** (b) **wouldn't be** (c) **aren't** so talented.

35 Do you know how she (a) **does feel** (b) **feels** (c) **feel**?

36 If I (a) **can** (b) **could** (c) **would** sing, I'd be in a band.

37 I wish I (a) **took** (b) **have taken** (c) **had taken** swimming lessons when I was at school.

38 If I (a) **'ve** (b) **'d** (c) **'d have** had a map, I wouldn't have got lost.

39 She's wearing (a) **an expensive white silk** (b) **a white expensive silk** c) **a silk white expensive** blouse.

40 I'm having my eyes (a) **test** (b) **tests** (c) **tested** tomorrow.

Score: __ /10

Glossary

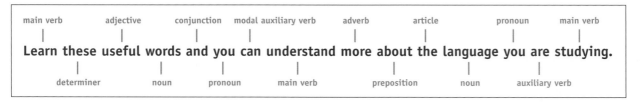

Learn these useful words and you can understand more about the language you are studying.

Agents are people or things that perform an action in a passive sentence.
*He was brought up by **his aunt and uncle**.*

Antonyms are words that mean the opposite of other words.
rich ≠ poor   dead ≠ alive   tall ≠ short

Back-shift is when a verb moves 'one tense back' in a conditional clause or reported statement.
*If you **were** a woman you'd understand.*
'I can't come.' ➔ *He said he **couldn't** come.*

Clauses are groups of words containing a subject and a verb.
main clause   subordinate clause   main clause   time (subordinate) clause
I waited   but she didn't come.   I'll phone   when I get there.
Note: Subordinate clauses are introduced by conjunctions.

Collocation refers to words that frequently occur together.
common sense   get on well   Merry Christmas

Complements refer to adjective or noun phrases which give more information about the subject of a clause.
*She was **very happy**.   It's **my fault**.   I feel **a complete idiot**.*
Note: Complements usually follow verbs like *be, seem, feel*.

Conjunctions show a connection between one clause and another.
***Just as** we were leaving the hotel, I spotted a friend.*

Consonants are all the letters of the English alphabet except for the five vowels *a, e, i, o* and *u*.
b, c, d, f, g, h, j, k, l, m, n, p, q, r, s, t, v, w, x, y, z

Expressions are groups of words that belong together where the words and word order never or rarely change.
black and white   That reminds me.   How do you do?

Idioms are groups of words with a meaning which cannot be understood by taking the meaning of each individual word.
*My father **footed the bill**.   Let's **play it by ear**, shall we?*

Intransitive verbs do not take an object.
*He's **arrived**.   Is Marta still **sleeping**?   Stop **shouting**!*
Note: Many verbs can be either intransitive or transitive. It depends on the meaning or context.
*He **opened** the door. (Transitive)   The door **opened**. (Intransitive)*

Linkers show a connection between one sentence and another.
*Many motorists drive too fast. **As a result**, there are more and more accidents.*

Numbers can be cardinal (*1, 2, 3, …*) or ordinal (*1st, 2nd, 3rd, …*).

Objects usually come after the verb and show who or what is affected by the verb.
*She closed **the door**.   My dog hates **me**.   I've made **a cup of tea**.*
Note: Some verbs take both a direct object (DO) and an indirect object (IO).
*She gave **him** (IO) **a kiss** (DO).   He sent **her** (IO) **some flowers** (DO).*
*I teach **students** (IO) **English** (DO).*

Participles are the forms of verbs used in compound tenses and as adjectives.
*What are you **doing**?   I've **finished**.   It's **freezing**!   He's **injured**.*

Particles are the adverbs or prepositions that form part of a phrasal verb.
*turn it **on**   take **off**   get **on with** her*

Partitives are words or expressions that show that only part of something is being referred to rather than all of it.
***a piece of** cake   **a packet of** crisps   **a bunch of** flowers*

The **phonetic alphabet** is a set of special symbols which shows speech sounds in writing.
mother = /ˈmʌðə/   television = /ˈtelɪvɪʒən/

Phrasal verbs are combinations of a verb and one or two particles.
switch on   come up with

Pronouns are words used in place of nouns or noun phrases. There are many classes of pronoun.
Subject pronouns: I, you, she, etc.
Object pronouns: me, you, her, etc.
Possessive pronouns: mine, yours, hers, etc.
Demonstrative pronouns: this, that, these, those

Proper nouns are words that refer to a particular person, place or institution.
Janet, Madrid, the United Nations

Proverbs or **sayings** are short, well-known statements that give practical advice about life.
When the cat's away, the mice will play.

Register describes a level and style of a piece of language which is appropriate for the circumstances in which it is used.
I am very grateful for your help. (More formal)
Cheers mate. (More informal)

Relative clauses are clauses that modify a noun or a noun phrase. They give additional information about the noun and are joined to a previous clause by words such as *who, that* or *which*.
*That's the man **who helped me**.   This the pen **(that) I lost**.*
*Everyone is well, **which is really great**.*

Synonyms are words or expressions which mean the same as another word or expression.
mad = crazy   tolerate sb = put up with sb   I'm off now. = I'm going now.

Transitive verbs take an object.
*You're wasting **your money**.   He's cut **his finger**.*
*I can't pronounce '**comfortable**'.*

Vowels are the letters *a, e, i, o* and *u*.

Recordings

Unit 1

🔘 **1.04–1.06**

(I = Interviewer; A = Adam; C = Carole;
S = Sharon)

Adam
I: Hi, excuse me – we're doing some research into how people use technology to talk to their friends. Do you mind if we ask you a couple of questions?
A: Well, I'm in a bit of a hurry.
I: It'll only take a few minutes.
A: Well, OK then.
I: Right, how do you usually contact your friends – by phone, email, text, …?
A: Um, I use my phone.
I: Do you usually use it to speak to friends, or do you text them?
A: I text from time to time, but I usually speak on the phone. It's so much quicker, and I'm very bad at texting.
I: Do you ever use email?
A: Yes, I check my personal emails twice a day, before I go to work and when I get back home.
I: Do you use messaging?
A: No, never.

Carole
I: Hi, excuse me – can I ask you a question for some research we're doing?
C: Certainly.
I: How do you usually contact your friends?
C: Oh, I pick up the phone.
I: And do you ever use email?
C: Yes, of course. I check my emails once a week. Oh, and I use Skype now and again. One of my grandchildren lives in Australia and she calls me on Skype every weekend.
I: When was the last time you wrote a letter?
C: Oh dear, I love receiving letters. But I must admit, I rarely write letters nowadays. It's a shame really, don't you think?

Sharon
I: Hi, excuse me – we're doing some research into how people use technology to talk to their friends. Do you mind if we ask you a couple of questions?
S: OK.
I: How do you usually contact your friends – by phone, email, text, …?
S: I never send emails. But I text all the time.
I: Do you speak on the phone?
S: Yes, but not very often – it's too expensive.
I: And what about when you're at home? Do you use your computer to communicate with friends?

S: Yeah, I use messaging. I'm always online so I chat with several friends every evening.
I: Do you use social networking?
S: What?
I: Facebook, MySpace, Bebo, …?
S: Oh yes, I've got 386 friends on Facebook. But I only contact about twenty of them regularly.

🔘 **1.07**

I suppose I've got five or six close friends, and most of them are really similar to me. But my friend, Jackie, is the exception. In many ways, we're opposites. We met about ten years ago in Paris. I was doing an intensive French language course, and she was doing a fashion course, but we were living in the same student accommodation. I arrived a few weeks after her, and she was really friendly. I guess we became friends because we were in the same situation and we were both from England. I'm amazed we got on so well, because we have nothing in common. For a start, we come from very different backgrounds. She grew up in the country on a farm with lots of brothers and sisters and dogs and horses. I grew up with my mother in a small apartment in the city with a pet hamster! We don't share the same taste in music, clothes, books, art, or anything really. Our personalities are very different – she's very artistic, and I'm not. I'm very tidy and organised, and she's not. We even look different – she's tall and dark, and I'm small and fair. But we do have one very important thing in common. We're both crazy about football, and we support the same team – Chelsea. We meet about three or four times a year and we usually go out for lunch and talk about football or the good old times in Paris.

Unit 2

🔘 **1.11**

a) It's very hot in here.
b) He's very angry.
c) She's very pretty.
d) My car's very dirty.
e) They're very tired.
f) This lesson is really interesting.

🔘 **1.12**

(I = Interviewer; A = Andy)
Andy
I: Have you ever had an injury?
A: Yes, I have. I was playing rugby for the local team, and it was just after kick-off. I was jumping up to catch the ball, when a player from the other team knocked me over, and I fell heavily on my left leg.
I: Oh dear. Were you badly hurt?
A: Yes, I twisted my ankle and couldn't play rugby for more than three months.

🔘 **1.13**

(I = Interviewer; B = Beth)
Beth
I: Have you ever been in a dangerous situation?
B: Yes I have. I was walking my dog one day with my sister, and we were crossing this field. There was a horse in it, and it suddenly started running towards us, looking really mad.
I: What did you do?
B: Well, I know you aren't supposed to run away from animals, because they can sense your fear. But we ran away as fast as we could.

🔘 **1.14**

(I = Interviewer; C = Cindy)
Cindy
I: Have you ever been really frightened?
C: Yes, I have. Last summer I was driving on the motorway in Spain. We were getting close to Barcelona so I started to slow down, ready to turn off the motorway. Suddenly, this black sports car appeared out of nowhere, pulled in front of me and stopped! I almost drove into the back of it, but I just managed to turn off the motorway in time. I've never been so frightened in my life.

🔘 **1.15**

(J = Jake; M = Mary)
J: Have I ever told you about the time a dog nearly attacked me?
M: No – what happened?
J: Oh well, it was a few years ago. I was still at school, actually, so I guess I was sixteen or seventeen. It was the weekend and it was summer – the sun was shining, and I was with some friends in the garden. We were playing football. Well, we weren't exactly playing football, because there were only three of us, but we were playing with a ball. In fact, we were using my older brother's football. Anyway, we were having a laugh and enjoying the game, when suddenly one of my friends kicked the ball really hard, and it went up in the air, over the fence and into my neighbour's garden. I couldn't believe it. My brother really loved that football and he never let me use it.
M: Oh no. What did you do?
J: Well, I went and knocked on the neighbour's door, but there was no answer. So I had to climb over the fence. It was really high, and my friends had to push me over. Anyway, as soon as I dropped down on the other side, I realised I wasn't alone.
M: The dog?
J: Yes, an enormous dog was running towards me, barking like mad. I've never been so frightened in my life!

M: What did you do?

J: I was absolutely terrified. I couldn't move. But then I noticed a chair near the fence, so I jumped up on it and managed to climb back over the fence.

M: What about the ball?

J: I didn't get the ball, but fortunately, the neighbours came back, before my brother did. So in the end, he never knew about it. Which is good because my brother is almost as frightening as the neighbour's dog!

 1.16

(I = Interviewer; T = Toby)

I: Toby, where did you learn?

T: I did a beginner's course in Spain. It's the most exciting thing I've ever done.

I: Is it hard?

T: Yes, you have to be strong and fit and also the kind of person who likes showing off!

I: What equipment do you need?

T: A wetsuit, a board, a kite and a harness.

I: Is it similar to wind surfing?

T: I think it's a bit more difficult than wind surfing. But it's similar, because you do it in the sea and you need the right amount of wind.

I: What's so good about it?

T: Everything! But hangtime is by far the best thing about it. That's when you jump, and try to stay suspended in the air for as long as possible. It's awesome.

 1.17

(I = Interviewer; K = Kate)

I: Kate, where do you do it?

K: Wherever there are good cliffs. One of the best places I've ever been is New Zealand. But I usually go to Wales. The cliffs are not as high as in New Zealand, but they're much closer to where I live.

I: Do many women do it?

K: No, there aren't as many women as there are men, but there are female-only courses to get women into the sport.

I: Is it very dangerous?

K: Yes, it is, so you must take the right equipment: waterproof clothes, climbing shoes and ropes.

I: Is it an expensive sport?

K: Not really. In fact, it's slightly less expensive than many other sports, because the mountains are free.

I: Why do you do it?

K: When you get to the top, it's the best feeling in the world.

Unit 3

 1.20

Ruth

Nobody thought we'd stay together, but we've just had our first wedding anniversary and we're very happily married. My mother-in-law hasn't spoken to us since the day we got married ... that's the good news! No, actually we're so upset about it that we've decided to move away

from our home town. It's not just because of Bill's mother, but the whole town knows about the competition. We've been trying to live a normal life but we can't walk down the street without people staring at us. Some people have even shouted horrible things, and the tabloid press have made our lives hell. They've been waiting for us to split up so that they can get a story, but it isn't going to happen. We've been together for a year now and we've been planning a big party to celebrate. Only this time, we're not inviting the press. Just our closest friends – the ones who have been there for us from the start.

 1.21

Clare

So it was about a year ago that I went to meet Stan at the airport. I felt really nervous but I couldn't wait to meet him. I spotted him immediately – he looked just like his photo. Over the next week or so, we got on really well and enjoyed one another's company, but unfortunately the relationship didn't work out. There was no real spark. In the end, we knew we weren't attracted to each other and we both agreed that we should just be friends. We stayed in touch for a while, when he went back to Canada, but then he met someone, and I haven't heard from him since they got married. I'm still looking for Mr Right.

Review A

 1.28

(N = Ned; A = Alicia)

N: Alicia! You're not going to believe what I've just seen.

A: What?

N: I was in the High Street and I saw Pete and Grace in the Grand Café. They were holding hands!

A: Oh, I thought you were going to tell me something I didn't know.

N: You knew?

A: Come on, Ned. You knew they liked each other, didn't you?

N: I knew Pete liked Grace but I had no idea she liked him.

A: You have to read the signs, Ned. They've liked each other for a long time.

N: But I thought Grace was going out with Dan.

A: Dan? That finished ages ago. They split up about six months ago.

N: Really? I knew they had their ups and downs but I thought they were still together.

A: OK, well they aren't. Anyway, why are you so excited? Are you interested in Grace?

N: Am I ... ? Of course not! I'm just surprised to see them together. That's all. Anyway, Pete told me he was seeing his parents this afternoon. I can't understand why he would say that.

A: Maybe he didn't want you to know about Grace. I think you need to find

a nice girlfriend, Ned. You and Pete spend too much time together.

N: Mm. Maybe you're right. What are you doing this evening?

A: Washing my hair.

N: Aha! For anyone special?

A: Oh, please!

Unit 4

 1.30

(I = Interviewer; H = Hua)

I: We're in Beijing, and it's mid-January. Hua, we've already celebrated New Year in England, but you don't celebrate New Year on 1st January, do you?

H: No, we don't. Our New Year usually takes place in early February but not always. It depends on the Chinese calendar.

I: I see. So how are you going to celebrate this year?

H: Well, everybody spends the month before New Year preparing for it. First of all, I'm going to help my mother to do the housework. We're going to sweep away all the bad luck and make room for good luck to come in.

I: Does everybody do that?

H: Yes, and some people paint their doors and windows, usually red.

I: Is red a lucky colour?

H: Yes, traditionally, red is the colour that frightens away bad luck. For New Year, we put red paper decorations on the walls.

I: And have you got plans for New Year's Eve?

H: Yes, we're having a big family dinner.

I: Is there a traditional New Year's Eve dinner?

H: Yes, we always eat jiaozi, which is dumplings cooked in boiling water.

I: Oh, I'm sure it's very nice. Are you going to a New Year's Eve party after dinner?

H: No, we always spend the New Year with our family. After dinner everybody watches television or plays cards or other board games, and at midnight, lots of fireworks and firecrackers go off. It's really exciting.

I: How long do the celebrations go on?

H: For about three days.

I: Do you make New Year's Resolutions?

H: Not exactly – we make wishes on New Year's Day.

I : What are you going to wish for?

H: I can't tell you, because it might not come true.

I: Well, I hope all your wishes come true. Happy New Year. How do you say that in Chinese?

H: Guo Nian Hao.

I: Guo Nian Hao!

 1.37

I went to a great party last summer. My friend, Maggie, was leaving our town and moving abroad to live. So she had a leaving party, but she also came up with a really good theme – it was fancy dress, and everybody had to dress up as something beginning with the letter M. She chose the letter M, because it's the first letter of her name. I thought it was a great idea, and people came dressed as all sorts of things – Mickey Mouse, Madonna, Medusa – I went as Marilyn Monroe. It was fun, but I didn't particularly enjoy wearing lipstick or high heels. I don't know how women do it all the time. The party was at Maggie's house, but it was summer, so we were in the garden a lot of the time. The garden looked really beautiful. They had fairy lights in the trees and lots of mirrors, so that the lights were reflected, and it made the garden look much bigger.

There must have been at least seventy people there. I think she invited everyone she knew. I didn't know everybody, but it didn't matter. The fancy dress was a perfect ice-breaker and everybody mixed really well. The food was great too – Maggie was moving to Thailand, so the food was Thai. She got the local Thai restaurant to do it, and it was delicious. We even had Thai beer to go with it. Maggie's brother is a DJ, so the music was fantastic, and I danced a lot – without my heels on.

Unit 5

🌐 **2.01**

Number 1. A little chocolate each day is good for your health. Chocolate contains antioxidants which help to protect the body against cancer. It also contains several minerals and some protein. In fact, one bar of chocolate contains more protein than a banana, so this statement is true.

Number 2. White chocolate doesn't contain any cocoa, so this statement is true.

Number 3. Chocolate contains chemicals that produce the same reaction in the body as falling in love, so this statement is true.

Number 4. The healthy part of chocolate is the cocoa, and dark chocolate has at least 50–70% cocoa. On the other hand, a lot of commercial milk chocolate bars have hardly any cocoa in them at all, so this statement is true.

Number 5. A little chocolate can make a dog sick. A lot of chocolate can kill it, so this statement is false.

Number 6. Americans consume a lot of chocolate, but per capita, the Swiss consume more. The Swiss consume ten kilograms per person per year, so this statement is false.

Number 7 is true.

Number 8. Chocolate contains much less caffeine than coffee, so this statement is false.

Number 9 is true.

Number 10 is true. In fact, they used a lot of chocolate sauce because the scene took seven days to shoot.

🌐 **2.03**

(I = Interviewer; M = Mark)
I: Mark, you've tasted some of the more unusual dishes from around the world. Can you tell us about them and what they taste like?
M: Yes, well, I've just come back from China where I ate cobra for the first time.
I: Cobra? I imagine it tastes fishy.
M: No, not at all. In fact tastes meaty, like chicken. It was a little tough and chewy, but delicious.
I: Really? I find that hard to imagine.
M: And before that I was in Thailand. I ate lots of fried grasshoppers there. They're really crisp and tasty.
I: Hm. I'm not sure I'd like to eat insects.
M: Well, that's because you're not used to them. In many parts of the world insects are a good source of protein and minerals. Last time I was in Indonesia, I had a feast of insects. In fact, for one meal, the main course was roasted cockroaches.
I: What did that taste like?
M: Well, they're crunchy on the outside, and on the inside there's a rich liquid which tastes quite sweet and fruity.
I: What other insects have you eaten?
M: While I was in Africa, I ate caterpillars. They boil them and dry them in the sun, so they taste a bit dry and bland. But they're really good for you.
I: Oh.
M: One of my favourite insects to eat is ants. Did you know that in Colombia, some cinemas serve roasted, chocolate-covered ants instead of popcorn?
I: Really? What are they like?
M: Sweet and crisp – like popcorn.
I: Oh.
M: What about you? Have you ever eaten anything unusual?
I: Well, I'm not as adventurous as you, and I haven't travelled much. But the strangest, and, I must say, the most revolting thing I've ever eaten was in Scotland recently. It was a deep-fried Mars Bar.
M: What? You mean, like fish and chips – Mars bar and chips?
I: That's right. Greasy and horribly sweet. Disgusting!

🌐 **2.04**

There were five of us at home when I was growing up – my father, my mother, my brother, my sister and me. My mother did most of the cooking, but we all helped her. Well, sort of helped her. We each had a special job: I used to chop vegetables, my brother helped with the washing up, and my sister set the table. I used to love everything my mother cooked, except for one thing – meat. I didn't like it, and that made life difficult for my mother, because everyone else liked it. So she used to cook meat for everyone else, and a vegetarian meal for me.

Teatime was always really important in my house – I think it's because my mother is half English. We'd have tea and cakes at about four o'clock in the afternoon. My mother would invite the neighbours round, and we'd have a tea party! I used to love those times. My father would come home from work at about seven o'clock in the evening, and then we used to have our dinner in the kitchen. Then we would help to clear the table, and we'd be in bed by 8.30. The weekends were a bit different. Every Saturday, we used to go to a restaurant for dinner, and on Sundays we'd have pasta as a treat. My father is of Italian origin, so pasta was his favourite dish. My favourite dish when I was a child was rice and beans – it's a popular dish in Brazil, but nobody makes it like my mum.

Unit 6

🌐 **2.11**

Job 1
I work in London for a big law firm. It's an American firm, and Head Office is in Washington DC, so I have to go to the States about once a month for meetings. Here in London, we're supposed to start work at nine, but I often start later and work until nine or ten o'clock at night. Unfortunately, we don't get extra money for working overtime. We have to dress smartly, so I always wear a suit and tie to work. Female lawyers aren't allowed to wear trousers or miniskirts. In London, we have to wear cloaks in court. Recently, Head Office brought in a new rule – we're not allowed to have relationships with people in the same company. I think it's ridiculous to ban office romance – where else are you going to meet somebody?

🌐 **2.12**

Job 2
This is the newsroom, where I work as a journalist. I'm actually responsible for foreign news. As you can see, we work in open-plan offices, so it can get quite noisy. We're allowed to work at home one day a week, so when I want to do some quiet work, I don't come into the office. We work flexible hours because news is coming in all the time. We're supposed to have a break every two hours, but when you're working to a deadline, you can't afford to take time for a break. Sometimes I work right through my lunch hour – it's mad really. In fact, you have to be mad to work here. As far as dress is concerned, we can wear anything we like.

🌐 **2.13**

Job 3
You have to be at least twenty-one to be a train driver, but you don't have to have any particular qualifications to get on a training course. I earn a good salary, but my job involves a lot of responsibility, and I work unsociable hours. I often work at night or at weekends and I'm supposed to work four or five shifts a week. You can't

work a shift of more than twelve hours and you have to have twelve hours off between shifts. My job affects my social life, because I can't have a few drinks and go to bed late in the evening if I'm driving the next day. We have to wear a uniform and we're supposed to wear our hats all the time, but it gets a bit hot.

Review B

 2.17

(C = Carol; R = Rob)

C What are you doing for Christmas this year? Are you staying here in London?

R: Oh, I don't know, actually.

C: Do you want to come and spend it in Somerset with my family?

R: Maybe. What are you planning?

C: Well, I'm going to take the day off and drive down on Christmas Eve, because Mum's having a little party. She always does. Everyone will be there – my brother, Ken, and his wife, Michelle, with their kids. And my sister, Di. My Granny – she's 92 now! And my mum's sister, Betty, with all my cousins.

R: Oh, right.

C: Then, we'll have dinner together. Dad always used to make it, but since they split up, Mum does it. We always have fish, usually salmon or something, with a light fruit dessert. Then, before bed, we're allowed to open one present each, from under the Christmas tree.

R: We always used to do that too, when we were kids! Do you go to church on Christmas Day?

C: Yes, we get up early and go to church. Then we'll have a smoked salmon and champagne breakfast before we spend the morning opening presents. After that we have lunch. I think Ken is going to cook it again this year. He's a brilliant cook. We usually have turkey, followed by Christmas pudding – you know, the traditional stuff.

R: What about the afternoon?

C: Dad's coming over in the afternoon, with his new wife. I'm a bit worried about it actually. I don't know what Mum's going to say. She isn't too happy about it. But she had to invite him, and Christmas just wouldn't be the same without Dad.

R: Oh.

C: Anyway, in the afternoon we'll all stay at home and play games, or watch a film on TV and eat chocolates.

R: And are you coming home the next day?

C: You mean Boxing Day? No, I'm staying for that. We always have a big lunch with friends. We eat cold meat and salad for lunch, with fresh fruit. Then we go for a walk, if it's not too cold or wet. I'll come back the next day.

R: That sounds lovely, Carol. But I think I'll stay at home on my own.

Unit 7

 2.19

(I = Interviewer; J = Jack)

I: People are increasingly obsessed with reading stories and looking at photographs of celebrities. Today there are more paparazzi on the street than ever, all of them trying to get the definitive celebrity photo. We talk to Jack, a paparazzo with fifteen years' experience, about his job. Jack, thank you for joining us.

J: You're welcome.

I: Jack, why are people so interested in reading about the private lives of celebrities?

J: Because they're young, beautiful, rich and photogenic and they lead glamorous lifestyles.

I: But the photos that appear in the tabloid press are not always glamorous. They're often unflattering photos of celebrities just trying to lead their lives. For example, I remember seeing a photo of Matt Damon getting a parking ticket. What's so interesting about that?

J: Well, people also want to think that these celebrities are just normal people, so they enjoy seeing photos of them doing ordinary things like shopping. I also think it's fine to take unflattering photos of them because it gives us hope when we realise that they're just like us really!

I: I understand that, but where do you draw the line?

J: Well, we're not completely insensitive. We try not to involve children. For example, Kate Moss asked us not to take photographs of her daughter, and we haven't. Do you remember seeing photos of her daughter in the press?

I: No, but I did read an interview with Kate Moss, where she said that she can't walk anywhere because the paparazzi follow her everywhere. That must be awful. In the same interview, she said that a female photographer was chasing her in New York and fell over a water hydrant. She cut her lip and was bleeding, so Kate stopped to ask her if she was OK. The woman just continued taking photographs! That's a bit desperate, isn't it?

J: The woman was just doing her job. Listen, so many of these celebrities refuse to cooperate with the paparazzi. We try reasoning with them. We explain that we don't want to upset them, but they shout and swear at us. So we follow them everywhere. It's a game. Have you ever seen a bad photo of Nicole Kidman in the press?

I: Er, no.

J: That's because she plays the game. She always agrees to smile for the camera, and we get our shot. Then we leave her alone. If you ask me, I think these celebrities are hypocritical. On the one hand they need to have their photos in the press, and on the other hand they tell us that we're invading their privacy. If they don't like the attention, I suggest that they change jobs.

 2.22

And here are the news headlines.

a)

Robert Holmes, Minister for the Environment, has resigned. The Prime Minister has ordered an investigation into the mysterious disappearance of a large sum of money. A spokesman for the Minister told us that he was out of the country and not available for comment.

b)

The total number of unemployed people in Britain has increased significantly. The opposition has called for the government to provide more jobs for school-leavers.

c)

Peace negotiations have ended after an argument broke out between delegates. According to our reporter at the conference, delegates were unable to agree on the order of matters to be discussed.

d)

A freak hailstorm has severely damaged fruit harvests in eastern regions of Spain. Meteorological experts have reported hailstones the size of footballs.

e)

Schoolgirl, Pauline Gates, has not been allowed back into school after the summer holidays because she has had her nose pierced. According to headmistress, Jean Bradley, Paula knew that piercing was against the school rules. The girl will be allowed back into school when she removes the offending nosering.

f)

And finally, to end on a happier note, wedding bells are ringing for 81-year-old Max Williams, who won £16 million in the lottery last month. He is going to marry 22-year-old dancer, Sally Lister. The happy couple posed for photographers outside the millionaire's luxury home in Essex, and Sally held out her hand to show off her £10,000 engagement ring for the cameras.

 2.25

a) We got engaged last week.

b) My internet's down again.

c) I'm going snowboarding for the first time at the weekend.

d) I've just won £1,000 in the lottery.

e) I'm reading Nelson Mandela's autobiography.

f) My wallet's been stolen.

g) My mum's going to give me her car.

h) I think my boyfriend might lose his job.

i) I passed all my English exams.

Unit 8

💿 2.26

(A = Amy; J = Joe)

A: Have you heard from Conrad lately? Is he still going round the world?

J: Yes, lucky thing. He's in South America now – I had a message from him yesterday.

A: How's he getting on?

J: He's having a great time – here, come and have a look at the photos on his web page.

A: Oh, great.

J: Right – here we are.

A: Oh wow! Look at those waterfalls. Where is that?

J: Well, he hasn't put the name of the place, but I suppose it could be Vietnam.

A: Or it could be India.

J: No, it can't be India, because he hasn't been there. I'm pretty sure it's Vietnam. I know he went trekking in the hills there.

A: Oh, I'd love to go to Vietnam.

J: Mm, me too. Now this one must be Singapore. Look at that skyline – it's so built-up.

A: Or it could be Hong Kong.

J: No, he didn't go to Hong Kong, but I know he stopped off in Singapore.

A: Ah. – Wow, look at these statues. They look really old. Is it a Buddhist temple?

J: Yes, I think so. That's probably Thailand. He was there for the New Year.

A: Lucky man. Now this is different – I didn't know Conrad could ride a horse.

J: He can't – I don't think that's him.

A: So where is this then?

J: I'm not sure, but it's probably southern Argentina.

A: Oh look here's a good one. What is he doing?!

💿 2.30

I once went on a trip through the Sinai desert in Egypt, from the Red Sea to a historical place called St Catherine's Monastery. I was actually on a windsurfing holiday with some friends in a small resort called Dahab. It's a perfect place for water sports, but one day, the weather was useless for windsurfing – basically, there was no wind at all. My friends decided to go diving, but I don't like being under the water, and I hate sunbathing. So I signed up for a trip to St Catherine's Monastery.

We left the hotel at about 10.00 a.m., and the weather was just beginning to get hot. There were ten of us in a minivan including eight tourists, one guide and one driver. Fortunately, the minivan was air-conditioned. The guide spoke five languages, so during the trip he told us the history of the monastery in English, Spanish, French and German.

The journey took about two hours, and as we drove through one of the driest deserts in the world, I just stared out of the window at the wonderful scenery.

The sandy colour of the mountains looked fantastic against the blue sky. We stopped once on the way at a place where the view is spectacular and everybody got out and took photographs. There were Bedouins selling souvenirs, and I bought a lovely necklace.

By the time we arrived at the monastery, it was really hot and there were loads of other tourists there, but I was glad I'd come. It's a very special place, and I'd love to do the trip again, but next time I'd hire a car and do it in my own time.

Unit 9

💿 2.34

1

A: Which is your favourite track on the album?

B: The last one – it's amazing. I can't wait to see them performing live.

2

C: What did you think of it?

D: I thought the acting was brilliant and the photography's superb. Apart from that, it was dead boring.

3

E: Have you finished it yet?

F: Nearly.

E: What's it like?

F: Really good. I reckon it's going to be a best-seller.

4

G: I enjoyed that. What did you think of it?

H: I thought it was rubbish – a sentimental tearjerker – and the ending was predictable.

G: Well, it made you cry anyway.

H: No, it didn't – I've got a cold.

5

I: Are you enjoying it?

J: Yes. I found it a bit difficult to get into, but now that I'm past the first few chapters, I can't put it down.

6

K: What did you think of the special effects?

L: What special effects?

K: It was all done with computers.

L: Oh no – I thought it was real. You've spoilt it now.

7

M: Did you have a good time?

N: Not really – I can't stand all that techno stuff. I like it when you can actually hear the lyrics.

M: Old hippy.

N: What did you say?

M: Nothing.

💿 2.36

One of my favourite films is *Forrest Gump*. I know it's quite an old film but I've never seen anything better. Actually, I've seen it three times. The last time I saw it was the other night on television, and it made me laugh and cry all over again. I love Tom Hanks and I think he's brilliant in this film. Robin Wright played the part of his girlfriend, and Sally Field was his mum. I can't remember who else was in it, or who directed it. But I do know that it won six Oscars including best film, best director and Tom Hanks got best leading actor. Apparently it's based on a novel, but I've no idea who wrote it.

There are so many things I love about this film. I suppose it's a drama, but it's historical and it's funny and it's really sad too. The character of Forrest Gump is brilliant – he's not very clever, and at the beginning of the film he can't walk properly, but he manages to succeed in life without meaning to, and without realising it. I particularly like the bits where he meets famous people like President Kennedy or Elvis Presley. It's so clever the way they mix old black and white footage from the 60s. It's hilarious when Forrest meets Elvis. Forrest has a strange way of walking, and when Elvis imitates him, it looks like the dance that he was famous for. The soundtrack is great too – there are all these classic pop songs including some by Elvis.

But the ending is a bit of a tearjerker – I cry my eyes out every time. I won't spoil it for you in case you haven't seen it – but you should see it because it's the best film of all time.

Review C

💿 2.42

(DR = Dan Rivero; L = Luke; M = Maria; J = Jason; C = Cathy)

DR: You're listening to WAZR on 98.6 FM, and I'm Dan Rivero. We're talking about Mika Brzezinski's refusal to cover the Paris Hilton story. What do you think? Give me a call and let me know. … We have our first caller. Is it Luke?

L: That's right.

DR: Go ahead, Luke.

L: Hi, Dan. I just want to congratulate Mika Brzezinski on taking a stand and for saying what most of America is thinking: we've had enough of hearing about these celebrities! That's not news! And what's the problem with Mika's co-hosts? They gave her no support at all when she really needed it.

DR: Thanks, Luke. Next up we have Maria.

M: You rock, Mika! It takes courage to do what you did. I wish there were more presenters like you. You're an inspiration. I'm going to tell my boss today what I think of him! Yeah! You know, Mika, you're a lot bigger and a lot better than those guys you have to work with.

DR: Thanks, Maria. We have Jason on the line. Jason?

J: Thanks, Dan. I have to say I was disappointed by Mika Brzezinski's refusal to cover the lead story. It's not up to her to decide which stories she does and doesn't cover. Her job is to read out what she's given. I think her co-presenters were right to tell her that her behaviour was unacceptable.

DR: OK, Jason. Thanks for your call. Time for one more. Let's hear from Cathy.

C: Hi, Dan. I don't know what your last caller was talking about. I agree with your other callers that Mika was right and the other guys on the show were trying to make her look stupid. And just because the paparazzi are running around taking pictures of Paris Hilton, it doesn't mean we're actually interested in her!

DR: OK, let's take a break. We'll be right back after the news with more reactions …

Unit 10

🔊 3.01

1 It's something that lived a very long time ago. It looks very scary.
A thing that lived a long time ago.
Um … It's a big monster.

2 It's a man and he lives in … , he lives up in space.
He's someone who lives … who's died and he looks down on people.
A person that helps people, in heaven.

3 It's something that's very cold and it's … it's a … it's a stone.
It's a sort of big piece of ice that cracks off a bigger piece.
It's a big ice cube.

4 A place where animals have been put up to show.
Somewhere where they show you things that are very old.
It's somewhere where people will show things like dinosaurs and olden days things.

5 It's a person who takes toys away.
It's someone that in the middle of the night … and it's got a … something around his face with round holes and he's got a T-shirt that's got black and white and he robs things.
It's someone who steals things when you're asleep.

🔊 3.03

(D = Dale; R = Rachel; G = George)

D: Welcome to *Dale's Dilemmas*. I'm Dale Rogers, and the subject of today's dilemma is pushy parents. Are today's parents too ambitious for their children? Should they let children be children and stop organising their lives? Should we congratulate them for developing their children's potential, or should we say 'back off and leave the kids alone'?
In the studio we have George and Rachel from Chicago. They disagree about how to bring up their daughter, and we're going to hear what they have to say. … George and Rachel, welcome to the show.

G and R: Thanks.

D: Rachel, if we could start with you. Can you tell us a little about your daughter?

R: Yes, my daughter Hayley is five years old, and I think she has what it takes to be a film star. So I'm doing everything I can to get her into films.

D: And what exactly does that involve?

R: Hayley goes to acting classes twice a week. She has a singing teacher who comes to the house once a week, and we watch a lot of movies together at home. Then at the weekends we go to auditions. Sometimes we have to travel to New York or Los Angeles, but I'm willing to do whatever it takes.

D: That's a lot of travelling. What do you think about it, George?

G: I think my wife is obsessed. I don't think she should make Hayley do this. It isn't Hayley's choice. Rachel wanted to be a child star, and that's why she's making Hayley go though this.

R: I'm not making her do anything against her will. Hayley loves it and she wants to be a star.

D: But at five years old, does she understand what it means?

G: No, of course not. I want to let Hayley grow up like a normal child. There's too much pressure in the film world. She's a kid – let her play, let her have friends.

D: It's true that being a child star can be a very isolating experience.

R: I know that, but if you don't try, you don't succeed. When Hayley is famous and she's doing movies, you're going to look back and thank me.

D: Thank you Rachel and George. In just a moment, we'll be meeting Mark and Charlene who want their two-year-old son to be the next Tiger Woods. But first, it's over to the studio audience. Who has a question for Rachel and George?

🔊 3.04

(D = Dale; W1, W2 = woman 1, woman 2; R = Rachel; G = George; M1, M2 = man 1, man 2)

D: Who has a question for Rachel and George? Yes, the woman in the red dress please …

W1: Do you know how Hayley feels?

R: She enjoys her life and she wants to be a film star.

G: I think she's too young to know how she feels. She says she's happy because she wants to please her mom.

D: Thank you. Another question now please. Yes, the woman with the blue shirt.

W2: Can you tell me what you're going to do when Hayley starts school?

G: I'd like her to stop doing auditions and focus on being a normal school kid.

R: Well, I think it would be wrong to stop now after all the time and money we've invested. After all, you don't invest in a business and then give up after six months if you're not making a profit.

G: But Hayley is not a business – she's a child. Our daughter.

D: OK, … let's have one from the man in the green jacket.

M1: Do you think you're depriving Hayley of a normal childhood?

G: Yeah. I worry about that.

R: Well, I don't. She's special and I want to help her to fulfil her potential.

D: Yes, the young man with the baseball cap.

M2: Could you tell me whether you have any other children and how they are affected?

G: We have a seven-year-old son, and he misses his mom.

R: He's very proud of his little sister.

D: The woman in the red dress again.

W1: Do you have any idea how stressful it is to be a film star?

G: Very stressful. I don't think my wife has thought about the negatives at all.

R: We can cope. I just hope that I can come back here in ten years' time and we can do a follow-up story when Hayley's a star.

D: Well, I'm afraid that's all we've got time for now. Thank you to …

🔊 3.06

My mother plays the piano really well, so she was very keen for me to learn the piano too. I had lessons for a while, but I was useless, and eventually my piano teacher begged my parents to stop sending me. So that was the end of my music career! But what I really wanted to do was martial arts, and my parents let me join a club when I was about nine. I used to love those kung fu movies – Bruce Lee was my hero, and I had posters of him all over my room, and that was how I got the idea. I was a bit disappointed at first, because our classes weren't like the films, but then I got quite obsessed with it and I was doing martial arts two or three times a week. We did it at a gym in the city centre, so my parents drove me there because it was quite far away from my house. But when I was about fourteen I decided that I didn't want my friends to see my parents dropping me off, so I took the bus instead. I'm still doing martial arts now after ten years, and I've started getting more and more interested in kick-boxing. I'd definitely encourage my own children to do martial arts. It's not just about fighting – of course, you learn self-defence – but you also learn other skills such as mental discipline and self-confidence.

Unit 11

🔊 3.12

(M = man; W = woman)

M: You look worried. What's on your mind?

W: Actually, there is something I've been meaning to tell you …

M: Look, if it's about last night, it really doesn't matter. I shouldn't have said anything.

W: No, no, it's nothing to do with that. Or rather I suppose it is, in a way.

M: I knew it – if only I'd kept my mouth shut.

W: Look, I agree with you – Bryan Adams *is* old-fashioned, and I wish I'd never put that CD on.

M: It's not a bad CD. It's my fault – I shouldn't have called him a boring old dinosaur.

W: No, it's my fault – I shouldn't have reacted like I did. It's just that that CD brings back special memories for me.

M: Look, I understand. *My* parents used to play Bryan Adams too.

W: No, you don't understand – I was in my teens when that record first came out.

M: Ah, right. I see what you mean. Well, you look very good for your age.

W: Oh, shut up.

M: No, what I mean is that I don't care how old you are – and anyway, I've got something to tell you. I'm not 31. I'm 26.

W: What?!

🔘 3.13

a) Of course I didn't say anything – I mean, the cashier should have asked to look in her bag, shouldn't she? If it had been a small shop, I probably would have said something, but a big supermarket like that can afford it.

b) Well, I picked it up, brushed the cat hairs off and served it. What you don't see you don't worry about, do you?

c) I don't know if he saw me, but I didn't want to embarrass him, so I just carried on walking. I often think about him and wonder how he ended up on the streets.

Unit 12

🔘 3.17

1 Al I'm really proud of my fabulous American snakeskin cowboy boots. Most of my friends hate them and wouldn't be seen dead in boots like these, but I like the fact that they're different. I wear them for work with a smart suit and tie and I think the contrast looks great. I like to stand out from the crowd.

2 Fran: I usually wear jeans and a hoody during the day, but for going out, my favourite thing is my red low-waisted miniskirt. I wear it with a wide black leather belt and short boots, and it looks fantastic with my old black leather jacket.

3 Jay: I have about twenty-five pairs of jeans, but my favourites are my old black skinny jeans. I play the guitar in a band and I always wear my black skinny jeans and a black polo-neck top when we're playing. It's like a uniform.

4 Bea: I'm really into vintage clothes and I've just bought a beautiful long blue silk evening dress. I haven't worn it yet – I'm waiting for the right occasion. It would look great on the red carpet at the Oscars.

🔘 3.19

I was invited to a friend's birthday party recently, and there were quite a few people there who I'd never met before. I'm not very good at introducing myself to strangers, so I just stayed with the people I knew, and that was nice because I hadn't seen them for a while. But then this woman came over and introduced herself, and asked who I was. I thought she seemed really friendly and very confident. She was tiny, with long curly black hair, and I remember she was wearing a beautiful turquoise necklace. I admired the necklace, and she told me that it was from Egypt. We talked about Egypt, and it turned out that we'd both been on holiday to the same Egyptian holiday resort, but not at the same time. Small world. I haven't seen her since then, but she works with my friend, so I think I'll probably bump into her again some time. I hope so.

🔘 3.20

(A = Annie; B = Betty)

A: Did you see *Ten Years Younger* last night?

B: No, I missed it. I had to work. Why, was it good?

A: It was brilliant. They had a man and a woman on, and honestly, the transformation was incredible.

B: What did they look like?

A: Well, the man looked about sixty, even though he was only forty-four.

B: Oh no!

A: He had this horrible long grey hair, and he dressed a bit like an old rock star.

B: Urgh!

A: Anyway, he had his hair cut and coloured and he had his teeth whitened.

B: Oh yes, that makes such a difference.

A: And I think he had his eyelids lifted.

B: Oh well, of course if you can afford to have plastic surgery, you're bound to look better.

A: Yes, but I think that's all he had done. Oh, and he had his clothes chosen by a stylist.

B: What about the woman? Did she have lots of plastic surgery?

A: No, she didn't actually. But she looked as if she'd had a major facelift, it was amazing. Before the makeover, everybody thought she was about fifty-five, and in fact the poor woman was only forty.

B: Oh dear. What did she have done?

A: She had her hair cut and coloured, of course. And she had her make-up done by an expert and her clothes chosen by a stylist.

B: Oh, I'd love that. How old did they think she was after the makeover?

A: Thirty-eight.

B: Oh, she must have been pleased. Hey, do you think I need to have my hair cut?

Review D

🔘 3.26

(I = Interviewer; C = Colin)

I: Colin, tell me about your childhood. You never knew your real parents, did you?

C: That's right. I was brought up in children's homes – I moved several times when I was very young – and then went to live with my foster parents, Flo and Isaac, when I was ten.

I: Was it a difficult childhood?

C: Well, some people might see it that way, but I have very good memories. In that part of London at that time, everyone there was poor – we never had any money – but we didn't complain. There was a real neighbourhood spirit. Everyone helped each other.

I: Can you tell me what your memories of that time are?

C: We used to make our own entertainment – there was no TV, no video games. We played in the fields and down by the canal. All the kids together.

I: And you left school quite young, didn't you?

C: Yes. I left school at fourteen and went to work in a factory. But I didn't like it. I only stayed there two years. I always wanted to work for myself, so I trained to be a taxi driver. I worked as a driver for ten years until I got married.

I: But you didn't stay a taxi driver?

C: No. I was ambitious! We already had two children, and another on the way. I wanted a good life for my kids, so I started my own business from nothing, but soon had fifty cars and drivers. I sold the business a few years ago, and made enough money to buy a holiday home in Spain.

I: How did you meet your wife?

C: We met at a dance. She was wearing a beautiful yellow silk dress. I thought she was the prettiest thing I'd ever seen. We got married six months later.

I: Any regrets? Would you change anything about your life?

C: Not a thing! I feel like the luckiest man in the world!

Phonetic symbols & Spelling

Single vowels

/ɪ/	ship	/ʃɪp/	(build, business, England, gym, lettuce, spinach, women)
/iː/	need	/niːd/	(bean, he, key, niece, people, sardine)
/ʊ/	put	/pʊt/	(could, foot, woman)
/uː/	pool	/puːl/	(flew, fruit, lose, rule, shoe, through, two)
/e/	egg	/eg/	(breakfast, friend, many, said)
/ə/	mother	/ˈmʌðə/	(arrive, colour, husband, lemon, nervous, police)
/ɜː/	verb	/vɜːb/	(learn, curly, skirt, word)
/ɔː/	saw	/sɔː/	(abroad, caught, four, horse, talk, thought, towards, water)
/æ/	back	/bæk/	—
/ʌ/	bus	/bʌs/	(blood, does, enough, onion)
/ɑː/	arm	/ɑːm/	(aunt, heart, laugh, past)
/ɒ/	top	/tɒp/	(cauliflower, what)

Diphthongs

/ɪə/	ear	/ɪə/	(beer, here, Italian, theatre)
/eɪ/	face	/feɪs/	(break, eight, fail, say, they)
/ʊə/	tour	/tʊə/	(plural, sure)
/ɔɪ/	boy	/bɔɪ/	(noise)
/əʊ/	nose	/nəʊz/	(aubergine, although, coat, know, shoulder)
/eə/	hair	/heə/	(careful, their, wear, where)
/aɪ/	white	/waɪt/	(buy, die, eye, height, high, my)
/aʊ/	mouth	/maʊθ/	(town)

Consonants

/p/	pen	/pen/	(happy)
/b/	bag	/bæg/	(rabbit)
/t/	tea	/tiː/	(ate, fatter, worked)
/d/	dog	/dɒg/	(address, played)
/tʃ/	chip	/tʃɪp/	(natural, watch)
/dʒ/	jazz	/dʒæz/	(age, bridge, generous)
/k/	cake	/keɪk/	(chemistry, kitchen, knock, toothache)
/g/	girl	/gɜːl/	(foggy)
/f/	film	/fɪlm/	(different, laugh, photograph)
/v/	very	/veri/	(of)
/θ/	thin	/θɪn/	—
/ð/	these	/ðiːz/	—
/s/	snake	/sneɪk/	(city, message, race)
/z/	zoo	/zuː/	(has)
/ʃ/	shop	/ʃɒp/	(description, machine, sugar)
/ʒ/	television	/ˈtelɪvɪʒən/	(garage, usual)
/m/	map	/mæp/	(summer)
/n/	name	/neɪm/	(sunny, knife)
/ŋ/	ring	/rɪŋ/	(thanks, tongue)
/h/	house	/haʊs/	(who)
/l/	leg	/leg/	(hill, possible)
/r/	road	/rəʊd/	(carry, write)
/w/	wine	/waɪn/	(one, why)
/j/	yes	/jes/	(used)

Stress

Word stress is shown by underlining the stressed syllable: <u>wa</u>ter, a<u>ma</u>zing, Japa<u>nese</u>.

Letters of the alphabet

/eɪ/	/iː/	/e/	/aɪ/	/əʊ/	/uː/	/ɑː/
Aa	Bb	Ff	Ii	Oo	Qq	Rr
Hh	Cc	Ll	Yy		Uu	
Jj	Dd	Mm			Ww	
Kk	Ee	Nn				
	Gg	Ss				
	Pp	Xx				
	Tt	Zz				
	Vv					

Irregular verbs

Infinitive	Past simple	Past participle	Infinitive	Past simple	Past participle
be	was/were	been	let	let	let
beat	beat	beaten	lie	lay/lied	lied/lain
become	became	become	light	lit/lighted	lit/lighted
begin	began	begun	lose	lost	lost
bend	bent	bent	make	made	made
bet	bet	bet	mean	meant /ment/	meant /ment/
bite	bit	bitten	meet	met	met
blow	blew	blown	must	had to	(had to)
break	broke	broken	pay	paid	paid
bring	brought /brɔːt/	brought /brɔːt/	put	put	put
build /bɪld/	built /bɪlt/	built /bɪlt/	read	read /red/	read /red/
burn	burnt/burned	burnt/burned	ride	rode	ridden
burst	burst	burst	ring	rang	rung
buy /baɪ/	bought /bɔːt/	bought /bɔːt/	rise	rose	risen
can	could /kʊd/	(been able)	run	ran	run
catch	caught /kɔːt/	caught /kɔːt/	say	said /sed/	said /sed/
choose	chose	chosen	see	saw /sɔː/	seen
come	came	come	sell	sold	sold
cost	cost	cost	send	sent	sent
cut	cut	cut	set	set	set
deal /diːl/	dealt /delt/	dealt /delt/	shake	shook	shaken
dig	dug	dug	shine	shone	shone
do	did	done	shoot	shot	shot
draw	drew	drawn	show	showed	shown
dream	dreamt/dreamed	dreamt/dreamed	shrink	shrank	shrunk
drink	drank	drunk	shut	shut	shut
drive	drove	driven	sing	sang	sung
eat	ate	eaten	sink	sank	sunk
fall	fell	fallen	sit	sat	sat
feed	fed	fed	sleep	slept	slept
feel	felt	felt	slide	slid	slid
fight	fought /fɔːt/	fought /fɔːt/	smell	smelt/smelled	smelt/smelled
find	found	found	speak	spoke	spoken
fly	flew	flown	spell	spelt/spelled	spelt/spelled
forget	forgot	forgotten	spend	spent	spent
forgive	forgave	forgiven	spill	spilt/spilled	spilt/spilled
freeze	froze	frozen	split	split	split
get	got	got	spoil	spoilt/spoiled	spoilt/spoiled
give	gave	given	spread	spread	spread
go	went	gone/been	stand	stood	stood
grow	grew	grown	steal	stole	stolen
hang	hung/hanged	hung/hanged	stick	stuck	stuck
have	had	had	swear	swore	sworn
hear	heard /hɜːd/	heard /hɜːd/	swell	swelled	swollen/swelled
hide	hid	hidden	swim	swam	swum
hit	hit	hit	take	took /tʊk/	taken
hold	held	held	teach	taught /tɔːt/	taught /tɔːt/
hurt /hɜːt/	hurt /hɜːt/	hurt /hɜːt/	tear	tore	torn
keep	kept	kept	tell	told	told
kneel	knelt/kneeled	knelt/kneeled	think	thought /θɔːt/	thought /θɔːt/
know	knew /njuː/	known	throw	threw	thrown
lay	laid	laid	understand	understood	understood
lead	led	led	wake	woke	woken
learn	learnt	learnt	wear	wore /wɔː/	worn
leave	left	left	win	won /wʌn/	won /wʌn/
lend	lent	lent	write	wrote	written

Macmillan Education
4 Crinan Street
London N1 9XW
A division of Macmillan Publishers Limited
Companies and representatives throughout the world

ISBN 978-1-4050-9972-1

Text © Sue Kay & Vaughan Jones 2009
Design and illustration © Macmillan Publishers Limited 2009

First published 2009

Review units by Peter Maggs and Catherine Smith

Project development by Desmond O'Sullivan, Quality Outcomes Limited

Designed by 320 Design Limited

Photographic research and editorial by Sally Cole, Perseverance Works Limited

Illustrated by Beach p91; Ed McLachlan pp10, 18, 26, 28, 29, 38, 46, 47, 54, 57, 66, 74, 82, 84, 94, 95, 99, 101, 102, 105, 110, 112, 117, 118, 119, 120, 122, 123, 124, 125, 127, 129, 131, 133, 135, 139, 141, 145, 147, 149; Adrian Valencia pp16, 113.

Cover design by Andrew Oliver
Dictionary extracts taken from the Macmillan Essential Dictionary © Macmillan Publishers limited 2003, used with permission.

Authors' acknowledgements

We would like to thank all our students and colleagues at the Oxford English Centre in Oxford as well as all our teaching colleagues around the world who are using Inside Out – your feedback has helped us identify what we should keep and what we could improve. Particular thanks go to the following people: Peter Tamkin, Phil Hopkins, Steve Jones, (English Language Centre, Brighton); Howard Smith (Oxford House College, Oxford); Kimberley Moss, Paul Steinly, Susan Beer, David Murphy (Anglo-Continental, Bournemouth); James Frith, Françoise Votocek, Chris Edgoose (Bell School, Cambridge); Alex Doyle, Ian Lawrence, Anne Lewis, Herman Robin, Linda Smith, Niall Abrahams (King's School of English, Bournemouth); Guy Wellman, Verna Green, Judith Barrow (BEET, Bournemouth); Rachel Bradley, Peter Walton, Daniel Hinkley, Marc Kets (Manchester Central School of English); Antonella Vecchione (Liceo Scientifico, Varese, Italy); Caroline Bütler (KV Zürich Business School, Switzerland); Philippe Brutsaert (nstitut Saint Henri Comines, Belgium); Aleksandra Sauermann (University of Szczecin, Poland); Hania Bociek Kantonsschule (Wiedikon, Switzerland); Suria Shukurova, Irina Kruglova (International Education Centre, Moscow); Renata Skrivankova (Anglictina Rehor, Czech Republic); Elizabeth Zherebtsova (Moscow State Pedagogical University); Irina Kulkova (Institute of Business Studies, Moscow); Elena Arbuzova (Academy of National Economy, Moscow); Begoña Garate, Ascención Luca, Javier Martinez Maestro, Dana Mihael Giurcá, Camern Prieto Domínguez, Alicia Cogollucio Sobrino, Roque Crespo Lorenzo, Anne-Marie Powell (Majahonda and EOI Parla, Madrid); Sally Fleming, Andy McNish (International House Zurbano, Madrid); Soňa Jersenská (A School, Czech Republic); Patricia Muradas (Academic Consultant. Macmillan Brasil) Ana Flavia da Veiga Gaia (Planet Idiomas)

We are especially grateful to Peter Maggs and Catherine Smith for their excellent Student's Book review units, to Julie Moore (author) and Penny Analytis (editor) for the excellent CD ROM, to Philip Kerr for the wonderful New Inside Out Workbook, and to Helena Gomm, Peter Maggs and Chris Dawson for their important contributions to the New Inside Out Teacher's Book. We're also grateful to Scott Thornbury for allowing us to use extracts from his excellent book, An A–Z of ELT.

At Macmillan Education, we would like to thank Rafael Alarcon-Gaeta, Jemma Hillyer, Mo Dutton, Karen White, Julie Brett, Katie Stephens, Penny Ashfield, Hazel Barrett, Stephen Bullon, Claire Sparkes and Stephanie Parker for all their hard work on our behalf. Stephanie, in particular, deserves a special mention for the invaluable contribution she has made and continues to make to the management of this project. We would also like to thank Sally Cole (freelance photo researcher), Alyson Maskell, Celia Bingham and Xanthe Sturt Taylor (freelance editors), as well as James Richardson (freelance audio producer).

Jackie Hill and Kim Williams – our wonderfully talented freelance designers – continue to work their magic. Inside Out would not be the stylish course it is without them, or without Andrew Oliver's fabulous cover design.

Many thanks also go to the Macmillan production and marketing teams around the world whose enthusiasm and encouragement have been such a support.

Our biggest thank you goes to Des O'Sullivan (freelance project developer). Always thorough, always considerate and always there for us. We realize how lucky we are to be working with such a consummate professional.

Last but not least, we are so grateful to our families for their ongoing support and understanding.

Inside Out Intermediate was the first book to be published in the original edition. Throughout the process of rewriting it we have been reminded of the debt we owe David Riley (1955-2007) who was our first editor at Macmillan. His vision, wit, enthusiasm and unique publishing flair were instrumental in shaping the course. We miss him very much.

The authors and publisher are grateful for permission to reprint the following copyright material:
Article on *Mika Brzezinski* used with permission of Associated Press, copyright © 2007. All Rights Reserved.
Extract from 'Come Together' by Josie Lloyd and Emily Rees (Arrow), reprinted by permission of The Random House Group and Curtis Brown Group Ltd.
Extract from 'To Mum the Kindest of Ladies' edited by Richard and Helen Exley (Exley Publications, 1976), reprinted by permission of the publisher.
Article on *David Schwimmer* by Rosanna Greenstreet, copyright © Rosanna Greenstreet first published in The Guardian Weekend Magazine 08.09.07, reproduced by permission of the author.
Extract from 'If this ain't lunch, why does it feel so good' by Rosie Swash, copyright © Guardian Newspapers Limited 2008, first published in Observer Food Monthly 28.01.07, reproduced by permission of the publisher.
Extract from 'How I get dressed' by Eva Wiseman, copyright © Guardian News & Media Limited 2007, first published in The Guardian 09.09.07, reprinted by permission of the publisher.
Extract from 'How I get dressed' by Neil Norman, copyright © Guardian News & Media Limited 2008, first published in The Guardian 10.02.08, reprinted by permission of the publisher.
Extract from 'Valencia burns and the people come out to party' by Nicholas Taylor, copyright © The Independent 1998, first published in The Independent 08.02.98, reprinted by permission of the publisher. Extract from 'Global Myths No. 6: Another Story from the Travellers' Grapevine' by Maxton Walker, copyright © The Independent 1998, first published in The Independent 22.02.98, reprinted by permission of the publisher. Extract from 'Ageism has withered her' copyright © The Independent 1996, first published in The Independent on Sunday 08.12.96, reprinted by permission of the publisher. Extracts from 'The Beach' by Alex Garland, copyright © Alex Garland 1997, reprinted by permission of the publisher. Extract about *Kate Moss*, reprinted by permission of Storm Model Management Ltd. Extract from 'I've got a little list' by Alice Hart-Davis, copyright © Telegraph Newspapers Limited 1997, first published in The Telegraph 13.12.97, reprinted by permission of the publisher. Article from website *www.deadmike.com*, copyright © Michael B. Vederman, reprinted by permission of the author.

These materials may contain links for third party websites. We have no control over, and are not responsible for, the contents of such third party websites. Please use care when accessing them.

The author and publishers would like to thank the following for permission to reproduce their photographs: **Alamy**/Acestock p43(e), Alamy/J.Collins p93, Alamy/A.Cooper p62(r), Alamy/N.Daly p14(mt), Alamy/A.Ekins p64(tm), Alamy/M.Friang p59(r), Alamy/S&R Greenhill p89(b), Alamy/M.Jenner p33, Alamy/Mira p59(tr), 59(l), Alamy/D.Noble Photography p65(b), Alamy/PCL p61, Alamy/J.Powell p92(b), Alamy/J.Sturrock p64(bl), Alamy/S.I.N p36(l), Alamy/Travelstock44 p69(t), Alamy/I.Trower p70(ml), Alamy/L.Turner p91, Alamy/M.Ventura p78(l), Alamy/A.Weingart p35(bl); **Aurora** p72; **Axiom** p69(m), Axiom/I.Cumming p85; **Blend Images** p45(b); **Corbis**/ D.Beeler/Transtock p68, Corbis/G.Brown p78(r), Corbis/Darkside Productions p64(tr), Corbis/R.Faris p106, Corbis/P.Giardino p37(tl), 60, Corbis/R.Gomez p16(l), Corbis/R.Holz/Zefa p73(t), Corbis/Image100 p49, Corbis/H.King p52(m), Corbis/Klawitter Productions p76, Corbis/S.Kumar p78(m), Corbis/Mango Productions p24(a), Corbis/R.Recker/Zefa p37(tr), Corbis/J.Sohm/Visions of America p70(b); **DK Stock** p114(t); **Gallo Images** p73(b); **Getty Images** /A.Collinge p36(r), Getty /E.Contreras p5(r), Getty/G.Faint p21, Getty/S.Gallup p52(r), Getty/E.Grasser p5(t), Getty/H von Hollben p6,Getty/J.Hollingsworth p45(t), Getty/T.Jones p14(mb), Getty/G. & M. David de Lossy p35(tr), Getty/R.McVay p24(d), 24(f), Getty/R.Mettifogo pp12-13(t), Getty/J.Naughton p51, Getty/National Geographic p71, Getty /J.Nicholson p5(l), Getty/Nordic Photos p58(t), Getty/T.Paviot p16(r), Getty/J.Pumfrey p7(m), Getty/A.Ryan p7(l), 24(b), Getty/C.Schiff p14(m), Getty/Stock Food Creative p40(b), Getty/Stone p98, Getty/M.Taylor p64(bm), Getty/D.Trood Pictures p⁰⁰⁰⁺, Getty/D.Tuson/AFP p32, Getty/B.Wilson p53; **Robert Harding**/M.Simoni p70(tl); **Icc** pp9(b),109; **Image Bank** p70(tr),100; **Sue Kay** p37(bl); **Kobal Collection**/Paramount p79(r); **Masterfile** pp23, 105(bm), Masterfile/K.Davies p20(mt), Masterfile/M.Ertman p14(t), Masterfile/ R.Gomez p22(br), Masterfile/M.Leibowitz p52(l), Masterfile/Shift p105(b); **Maverick Television** pp108(a),(b),(c),(d); **PA/Photos/UK Press** p4, PA/AP/A.Harvey p116; **Panos Pictures**/M.Ostergaard p20(b); **Photoalto** p30(mt); **Photographers Choice** pp40-41(m), 41(tr), 88(b), 90, 114(r); **Photolibrary.com**/Nonstock p7(r), Photolibrary/Mauritius p24(e), Photolibrary/Japan Travel Bureau p42, Photolibrary/D.Herrmann p42-43(a), Photolibrary/J.Young p43(b), Photolibrary/G.Bryce p43(c), Photolibrary/M.Fogden p43(d), Photolibrary/R.Toft p43(f), Photolibrary/L.Williams p48, Photolibrary/The Irish Image Collection p58(b), Photolibrary/S.Pacho p105(tm), Photolibrary/L.Bobbe p114(b), Photolibrary/M.Prince p143; **Photonica** p64(tl), 87(l), 88(t); **Plainpicture**/Folio p80(b), /A.Lechner p22(l), Plainpicture/LP p80(t), Plainpicture/N.Renninger p24(c), Plainpicture/S.Schrunder p80(bm), Plainpicture/K.Sonnewend p30(b); **Reuters Pictures**/C.Cortes p34; **Retrofile** p114(tl); **Rex Features** pp63, 79(t),96, Rex/P.Carrette p97, Rex/© W.Disney/Everett p107(r), Rex/Everett Collection pp81, 107(m), Rex/20thcentury Fox/Everett p107(ml), Rex/S.Jaye p86(r), Rex/D.Rothenberg p107(l), Rex/Sipa Press p104(l); **Riser** pp 9(t), 15, 35(tl), 80(m), 80(mb), 113(b), 114(bt); **Stone** pp 12-13(b), 17, 30(m), 62(m),64(br), 65(t), 69(b), 70(b), 87(r), 92(t), 92(m), 105(t), 115(br); **Taxi** pp 22(tr), 62(l), 80(mt), 107(bl), 113(t), 115(bl); **TVHeads.com** p86(tl); **Wire Image** pp44, 86(m), 104(t).

Commissioned photographs by Lisa Payne pp20, 30 (Pete, Grace), 31, 50.

Printed and bound in Spain GZ Printek

2022 2021 2020 2019 2018
24 23 22 21 20 19 18 17 16